The WORLDING of JEAN RHYS

Recent Titles in
Contributions to the Study of World Literature

The WORLDING *of* JEAN RHYS

Sue Thomas

Contributions to the Study of World Literature, Number 96

GREENWOOD PRESS
Westport, Connecticut • London

Library of Congress Cataloging-in-Publication Data

Thomas, Sue, 1955–
    The worlding of Jean Rhys / Sue Thomas.
        p.   cm.—(Contributions to the study of world literature,
    ISSN 0738–9345 ; no. 96)
    Includes bibliographical references and index.
    ISBN 0–313–31092–0 (alk. paper)
        1. Rhys, Jean—Criticism and interpretation.   2. Autobiographical
fiction, English—History and criticism.   3. Women and literature—
West Indies—History—20th century.   4. Women and literature—
England—History—20th century.   I. Title.   II. Series.
PR6035.H96Z9   1999
823′.912—dc21   99–17846

British Library Cataloguing in Publication Data is available.

Library of Congress Catalog Card Number: 99–17846
ISBN: 0–313–31092–0
ISSN: 0738–9345

First published in 1999

Greenwood Press, 88 Post Road West, Westport, CT 06881
An imprint of Greenwood Publishing Group, Inc.
www.greenwood.com

Printed in the United States of America

The paper used in this book complies with the
Permanent Paper Standard issued by the National
Information Standards Organization (Z39.48–1984).

10 9 8 7 6 5 4 3 2 1

Copyright Acknowledgments

The author and publisher gratefully acknowledge permission for the use of the following material:

From the following works by Jean Rhys: *Wide Sargasso Sea* (Harmondsworth: Penguin, [1966] 1969); "The Imperial Road" (Ts., Jean Rhys Papers); *Voyage in the Dark* (Harmondsworth: Penguin, [1934] 1969); Letter to Peggy Kirkaldy (30 July [1957], Jean Rhys Papers); Black Exercise Book (Ms., Jean Rhys Papers); "The Birthday" (Ts., Jean Rhys Papers); *The Left Bank and Other Stories* (Freeport, NY: Books for Libraries Press, [1927] 1970); "Triple Sec" (Ts., Jean Rhys Papers); *Quartet* (Harmondsworth: Penguin, [1928] 1973); *After Leaving Mr Mackenzie* (Harmondsworth: Penguin, [1930] 1971); "Lost Island. A Childhood: Fragments of Autobiography" (Ts., Jean Rhys Papers); Add. Mss. 57856 (Department of Manuscripts, British Library, London); *Good Morning, Midnight* (Harmondsworth: Penguin, [1939] 1969); "Temps Perdi," in *Tales of the Wide Caribbean*, ed. Kenneth Ramchand (London: Heinemann [1986]); Add. Mss. 57859 (Department of Manuscripts, British Library, London); Annotation on "Mr Howard's House./CREOLE" (Ts., Jean Rhys Papers). All material is used by permission of the Jean Rhys Estate. Selections from the Jean Rhys Papers are used by permission of the Department of Special Collections, McFarlin Library, University of Tulsa, Oklahoma.

Chapter 1, "Jean Rhys and Dominican Autoethnography," is an expanded version of the author's essay of the same name in *Victorian Journalism: Exotic and Domestic. Essays in Honour of P. D. Edwards*, ed. Margaret Harris and Barbara Garlick (St Lucia: University of Queensland Press, 1998, pp. 171–96). Used by permission of the University of Queensland Press.

Chapter 2, " 'Grilled Sole' and an Experience of 'Mental Seduction,' " is an expanded version of the author's essay of the same name in *New Literatures Review: Decolonising Literatures* 28/29 (Winter 1994/Summer 1995): pp. 65–84. Used by permission of the *New Literatures Review*.

Chapter 7, "The Labyrinths of 'a Savage Person—a Real Carib,' " is a revised version of the author's essay, "The Labyrinths of 'a Savage Person—a Real Carib': The Amerindian in Jean Rhys's Fiction," which appeared in *Journal of West Indian Literature* 7.1 (May 1996): pp. 82–96. Used by permission of the *Journal of West Indian Literature*.

Chapter 8, "A Place-to-Be-From," includes a slightly shorter and revised version of the author's essay, "James Potter Lockhart and the 'Letter of the Law,' " which appeared in *Jean Rhys Review: An International Journal* 9.1–2 (1998): pp. 36–43. Used by permission of the *Jean Rhys Review*.

for my son Brendan, my love—
our relationship has joyed, sustained, and enriched me

Contents

Acknowledgments

The research that informs *The Worlding of Jean Rhys* was funded by an Australian Research Council small grant for 1993–1994 and Outside Studies Program travel grants from La Trobe University in 1993 and 1997. The Faculty of Humanities and Social Sciences at La Trobe provided conference travel grants. In particular I want to thank my research assistants, Jennifer Laurence, Catriona Elder, and Keryn Carter, who helped in the early stages of the project; Fred Smith, La Trobe's deputy vice-chancellor (Research); interlibrary loan and reference staff at La Trobe's Borchardt Library; and Lori Curtis, associate curator, Department of Special Collections, University of Tulsa. Francis Wyndham, Jean Rhys's literary executor, has facilitated my work in various ways. Lucy Frost, Richard Freadman, and Christopher Palmer, as heads of the School of English at La Trobe, have been unflaggingly and warmly supportive.

The encouragement of Rhys scholars Helen Tiffin, Peter Hulme, Nora Gaines, and Elaine Savory has vitally maintained my morale. A discussion with Helen about some of the general issues raised by the seduction narrative in the Black Exercise Book helped me extend my argument in chapter 2. Peter kindly offered to read the full manuscript.

I have presented papers based on this Rhys project in Australia, New Zealand, Singapore, and England. I thank the organizers of the following conferences for giving me the opportunity to speak: 1st and 2nd Biennial Australian Association for Caribbean Studies Conferences; Constructing British Identities: Texts, Sub-Texts, and Contexts; De-scribing Empire: Colonialism and Textuality; Factions and Frictions: Literature, History and Other Contra-Dictions; Narrative and Metaphor across the Disciplines; Post-Colonial Fictions; and The Victorians and Science. I much appreciated, too, the speaking engagements set up by and the hospitality of Cora Kaplan, David Glover, Peter Hulme, Elaine Jordan, John

Thieme, and Marilyn Lake.

   Staff at Greenwood Publishing—especially George Butler, Rebecca Ardwin, and Marilyn Brownstein—have handled my project with admirable promptness, courtesy and efficiency. At La Trobe University Mary Mulroney, Paul Salzman, and staff at the Computer Help Desk have provided valuable technical support with and advice on wordprocessing.

   The support and love of my family in Brisbane—Hazel and Ray Smith; Christine, Greg, Jennifer, and Malcolm Bartlett; and Robyn, Peter, and Andrew Kinne—have also proved sustaining. Thanks, too, to Anne Hannington.

Abbreviations

ALMM	*After Leaving Mr Mackenzie*
BEB	Black Exercise Book
GM,GR	"Good-bye Marcus, Good-bye Rose"
GM,M	*Good Morning, Midnight*
Letters	*Letters 1931–66*
SP	*Smile Please: An Unfinished Autobiography*
TS	"Triple Sec"
TWC	*Tales of the Wide Caribbean*
Tigers	*Tigers Are Better-Looking: With a Selection from* The Left Bank
V	"Vienne" [1927 version]
Voyage	*Voyage in the Dark*
Voyage IV	*Voyage in the Dark* Part IV [original ending]
WSS	*Wide Sargasso Sea*

The publishing details of the editions used are given in Works Cited. Rhys often uses ellipses as a stylistic device. I distinguish between her ellipses and mine in quoting from her writing. My ellipses are indicated with square brackets: [. . .].

The WORLDING
of JEAN RHYS

Introduction

"[T]o a certain extent, [Jean] Rhys functions as the **archetypal** post-colonial woman writer," comments Denise de Caires Narain in a review of *Motherlands*, a collection of scholarly essays on *Black Women's Writing from Africa, the Caribbean and South Asia*, in which Rhys "is discussed in detail in three of the essays and is cited extensively in other essays and in the introduction" (113). Rhys, a white Creole, a racial category with a specific historical provenance, was born Ella Gwendolen (or Gwendoline) Rees Williams in 1890 in Dominica (Wai'tukubuli, "tall is her body," in Carib), an island then a tropical colony of Britain, part of the Leeward Islands Federation. She was educated there at the Convent of the Faithful Virgin in Roseau, her birthplace, and sent to England in 1907 to continue her studies at the Perse School for Girls in Cambridge and very briefly at the Academy of Dramatic Art in London. In 1909, George Bancroft, the academy's administrator, advised her father that her (Caribbean) accent needed to be "conquer[ed]," "overcome," for her to make a success of her training and a stage career (qtd. in Angier 49). Apart from one short return visit to Dominica in 1936, Rhys would live the rest of her long life—she died in 1979—as an expatriate, in a usually "cold, dreary and beastly" England (Rhys, *Letters* 247), and, during her marriage to Jean Lenglet, in continental Europe from 1919 to 1928. Rhys's Creole mother, Minna, was from the formerly slaveowning Lockhart family, holders of Geneva estate, described mordantly in the Dominican press in 1886 as "decayed" ([Davies], "Their Photographs" [2]). Her father, William Rees Williams, was a government medical officer, a Welsh settler. In a 1959 letter to Francis Wyndham, Rhys wrote, "As far as I know I am white—but I have no country really now" (*Letters* 172). Recently Helen Carr has suggested that "'homelessness' is the terrain of Rhys's fiction," "dealing as it does with those who belong nowhere, between cultures, between histories" (xiv).[1]

The paradoxes of Rhys's belonging in her world, of her protagonists' belonging in theirs, and of where Rhys fits in postcolonial, Caribbean, feminist, and modernist literary and cultural histories are staple themes of Rhys criticism and debate generated by and around her work. My interest in writing a book on Rhys was whetted by my sense of the unread, the gaps, silences, and blind spots in the scholarly recovery of Rhys's voice, an awareness, based at first on prior research on early twentieth-century women's writing, that the historical propositions informing much Rhys criticism are so general that, as Peter Hulme remarks, "the particular conditions that produced particular books can remain ignored, indeed even unavailable" ("Locked Hearts" 21). Having lived for my first thirty years in Queensland, a tropical and subtropical ex-colony of Britain, I am also familiar with many of the ways in which the tropics and their peoples have been mythologized and gothicized. I wanted to begin to understand Rhys's locations, the manner in which she situates her authorial and narrative voices politically and ethically in relation to the worlds of her fiction and autobiographical writing. In taking Rhys and her writing as my subjects of study, I emphasize her part as "actor and agent," rather than as merely "a screen or a ground or a resource" in my production of knowledge (Haraway 198). I focus, for instance, on the means by and methods through which she engages with discourses of empire, gender, sex, race, class, and desire that shaped her sense of world. Jan Pettman in her recent examination of *A Feminist International Politics* uses the term "worlding" in her main title, *Worlding Women*. For her, the term "means taking women's experiences of the international seriously, while not assuming that any experiences are transparent or politically innocent" (x). I use the term, though I had settled on it before Pettman's book was published, to signal also my effort to engage a range of meanings of Rhys's experiences and representations of the international, while not assuming their transparency or political simplicity. Gayatri Chakravorty Spivak, too, has developed the concept of "worlding" to describe the "necessarily heterogenous" processes ("Rani" 133) by which colonized space and peoples are absorbed into "the consolidation of Europe as sovereign subject, indeed sovereign and subject" ("Rani" 128). My concept of worlding is more multifarious.

My own critical voice is contingent on historically specific theoretical approaches to literary and cultural production, while also engaging with them. My approach to the "dense particularity" of Rhys's work (Hulme, "Locked Hearts" 23) is intertextual. John Frow proposes: "The concept of intertextuality requires that we understand the concept of text not as a self-contained structure but as differential and historical. Texts are shaped not by an immanent time but by the play of divergent temporalities. . . . They are shaped by the repetition and the transformation of other textual structures" (45). Rhys's textual strategy of rewriting "*European* tropes, forms, themes, myths and the ways in which these operate" (Brydon and Tiffin 78, italics added) is widely acknowledged in postcolonial and feminist criticism. In Veronica Marie Gregg's *Jean Rhys's Historical Imagination* (1995), a largely exemplary situation of Rhys's writing in relation to

European narrativizations of post-Emancipation Caribbean history and recent
Caribbean rewriting and contestation of them, Dominica is an object of history
or travel writing, not a site of cultural production and traffic. In this study, I
situate Rhys's writing, locate it historically, in relation to texts as diverse as
Dominican journalism of the late nineteenth and early twentieth century, moral
panics around the "amateur" prostitute in England in the 1910s and 1920s and
around Obeah in Dominica circa 1904, modernist primitivism, European ethnographic discourses about the white Creole, the "Letter of the Law" in 1830s Jamaica and Dominica, and inscriptions of the "Carib War" of 1930.

   Rhys's fiction has been productively researched and analyzed through approaches emphasizing, like mine, her representations of gender and sexuality,
modernism and the Caribbean (Emery, Howells, Carr); but in the popular feminist imaginary of the 1990s, Rhys is still renowned and denigrated for her fictional studies of "the Rhys woman," a composite protagonist assuming various
guises in her novels, "hopelessly and helplessly at sea in her relations with men,
a passive victim doomed to destruction" (Allen 5). "The Rhys woman" is a figure of narcissistic self-absorption and is pathologized as a sign of Rhys's own,
for she is usually read autobiographically. This last assumption has been abetted
in the 1990s by Rhys's prizewinning biographer Carole Angier, who writes that
"one of the most intriguing of all the paradoxes about Jean Rhys" is "that she
knew so little, and wrote only about herself, and yet . . . managed to write novels which were completely modern" (218). Angier routinely conflates the life and
the fiction. I write against the customary assumption of confessional transparency in autobiographical reading practices and the reductiveness of the concept of
"the Rhys woman." The concept is based on an implicitly prescriptive images-
of-woman analysis. In "Representation and the Colonial Text," Homi Bhabha
makes a range of points about black-image analysis carried out by nationalist
critics, which may be applied to images-of-woman analysis. The images-of-
woman critic implicitly demands that the negative image be replaced by ones
"more complex, less hidden from history and vividly distinct in its textual figuration" (105), ones that elaborate a given historically contingent ideology of
women's liberation—that liberation resides in autonomy, will, purposiveness,
and individualism. The aesthetic demanded of the author is the provision of female role models as understood in late twentieth-century "Western" feminist
terms.

   My first two chapters focus on Rhys's worlding as a Dominican. In chapter
1, I examine Rhys's representations of white Creole culture and people and Dominica in relation to late nineteenth- and early twentieth-century Dominican
autoethnographic inscriptions of nature and tropes of place. Nineteenth-century
historian James Anthony Froude reworks Dominican discourses of nature and
place in *The English in the West Indies or, The Bow of Ulysses* (1888). In *Voyage in the Dark* (1934) and also in *Wide Sargasso Sea* (1966), her best known
novel, Rhys transculturates for a metropolitan audience the historical narrative
that Froude develops through motifs of drift and indifference, in the process also

engaging with and "rewriting" or "writing back" to Dominican autoethnographic expression familiar from her childhood and adolescence. In 1938 Rhys wrote an autobiographical narrative about having been mentally seduced as a fourteen-year-old in Dominica by an elderly English gentleman, "Mr. Howard." Rhys's narrative, which she experiences difficulties in telling, is a recovered and contextualized memory of a series of incidents that constitute a sexual rite of passage from naive girlhood to "doomed" womanhood (BEB). In analyzing this account, which is found in what is termed the Black Exercise Book, and Rhys's fictional treatments of themes drawn from it in "The Birthday" and "Good-bye Marcus, Good-bye Rose," I highlight in chapter 2, "'Grilled Sole' and an Experience of 'Mental' Seduction," some of the complexities, crises of figuration, and blind spots of Rhys's gendered Creole subjectivity. The narrative in the Black Exercise Book is normally simply mined for biographical "information" about Rhys; I problematize more the nuances of Rhys's storytelling.

Motifs, thematics, tropological patterns, and narrative strategies opened out for discussion in these chapters are elaborated further in later parts of this study. In my analyses of "Triple Sec," *Quartet* (1928), and *After Leaving Mr Mackenzie* (1930) in chapter 4, and *Good Morning, Midnight* (1939) in chapter 6, for example, I also draw out in a secondary argument thematics of indifference, which Rhys develops in relation to different sets of intertexts. Chapters 3 to 6 largely follow the chronological publication of Rhys's pre–Second World War fiction; I group "Triple Sec," Rhys's unpublished first novel, thematically, however, and analyze aspects of *Smile Please: An Unfinished Autobiography* (1979) in relation to the modernist primitivisms of *Voyage in the Dark*.

Ford Madox Ford identifies Rhys's voice as Antillean in his preface to her first published book, *The Left Bank and Other Stories* (1927). In chapter 3, I examine Rhys's negotiations of Dominican autoethnographic expression in finding a female white Creole speaking/writing position in her stories; the way Ford's description of Rhys's background and its realization in perspective and sympathy with particular character types shaped the reception of the book; and the play of empathy between the authorial and narrative voices in "Vienne," the longest story in the collection.

In early twentieth-century Britain, Rhys's protagonists in *Quartet*, *After Leaving Mr Mackenzie*, and *Voyage in the Dark* would have been classified "amateur" prostitutes, a pejorative term for women sexually active outside marriage. The "amateur" was the object of moral panics during the First World War and the 1920s. In chapter 4, I argue that in "Triple Sec," *Quartet*, and *After Leaving Mr Mackenzie*, Rhys engages with the public discourses that circulated around the amateur. Stella Bowen, Ford Madox Ford's partner when he and Rhys first met, describes Rhys as having "written an unpublishably sordid novel of great sensitiveness and persuasiveness" (166). That novel, "Triple Sec," has only recently been made available to scholars. It is an important document. The contrast between its generic styles and Rhys's later fiction throws light on the narrative possibilities opened by more modernist writing practices. "Triple Sec" also contains graphic narratives about the procurement of an abortion in 1913 London and a major depressive episode.

In *Smile Please*, Rhys writes about "Triple Sec." Her story is that she approached H. Pearl Adam, an "experienced journalist" and wife of the *Times* correspondent in Paris, about placing three stories by her Dutch-French husband, Jean Lenglet, which she had translated into English. Mrs. Adam asked her about her own writing, and hesitantly Rhys showed her exercise books in which she had begun writing in London after the end of an affair (with, Angier reveals, Lancelot Hugh Smith), telling Adam they were "'a sort of thing I wrote years ago—a diary, or rather I wrote it in diary form'" (155). "I pulled a chair up to the table, opened an exercise book, and wrote *This is my Diary*. But it wasn't a diary. I remembered everything that had happened to me in the last year and a half. I remembered what he'd said, what I'd felt," Rhys recalls of her days in Fulham (129). After reading the exercise books, Adam thought Ford Madox Ford, who was "famous for spotting and helping young authors," might be interested in Rhys's writing. She offered to type the material, asking, "'You don't mind if I change parts of it in the typing, do you? [. . .] It's perhaps a bit naïve here and there.'" Rhys agreed to Adam's proposal, but says she "didn't really like" the "typed manuscript." Adam "had divided it up into several parts, the name of a man heading each part" (155–56). While the typescript of "Triple Sec," now in the Department of Special Collections of the McFarlin Library at the University of Tulsa, is divided into parts, the headings are not all names of men. The exercise books became the "foundation" for the writing of *Voyage in the Dark* (Rhys, *SP* 156).

"The Equivoice of Caribbean Patois and Song," chapter 5, opens with an analysis of the ambivalences of Rhys's representations of African/white Creole difference in *Smile Please* and *Voyage in the Dark*. Caribbean patois and song, I suggest, occupy an equivocal site in Rhys's representations of the possibility of cross-racial community among women. This site also fits Hélène Cixous's space of the maternal equivoice, her "privileged metaphor for 'femininity in writing.'" I argue secondarily that the mirroring of Cixous's theory in Rhys's representations of African Caribbean difference reflects the primitivisms of Cixous's and other recent feminist rehabilitations of the pre-Oedipal mother/daughter bond. One of the stark differences between Rhys's representations of Suzy Gray in "Triple Sec" and Anna Morgan in *Voyage in the Dark* is Rhys's modernist interest in the latter novel in the constitutive function of memory and especially corporeal memory. Anna's corporeal memory acts as her transcendental anchor in modernity. Like Proust in *Á la recherche du temps perdu* (*Remembrance of Things Past*), Rhys is "overwhelmingly concerned with the interaction of different temporalities," which "acquire value in so far as they embody infinitely complex strata of the inner self" (Nicholls 263–64). I elucidate the metaphorical resonances of blackness in the play of temporalities in *Voyage in the Dark*.

The sexological, evolutionary, and literary discourses that circulated in the early twentieth century around the *cérébrale* and the dreaming woman, types of the intellectual woman, are, to date, unrecognized intertexts of *Good Morning, Midnight*. In chapter 6, I link Rhys's negotiation of these discourses to her representation of Sasha's responses to the modernist primitivist tastes of Serge, a Russian-Jewish artist. I compare Rhys's invocation of weeping women and a grieving mother with a dead baby with Pablo Picasso's use of such figures in *Guernica* and his studies for it. *Good Morning, Midnight* is set in Paris during the 1937 Exhibition at which *Guernica* was first shown. The literary treatments of the dreaming woman to which I relate *Good Morning, Midnight* are D. H. Lawrence's *The Trespasser* (1912), Helen Corke's *Neutral Ground* (1933), and Rachel Annand Taylor's *The Hours of Fiammetta* (1910).

Dominica has one of the two significant Carib Indian communities of island Caribbean countries. Rhys's representations of Carib Indians in *Voyage in the Dark* and "Temps Perdi" (1967) are integral to the racially inflected formation of her modernism, a formation highlighted in particular in chapters 5 and 6. She uses Carib Indians, I argue in chapter 7, to figure issues associated with transcendence of womanly embodiment, the relation of Dominican women to writing, and feminine colonial mobility.

In my final chapter, "A Place-to-Be-From," I return to *Wide Sargasso Sea*, reading the intersubjective relationships in the novel in relation to a number of Rhys's historical intertexts. I read the relationships among Christophine, Antoinette, and Rochester in relation to a turn-of-the-century Dominican Obeah case and the "Letter of the Law" in the British Caribbean of the 1830s; and the relationships among Rochester, Daniel, Amélie, and Antoinette in relation to Shakespeare's *Othello* and the historical narratives surrounding Indian Warner, who was killed at Massacre, the named Dominican village in *Wide Sargasso Sea*. I analyze closely Antoinette's three dreams. Throughout the chapter, I critique, in particular, Gayatri Chakravorty Spivak's influential account of the relation between self and "Other" in *Wide Sargasso Sea* in her essay "Three Women's Texts and a Critique of Imperialism."

Rhys grew up in a culture stratified on racial lines and lived in a period in which questions of ethnicity were often referred to "bloodlines." Throughout *The Worlding of Jean Rhys*, I elucidate the racial consciousness of Rhys's characters, of Rhys herself, and of turn-of-the-century Dominicans in relation to historical stereotypes, ideas, and understandings of "race." This commits me to using descriptors that are part of that consciousness.

Regrettably, because of considerations of space, I have been able to discuss in detail here only three of Rhys's late short stories: "The Imperial Road," "Goodbye Marcus, Good-bye Rose," and "Temps Perdi." I have written about several more of them elsewhere: "Let Them Call It Jazz" in *De-scribing Empire*, edited by Chris Tiffin and Alan Lawson, and "The Insect World" and "Heat" in *A Talent(ed) Digger*, edited by Hena Maes-Jelinek, Gordon Collier, and Geoffrey V. Davis. I will be discussing a wider range of the late short stories in a chapter on Rhys I am writing for *England in Twentieth Century Fiction through Colonial Eyes*, a book I am coauthoring with Ann Blake and Leela Gandhi.

NOTE

1. When I visited Roseau in 1997 to do archival research, I was directed to the former Rees Williams family house; Rhys's Dominican childhood was acknowledged, but a qualification was added, "Rhys called England home." Colonial pieties were often modeled on family loyalties (the imperial power as the mother country, parent culture, or home), but the sharpness in the rider referred more to the politics of Rhys's perceived *choice* of continuing expatriation than to her colonial sensibility.

Chapter 1 ———————————————

Jean Rhys and Dominican Autoethnography

In the theoretical preamble to "Three Women's Texts and a Critique of Imperialism," Gayatri Chakravorty Spivak takes as her object of investigation an "abject" "imperialist narrativization of history," strategically eschewing a reading that would "touch" the "bio-graphy" of the author. She does, however, cursorily implicate Jean Rhys's biography in her "reinscription" of *Jane Eyre*: she suggests that *Wide Sargasso Sea* is the "'scene of writing'" (244) of Rhys's origins, birth in Dominica (249), and of "the interest of the white Creole" (253). Spivak assumes the transparency of these signifiers of a "named life" (244). As Laura Chrisman argues, in Spivak's essay "one colony, India, inadvertently begins to occupy a privileged site of representativeness, of conceptual supremacy for imperial 'worlding,' at the expense of other colonies such as those in Africa and the Caribbean" (Chrisman 39). My project in this chapter is to begin comprehending Rhys's "worlding" as a Dominican and suggesting where Rhys writes her novels and herself "into history by means of . . . narrative" (Erwin 143) and tropology. I situate Rhys's representations of white Creole culture and people and Dominica in relation to late nineteenth- and early twentieth-century Dominican autoethnographic inscriptions of nature and tropes of place.

"Autoethnography" is a concept developed by Mary Louise Pratt in *Imperial Eyes: Travel Writing and Transculturation*: "If ethnographic texts are a means by which Europeans represent to themselves their (usually subjugated) others, autoethnographic texts are those the others construct in relation to or in dialogue with those metropolitan representations." Autoethnography is integral to "transculturation"—"how subordinated or marginal groups select and invent from materials transmitted to them by a dominant or metropolitan culture"—and the questions it raises: "How are metropolitan modes of representation received and appropriated on the periphery? . . . with respect to representation, how does one speak of transculturation from the colonies to the metropolis? . . . How have Europe's constructions of subordinated others been shaped by those others, by the constructions of themselves and their habitats that they presented to the Europeans?" (6–7).

James Anthony Froude reworked Dominican discourses of nature and place in *The English in the West Indies or, The Bow of Ulysses* (1888), a provocative travel book that had an important place in Rhys's family history and colonial British Caribbean educational curricula. In 1892 Froude was appointed Regius professor of modern history at Oxford. The anxieties evoked for Froude by his 1887 visit to Dominica are apparent in two insistently repeated motifs—drift and indifference—both related to the spectre of England's mere "titular dominion" (142). In *Voyage in the Dark* (1934) and *Wide Sargasso Sea* (1966), Rhys transculturated for a metropolitan audience the historical master narrative Froude developed through these motifs, in the process also engaging with and "rewriting" or "writing back" to Dominican autoethnographic discourses familiar from her childhood and adolescence. Indifference, too, is part of Rhys's autobiographical figuration of oceanic desire for maternal solace and favor and attachment to place.

Dominican journalism published between 1880 and 1907 is my main source of autoethnographic expression. The principal language spoken in Dominica was a Normandy-based French patois. English was the language of government, education, the press, and a significant portion of trade and commerce. The editor-proprietors of the Dominican papers, four-page weeklies for most of the period, were "colored" Creoles, members of a class termed the "Mulatto Ascendency" in Dominican history. Their proprietorships follow colonial American patterns of Creole editor-proprietorship, the printer-journalist (Febvre and Martin 210–212, Anderson 61–62), the politician-journalist (Lent *passim*), and the journalist-editor models. The *Dominican* (1839–1907) was edited by Alexander Rumsey Lockhart from 1872 until 1880 and by Augustus Theodore Righton, known popularly as Papa Dom, from 1880 until his death in 1907. Rhys has a journalist-editor character, Papa Dom, in "Again the Antilles" (1927), and in two late stories, "Fishy Waters" and "Pioneers, O Pioneers," published in *Sleep It Off Lady: Stories* (1976). Lockhart and Righton were government printers. Lockhart was probably a descendant of Rhys's slaveowning great-grandfather James Potter Lockhart.[1] The *Dominica Dial* (1882–1893) was edited by William Davies, influential leader of the Ascendency in the 1880s and 1890s, and the *Dominica Guardian* (1893–1924) was owned initially by William Davies, Sholto Pemberton, A. R. Lockhart, and Henry Hamilton, the elective members of the Dominican Assembly until the imposition of Crown Colony rule in 1898, with Joseph Hilton Steber as subeditor and manager. (The assembly before its abolition consisted of elected members—called "electives"—and members nominated by the governor, who were usually drawn from the very small class of white public officials.) Davies took over the editorship of the *Dominica Guardian* to campaign against Crown Colony rule. Steber, a professional journalist, became editor in his own right. Righton and Steber had received early training under A. R. Lock-hart.

In 1880 Lockhart published in the *Dominican* an article he thought "highly interesting and graphic," designed "to bring the resources of the country to the notice of persons abroad as a means of inviting settlement and capital."[2] The article, called "Dominica & Its Boiling Lake," by two locals, Dr. H. A. Alford Nicholls and Edmund Watt, conflates three standard late nineteenth-century Dominican discourses about "nature": scientific systematization, the picturesque sublime, and capitalist invigoration. The explicit purpose of the writers is to make "the loveliest, the most interesting, but one of the least known islands of the New World" and its "advantages" more "generally known." Nicholls and Watt associate the presence of English authority in Dominica after 1770 with "fresh survey." They implicitly situate themselves in a line of knowledge-production and discovery: chart making; uncovering of "submerged" geological history; interior survey of geological formation, vegetation, animals, climate ([3]). The local scientific authority cited is the highly esteemed Dr. John Imray, who practiced in Dominica from 1832 until his death in 1880. The obituary in the *Dominican* memorialized his political integrity and his botanical work: bringing to "scientific notice" through his correspondence and collaboration with Sir John Hooker of Kew Gardens "our rare and curious plants and flowers" and the introduction of "new and valuable plants," including limes and Liberian coffee for commercial cultivation on his plantations ([Lockhart], "In Memoriam!").[3] He is constructed as a "benign, decidedly literate . . . 'herborizer'"; Pratt associates such figures with the expansion of "Europe's 'planetary consciousness' . . . marked by an orientation toward inner exploration and the construction of global-scale meaning through the descriptive apparatuses of natural history" (15). Imray's protégé Nicholls continued his botanical work, concentrating on scientific agriculture, his labors culminating in the prizewinning *A Text-book of Tropical Agriculture* (1892), reprinted eight times by 1926; scholarly recognition in the United Kingdom, the United States, and the Caribbean; and knighthood.[4] In their 1880 sketch, Nicholls and Watt draw attention to "many plants of economic value" in the "primeval forest," the "large tracts of virgin soil, as rich as can be found any where in the tropics," waiting to be "mapped out in thriving plantations," and the commercial possibilities of "systematic" sulphur and silver mining ([3]). Primeval forest and virgin soil are the canonical local images of Dominica.

Nicholls and Watt's transformative vision of economic modernization entails a reinvigoration of the planter class by "a portion of the tide of wealth in men and money now turned to the East" ([3]); they seek to entice what Pratt calls the "extractive vision" of a European "capitalist vanguard" (150). Editorials and letters to the editor in all local papers, and evidence to the 1893 British Royal Commission on the condition and affairs of Dominica published in the *Dominica Guardian* show that the colored middle class and small landholders generally shared this desire for recapitalization. Tradesmen and laborers were keen for the work supplied by plantation owners; irregular employment in that sector meant by 1893 that they had difficulty paying the road tax.[5] As planters rather than politicians, William Davies and A. R. Lockhart gave evidence to the 1897 West India Royal Commission, which enquired into depression in the sugar industry: Davies urged more popular representation in government; Lockhart, immigration and capital. Both proposed credit schemes. In Nicholls's elaboration of his vision of modernization before the 1897 commission, he lauded "scientific principles of agriculture" as opposed to the "primitive," "wasteful," and "unwise" farming practices of predominantly black small landholders.[6]

Pratt observes that the "concrete relations of labor and property" seldom figure in the writing of the capitalist vanguard or in (white) Creole civic consciousness: "In the esthetic (as in the political) realm, the unquiet American multitudes [of subjugated peoples] could not be dealt with" (180). Nineteenth-century travelers to Dominica often presented it in their writing as a twin spectacle: naturally picturesque from a distance, but the human transformation of the landscape in a state of decay. For Anthony Trollope the decay was graphically emblematized in the "thick, rank grass" growing through the cobblestone roads of Roseau, the capital. Froude was also disturbed by this spectacle. Trollope, like others, essentialized and pathologized the decay as a failure of civic character, an entropic reversion of all racial groups to the stereotypical "nature" of black people: "chattering, idle, and listless" (161).

Nicholls and Watt present subjugated peoples in negative and positive aesthetic registers. Epitomized and delegitimated as the "Crown Land squatter," the small landholder is represented as a rapacious and unsystematic despoiler of the "riches" of the forests. Pacification is presented approvingly: once "warlike" Carib Indians "now gentle in demeanour and timid in nature" are contained in duly allotted "Indian Country," yet still "skilled" in hunting and seafaring; and bucolic fishermen ply "the gentle art" with "intense satisfaction and great good humour," turning to (white) spectators with a "'Look you, Master, what I have done!'" ([3]).[7] The dialect speech, a sharp contrast to the language and stylistic registers of the authors, essentializes in linguistic caricature "the difference that separated white from black" (Gates 6). Nicholls and Watt do not refer to the colored and black middle class, with whom the Crown and white officials were engaged in a fierce contest over political authority and financial responsibility. Unequal relations of labor and property, particularly as they concerned ability to pay land, horse, and road taxes, were forcefully articulated by small landholders William Gabriel Marie, Henry Le Blanc, and Fagan Pinard at the 1893 Royal Commission.[8] The commission was held in the aftermath of the La Plaine uprising against land tax, in which four men were killed and two women wounded (Honychurch 144).

The ambitions and sense of propriety of the middle class produced some alternative visions of political, social, and economic modernization. To the colored journalists the stock historical image of the colored or black person in a state of "nature" was the "beast of burden" under slavery;[9] the contemporary image was of the rowdy "'pests'" who "infected" the streets of Roseau and confirmed the racially traducing prejudices of "morbid" white minds ("Moralizing" [2]–[3]). In his 1896 obituary of Joseph Fadelle, Righton lauded the free middle class of the 1820s and 1830s who contributed to the "regeneration of their race" by acquiring the "essentials" of *knowledge, morals,* and wealth" in order to enter political and legal contest with white authorities. (After the passing of the Brown Privilege Bill in 1831, the qualifications for enfranchisement were maleness and a specified measure of property.) The activities of the Young Men's Mutual Improvement Society (for nonwhite men) in March and April 1888 indicate the kinds of knowledge valued: reading of essays in English, grammatical exercises, dictation, and classes on "Arithmetic, Synonyms and Geography."[10] Obeah (a metonym for African religion) was represented as "barbaric";[11] and the clergy and the press were extolled as the "two most powerful agents fighting towards the advancement of civilization" ("Moralizing" [3]). Civic space is mapped such that metaphorically filth, "unhallowed mire," comes to stand for those outside "a thrifty, industrious, and moralized class" of people fit for orderly and "healthy occupations" ("Moralizing" [2]).[12] A. R. Lockhart read to Sir Robert Hamilton's 1893 Royal Commission a brief legislative history of the island from 1775: modernization ("advance") is linked with the relief of "social and political disabilities" from the population of "African descent," popular education, the emergence of a class of "peasant free-holders," and restoration of fiscal responsibility through increasing the number of elected members of the Legislative Assembly in relation to government-nominated members. Speaking for the electives, he associated the arresting of progress with the "hybrid constitution" of 1865, which was offered as an alternative to Crown Colony rule and was designed to curb the increasing political power of the colored population ("The Special Inquiry" [2]).[13]

Crown Colony rule was imposed in 1898, with the promise of a substantial grant of £15,000 for roadbuilding to "open up" virgin soil. The bulk of the grant was used by Administrator Henry Hesketh Bell to build the Imperial Road. Davies called Crown Colony rule a *"coup d'état"* [sic], engineered by "a conspiracy of the Government and the white section" of the people, "mostly new comers from Europe" disturbed by a seeming "(dis)order" of "Providence": finding "nearly the whole mercantile body and the local proprietary composed of black and coloured men," instead of "an upper crust of whites and a lower crust of subservient blacks" as in the "gorgeous East" ("The *Mot d'Ordre*"). In 1899 Steber published in the *Dominica Guardian*, which had led the campaign against Crown Colony rule, "The Real 'White Man's Burden,'" a parody of Rudyard Kipling's infamous poem, by Ernest H. Crosby, a white U.S. socialist. The first and last verses indicate the tone Crosby adopts in critiquing the imperialist project of "civilizing savage hordes":

Take up the White Man's Burden;
  Send forth your sturdy sons,
And load them down with whisky

And Testaments and guns.
Throw in a few diseases
    To spread in tropic climes,
For there the healthy niggers
    Are quite behind the times. . . .

Take up the White Man's burden,
    And if you write in verse,
Flatter your Nation's vices
    And strive to make them worse
Then learn that if with pious words
    You ornament each phrase,
In a world of canting hypocrited [sic]
    This kind of business pays.[14]

Crosby's use of the term "niggers" to cite racism accords with the practice of Steber and the elective members of the assembly.[15]

To describe Dominica's beauty, Nicholls and Watt use a vocabulary of the picturesque sublime and quote W. Gifford Palgrave's representation of the island within this compositional tradition. Palgrave is effusive: "[I]n the wild grandeur of its towering mountains, . . . in the majesty of its almost impenetrable forests; in the gorgeousness of its vegetation, the abruptness of its precipices, the calm of its lakes, the violence of its torrents, the sublimity of its waterfalls, it stands without a rival, not in the West Indies only, but, I should think, throughout the whole island catalogue of the Atlantic and Pacific combined." Nicholls and Watt's epithets are generally formulaic: a plateau is "magnificent," trees "lofty," the island in "many parts . . . indescribably rugged," volcanoes "slumbering" ([3]). A shift to a "heightened or intensified consciousness" (Weiskel 13)—a hallmark of the Romantic sublime—is effected by the transcendent prospect of the "virgin soil" being "mapped out in thriving plantations" and a latent anxiety that imperial capital may remain "turned to the East": Dominica is then summed up as "the richest, the loveliest, and the grandest island of the Carribean [sic] Archipelago" (Nicholls and Watt [3]). Andrew Wilton argues that the emergence of the sublime in landscape representation in the late eighteenth century was to enable the painter "to accomplish the leap from the 'local' and trivial to the grand and universal" (20). The picturesque sublime and an Edenic discourse facilitate this kind of leap in Dominican autoethnography. Nicholls and Watt's language genders the soil and island feminine. It is "loveliest," virgin and passive, waiting for the "tide of wealth in men and money," which will revive a colonial plantation economy ([3]). In "Acrostics," an anonymous poem published in the *Dominican* in 1880, the island's prosperity, ordained by "Nature," is "[a]n Eden of old," the agent of lapse has been "[c]ruel man," and a "hope sublime" of restored "bliss" is contingent on fertile Dominica being "made" its "hidden treasure to unfold" ([3]). In these gendered discourses Dominica's richness or treasure is not widely enough known, waiting to be opened up, or hidden.

Hidden treasure is a common motif in Rhys's representations of Dominica. Both the unnamed female protagonist of "Mixing Cocktails," first published in *The Left Bank and Other Stories* (1927), and Rochester in *Wide Sargasso Sea* contemplate the landscape through the historical romance of buried pirate treasure. Farewelling Dominica, Rochester explains the "law of treasure": "the finders never tell, because you see they'd only get one-third then," the law taking the rest. The desire for Antoinette, which violates his masculine English reserve, is, then, through a process of association, constructed as the treasure he has found. He has persistently conflated Antoinette's un-Englishness with the tropical landscape. In his mind he proposes they behave "[l]ike the swaggering pirates," "[k]eep[ing] nothing back," before his "sickening swing back to hate" (*WSS* 139). His hate is honed by the sense that he has been purchased with the Mason money, implying sexual enslavement. In Rochester's English home, Antoinette's keepers try to contain her difference in a "grey wrapper" (152), a "cardboard world" (148), metonymic of the book *Jane Eyre*. Antoinette's desire and otherness are emblematized in the red dress she worries they have hidden. She reports Rochester's comment that the dress makes her "look intemperate and unchaste" (152); the words may also be read as his disgust with his former desire for her, for him a suffocating reversion to nature, coded in Rhys's poem "Obeah Night" through stock signifiers of blackness—"Obeah," "dark," "Angry," "Blind fierce avenging," "shameless," "Hating and hated" (*Letters* 264–65). Rhys alludes to the story of Ali Baba and the forty thieves in "Temps Perdi" (1967); the treasure to which the expatriate white Creole protagonist wants the "Open Sesame" on her return visit in 1936 is the ability to make sense of her experience (*TWC* 161).

Rhys's engagement with the discourse of capitalist invigoration to open up the land is entwined in complex and conflicted ways with the Imperial Road and her witness of change during her own brief return visit to Dominica in 1936. The change is thematized in her writing as ingratitude and hostility towards white Creole people on the part of nonwhite Dominicans and as corruption. Concerned about the racist tone of "The Imperial Road," Rhys's publishers reportedly refused it for *Sleep It Off Lady* (1976) (Guide to the Jean Rhys Papers). Her representations of nonwhite people are certainly stereotypical; Gregg rightly points out that in this story Rhys "fetishizes black people as sullen, hostile servants and laborers" and that she "could only perceive [them] as servants, caretakers, and props" (195).

Rhys understands capitalist invigoration of turn-of-the-century Dominica as the policy of Henry Hesketh Bell, the administrator from 1899 until 1905. In "Pioneers, O Pioneers" and "Fishy Waters," Rhys thematizes the failure of the policy, as settlers have difficulty coping with the forest, racialized politics (illustrated by newspaper editorials and letters to the editor), and damaging gossip. During Bell's term as administrator he managed to attract new investment and white settlers; most of the £12,000 left from Joseph Chamberlain's road grant[16] was committed to the Imperial Road. In 1904 Bell represented the grant as having been in "aid of roads and land settlement" and the Imperial Road as having rendered "accessible a part of the fertile area that has been, for so long, lying waste and unproductive." The road, he reported in the *West India Committee Circular*,

runs for seventeen miles to a point in the very centre of the island, known as Bassinville. For the first five or six miles of its course, it is practicable for wheeled traffic, while the remainder is what may be termed a first class bridle-road, having such a gradient as to be ultimately fit for wheeled traffic. . . . The Imperial Road . . . will be extended when the demand for more land arises. In the meantime, another road, starting from Layou, a good shipping-place on the leeward coast, is being constructed and pushed up the Layou valley towards Bassinville, where it will ultimately connect with the Imperial road [sic]. ("The Imperial Road in Dominica" 259)

To Dominican people the Imperial Road would represent many things, including the promise of development contingent on Crown Colony rule, a vision of opening up crown land in the interior for cultivation, or, to draw out the implications of an allusion in the *Dominica Guardian*, the mess of pottage for which the "birthright" of representative government was sold or bartered ("Free Will or Compulsion?" [2]). The road was never completed, because of "bad conditions and costs" (O'Connor, "Jean Rhys" 409) and the failure of sustained investment in the interior (Boromé 51).

In "The Imperial Road," the narrator returns to Dominica, having lived abroad since she was "about sixteen" ("The Imperial Road," Jean Rhys Papers, [1]). The narrator is determined that she and her husband, Lee, walk back to Roseau from Portsmouth along the Imperial Road; she discovers that "[t]here wasn't a vestige left of the Imperial Road" (15). Drawing on memories of turn-of-the-century Dominica, including the ceremony to mark the opening of the road, she insists to herself that "the Imperial Road couldn't have disappeared without trace, it just wasn't possible. No Imperial Road or a trace of it. Just darkness, cut trees, creepers and it just wasn't possible" (18). The "darkness" emblematizes the unsustainability of the economic modernization project and the planter class, the narrator's depression, and the difficulty of access to the interior of place and people. The expatriate narrator's local knowledge is outdated; she needs local guides, but finds them hostile to her race, class, and Dominican past, and doubts their reliability. She shares little common ground of referentiality with local people. Her experience of the "new" is superficial; its only depths are bewilderment and a sense of loss. The rain on her journey through the forest functions textually as pathetic fallacy for her despair.

Froude invokes the picturesque sublime to represent the geography of Dominica, personifying the island as a beauty, once treasured as "the choicest jewel in the necklace of the Antilles" (153). He engages intertextually with local discourses: capitalist invigoration, scientific systematization, treasure, and Eden. Nicholls, praised as a scientific agriculturalist and "the only man in the island of really superior attainments," was one of Froude's key informants (165). Dominica is for Froude an available sexualized beauty "insolent" (169) and "conscious" of her "charms," scorned by the "enterprising youth of England," who take "their energy and their capital" elsewhere (160). The land is "fertile as Adam's paradise, still waiting for the day when 'the barren woman shall bear children'" (171). The scorn is returned as "indifference" (161, 173) and "scornful feeling towards English authority" (163). The local economy had declined to such an extent that the tax revenues could not support the public service—eulogized as the implementation by English authority of the "'latest discoveries of *political science*'" (144) [italics added]—and the plantation system and its monuments were in a state of "ruin" (173), "desolation" (153) and "neglect." He is not comforted by the "industry of the black peasantry": alongside the ruin and the demoralization of the English white people a "state of things more helplessly provoking was never seen" (159). "Neglect" became during the nineteenth century, Pratt argues, "the touchstone of a negative aesthetic that legitimated European interventionism." Like Robert Proctor in his 1825 view of Chile cited by Pratt, Froude "encodes" his "letdown in terms of money and dominance" (Pratt 149). For him the local indifference and scorn were symptomatic of a degenerative "drift" back to an uncapitalized barbarism: "the island drifts along, without credit to borrow money and therefore escaping bankruptcy"; the general mood is one of "torpid content" interrupted only by the agitations of the "elected members" (145); the "black boys . . . deserve a better fate than to be sent drifting before constitutional whirlwinds back into barbarism, because we, on whom their fate depends, are too ignorant or careless to provide them with a tolerable government" (158); the English whites (settlers and Creoles) "have lost heart, and cease to struggle against the stream" (159); and the "poor black," if "denied the chance of developing under guidance the better qualities which are in him, . . . will drift back into a mangy cur" (161). Froude's remedy for "drift" in this extremity of the English body politic that may "mortify and drop off" (173) is intervention to abolish the measure of representative government in the island's constitution. As Trinidadian John Jacob Thomas points out in *Froudacity* (1889), the best-known piece of nineteenth-century British Caribbean autoethnography, Froude's large project is the thwarting of "political aspiration in the Antilles" by recommending against elective local legislatures or elective elements in those legislatures, in effect the "exclusion of the Negro vote." (51). Thomas draws attention to Froude's "one-sided course" of relying on "'Anglo–West Indian'" political and racial views to form his opinions (73).

Thomas places his countering of Froude as the more enduring part of a wider "Ethiopic West Indian" project of refuting negrophobia (56). In Dominica that project had been undertaken in print by William Davies, then leader of the Mulatto Ascendency.[17] Locals reportedly mocked Froude's opinion of Nicholls by fabricating inflated market reports about the prices his scientifically cultivated produce was fetching ("An Ungrateful Munchausen" [sic] [2]). Davies published in the *Dominica Dial*, evidently without copyright permission, Froude's chapters on Dominica, judging that the cost of the book would prohibit a wide local read-

ership of the "tissue of misstatements," "wicked and impolitic" in its inflaming
of past racial hatreds ("Rubbish on the West Indies" [3]). He posted to Froude the
issues in which he editorialized against the book and Froude's informants and
those in which the chapters were republished ("Mr. Froude's Friends" [3]). The
Dial also featured "Negrophobia," a long review of Darnell Davis's pamphlet
Mr. Froude's Negrophobia, or Don Quixote as a Cook's Tourist, published in
Demerera, and reprinted a critique of Froude's book from the *Voice* (St. Lucia).
Davies notes before publication of *The English in the West Indies* Froude's connection with Thomas Carlyle, anticipating "an exaggerated and fanciful record . . .
largely tinctured with a leaven of the 'damned nigger' theory of civilization as
propounded by the cynical sage of Chelsea" ("1887: A Retrospect" [2]).

After publication Davies concentrates his attack on Froude's interpretation of
local history and on his informants, "negrophobist whites sighing for a past
which cannot be recalled" ("Froude Localised" [2]), who are said to have
"poisoned his ear" ("Rubbish on the West Indies" [3]). Froude's hosts had been
Captain John Spencer Churchill, the island's administrator, and his wife, Edith,
nee Lockhart, later to become Rhys's uncle and aunt. Davies identified Froude's
local guide, Mr. F—, as Acton Don Lockhart, another uncle ("Rubbish on the
West Indies" [3]). Rhys's parents, William and Minna Rees Williams, were part
of the "upper ten" in the administrator's social circle at this time ("The Queen's
Jubilee" [3]). "[L]ost heart," Froude's naming of the malady of the English white
people (numbering fewer than a hundred in a population of about 27,000), is
almost certainly a pun on Lockhart: the phrase occurs in a paragraph describing
tours with Mr. F —. Throughout the 1890s until the imposition of Crown Colony rule, Nicholls, Acton Don Lockhart, and William Rees Williams were political allies against the demands and influence of the elective members. Their
political principles were on tense occasions cited by the electives using the term
for racism—"nigger" ("The Garrison on Parade" [2])—or through mordant comment on a Rees Williams speech mannerism: overuse of the epithet "beastly," as
in the phrase "those *beastly* mulattos" ("The Saint; the Sawbones and the Speculator" [3]).

Rhys resists Charlotte Brontë's bestialization of Bertha Mason in *Wide Sargasso Sea*; and in *Voyage in the Dark* she registers as bestialization English
class, gender, and ethnic prejudice against the white Creole protagonist, Anna
Morgan, and her loss of class and ethnic privilege. After the death of her father,
Anna Morgan is dispossessed of her inheritance by her English stepmother, Hester, who is unwilling to sacrifice any of her own caste by making Anna an al-
lowance from the proceeds of the sale of the family's Dominican estate. Hester
suggests her husband made a bad investment; he had practiced scientific agriculture with Anna's help.[18] In England, Anna, who was expected in Dominica to be
a lady, struggles to make a living as a chorus girl. Contemplating her own poverty and "cheap" clothes through a conflated class and racial signifier with Dominican and English resonances before her affair with Walter Jeffries, Anna
thinks of "[t]he ones without any money, the ones with beastly lives. Perhaps

I'm going to be one of the ones with beastly lives. They swarm like woodlice when you push a stick into a woodlice-nest at home. And their faces are the colour of woodlice" (*Voyage* 23).

Peter Stallybrass and Allon White chart the Victorian production of desire through the association of the working class and the colonial Irish with the bestial in *The Politics and Poetics of Transgression*, arguing that "[i]t was above all around the figure of the prostitute that the gaze and touch, the desires and contaminations, of the bourgeois male were articulated" and that the smell of the "low" was a cause of particular anxiety, because smell "had a pervasive and invisible presence difficult to regulate" (126–34, 137, 139). Vincent Jeffries describes the affair Anna has had with his brother Walter as "rather beastly sort of love" that "simply doesn't matter," when "you get into a[n English] garden and smell the flowers" (*Voyage* 80). Anna is objectified sexually by anonymous men as a "fair baboon [. . .] worse than a dark one every time" (126), "swine" and "bitch" (128). Anna's xenophobic flatmate, Ethel, a masseuse who wanted Anna as manicurist to charm her clients, puts her in a room with "white furniture, and over the bed the picture of the dog sitting up begging—*Loyal Heart*" (127). These assertions of superiority are structured by "triangulated" analogies "among racial, class and gender degeneration" (McClintock 44). After withdrawing her consent during one sexual encounter, Anna retaliates against the implications of being positioned as a begging dog by smashing the picture.

Davies's contestation of Froude through metaphoricity, a dichotomy between native and exotic botanical species, is particularly pertinent to Rhys's representations of white Creole culture, English attitudes toward the white Creole, and Dominican attitudes toward white settlers. In nineteenth-century imperial discourse colonies were "planted."[19] Froude speaks of "whites whom we planted as our representatives . . . drifting into ruin" (121). Taking his cues from this discourse, Froude's metaphoricity of ill-health, and the discourse of scientific systematization, Davies distinguishes between native and exotic species to contest Froude's historical master narrative of drift. For Davies, nonwhite Dominicans are the generality of the "sons of the soil" ("The Medical Question" [3]), and "trade and the soil" are in their "hands" ("Froude Localised" [2]). "The white man," he writes, "is an exotic requiring at the best of times the forced conditions of the atmosphere of slavery and the high price of sugar to enjoy a sickly existence. What with the abolition of slavery, the competition of the beetroot [sic] industry, and the operation of the bounty, he has been going from bad to worse" ("Rubbish on the West Indies" [3]). Here he is also engaging a Darwinian discourse of the survival of the fittest and a European ethnographic discourse about the degeneration of the white race in the tropics. Davies naturalizes the inevitability of both the decay of white political, economic, and social privilege and the upward class mobility of the colored and black population and indigenizes that population. In the nineteenth-century British Caribbean, Creole was the term used to describe people born in the region, but not of indigenous Carib or Arawak ancestry. Distinctions were made between white, colored, and negro or black Creoles. Froude explains his racial description of Edith Spencer Churchill: "English Creole—that is, of pure English blood, but born in the island" (147). "Creole of pure English descent she may be, but they are not English or European either," Rhys's Rochester thinks of Antoinette in *Wide Sargasso Sea* (56). Davies prescribes different remedies for indifference and the "unprosperous condition" Froude diagnoses as drift: the black man's "equality before the law, and equality in citizenship" for indifference; and trusting to the "local experience" and financial responsibility of the "representatives of the people" for drift ("Froude Localised" [2]).

In her representations of white Creole people Rhys usually "writes back" to Davies's horticultural trope, and uses the English response to native species to expose the racism of anxieties about "purity" of "blood" or "descent." The gardens of the Dominican estates of local white families in Rhys's "Mixing Cocktails," *Voyage in the Dark*, and *Wide Sargasso Sea*, include both *native and exotic* species of plants. The mixed gardens are metonymic of a syncretic merging of cultures, the local and the European. Rhys represents Englishness in the mix by the presence of roses. (England and the English are represented on the silver mace that symbolized the authority of the British Crown in colonial Dominica by a rose.[20] In 1839 a local poet, William Satchell, bemoaned the changes brought about by the abolition of slavery by contrasting a "modest Rose" and an "other flower of upstart race" that was in the "*mode*" [4].) In "The Birthday," an unpublished story, Rhys indicates the syncretism of Dominican culture by Phoebe's wearing of a rose behind her ear, a Creole custom. Her English aunt is disgusted, linking the custom with what she perceives as the taint of Spanish Creole blood in her sister-in-law's family (Jean Rhys Papers).[21]

Rhys's response in the 1970s to the black nationalism of the Rastafarian movement, as reported by David Plante, is registered through the rose trope: "No roses in Dominica. Who got rid of them? I know. I know. Up the Dreads. Yeah, the dreads. They're in London, too, and they wear dark glasses. In Dominica they live in the forests. They're taking over" (Plante 274). (Rhys would appear to be confusing Rastafarians in London and a Dominican black-power group called the Dreads, which was linked during the 1970s with the murders of several white residents [Baker 182–83].)[22] Her hostility is integral to her sense that an element of the syncretism of Dominican culture and its history is being uprooted. Anna Morgan's English stepmother, Hester, a newcomer to Dominica, cannot bear the smell of the flowers—the mix gives her the "creeps" (*Voyage* 71), and one native species, the pop-flower, makes her faint (77). She pointedly has roses on her dining table (61) and is obsessed that Anna is "growing up more like a nigger every day" (54), linking her turning "out badly" with contamination by the black servant Francine, the possibility of "coloured" blood in and the "[u]nfortunate propensities" of her Creole family, and resistance to her own improving influence by mixing with Francine. Her disgust at Anna's relationship with Francine and Anna's Creole culture becomes focused on Anna's "awful sing-song" Caribbean accent in speaking English (56).

In the convent Antoinette Cosway Mason has as a sewing exercise "cross-stitching silk roses on a pale background." Allowed to color the roses as she sees fit, she stitches them in the colors of Dominica, "green, blue and purple" (*WSS* 44). (Rochester will later complain that Dominica is "[t]oo much blue, too much purple, too much green" [59].) The "fire red" of her signature under the roses is the color of the Dominican flowers that disturb Rochester and the earth around Granbois, her family's Dominican estate. She stitches her Dominican difference from Englishness in the colors of her sampler. On the breakfast tray served in Antoinette and Rochester's marital bedroom are "two pink roses," "each in a small brown jug" (72). The pattern of "two roses on the tray," signifying normative upper-middle-class English heterosexual marital love, is continued (75). On the first day Rochester touches the full-blown of the roses, and the petals fall away. What Rochester does not say directly is that the action starkly exposes the yellow and yellowish brown reproductive parts of the plant. "'Have all beautiful things sad destinies?'" Rochester asks Antoinette (72). For Hester and for Rochester flowers serve "as objects onto which fantasies of gender, sexuality, and race (not to mention class) could be projected" (Looby 125). For Rochester, reproductive sexuality is always already racially coded through color.

Rhys signifies the racialized difference of Anna Morgan and Antoinette Cosway Mason, expatriate white Creole women in England, in their sustaining corporeal memories of Dominica, in which the intensely pleasurable smell, spectacle, and color of native species figure strongly. Anna Morgan's origin, memories, and response to an English forest are the markers of non-English ethnicity. The chorus girls she tours with before her affair with Walter rechristen her "the Hottentot" because she was born in a tropical place (*Voyage* 12). Sander Gilman has shown that by the late nineteenth century the "Hottentot" woman had become a European "icon of pathologically corrupted sexuality" whose physiological features were incorporated into representations of prostitutes and promiscuous women (*Difference* 255, n. 16). Walter, Anna's first lover, whose terms of endearment are "rum child, rum little devil," remarks that the "tropics would be altogether too lush" for him (*Voyage* 48, 46). He encapsulates her difference in an epithet normally descriptive of vegetation, which implies uncontrolled fertility, excess in relation to his own acculturated sense of restraint, and drunkenness. Anna, by comparison, thinks the Savernake Forest, which Walter shows her, "beautiful," "[b]ut something had happened to it. It was as if the wildness had gone out of it" (67). Maudie, an English friend from the chorus line, is disturbed by Anna's approving reading of a poem left in her Adelaide Road boarding room by a former tenant in which London is described as a "vile and stinking hole"; Maudie's discomfort is apparent in her complaints about the "blasted pineapples" among other plant motifs in the "very dirty" moulding around the walls—they make her feel the room "isn't cosy" (41).

Antoinette's red dress, glossed as making her "look intemperate and unchaste" by Rochester, is the "colour of flamboyant flowers" (of the tropical flame tree), and it gives off a scent—the "smell of vetivert and frangipanni, of cinnamon and dust and lime trees when they are flowering. The smell of the sun and the smell of the rain" (*WSS* 152, 151). Rhys implies that her otherness among the English is experiential, internalized as corporeal memory and a differently acculturated structure of desire and pleasure, and that the otherness is racialized as degeneracy. Frangipani wreaths are laid out for the bridal couple; Rochester steps on his without compunction, an action which implies his contempt for Antoinette's cultural difference. In Rochester's narrative, the wreath, like tropical flowers from the 1820s onwards, becomes metonymic of "the primitive, the exotic, and the perverse" (Looby 118). For Rochester, at the Dominican estate Granbois Antoinette embodies the "wild, untouched, above all untouched" land with its "alien, disturbing, secret loveliness," and excess (especially of floral scent). At the core of both Antoinette and the land Rochester senses a mystery, a secret of otherness, which unsettles him: "'What I see is nothing—I want what it *hides*—that is not nothing'" (*WSS* 73). To use an Irigarayan formulation, he is "threatened by 'castration,' by anything he cannot see directly, anything he cannot perceive as like himself" (Irigaray, *Speculum* 138). Rhys figures his eroticized racial anxieties through his presumptions of a recoding of a European garden of rose and orange trees. He finds "a large clear space" in the "virgin" forest he personifies as "hostile." A priest's house is in ruin, the trees in its garden have grown wild. The place has, Rochester assumes, become a site for the practice of Obeah. He becomes "lost and afraid among" the "enemy trees" of the forest, which close over his head, while "the undergrowth and creepers" catch at his legs. Rhys encodes his disorientation and sense of danger through a vertical hierarchy of the body in which the head represents rational, Christian self-command, and the plant emblems of the "native" threaten to tangle the lower body, bringing him down (*WSS* 86–87). Daniel Cosway, an Iago figure in Rhys's reinscription of *Othello* motifs,[23] plays on Rochester's racial prejudices and anxieties. The secret Rochester credulously wants to believe is a taint of promiscuity—"indiscriminate mingling"[24] he labels "intemperance and unchastity"—inherited from a white Creole ancestry.

Rhys figures Anna's state after having been scorned and abandoned by Walter as drift. Her early numbness (indifferently, "I didn't care any more" [*Voyage* 84]) is troped as drowning; she survives. Gregg writes of the sensation of drowning as "an effect of Walter's rejection and his enabling contexts—imperial history and the interlocking formations of class, gender and racial hierarchies" (131). Having complained of illness to her next landlady, Anna sings a song she had heard performed in a Glasgow music hall. The lyrics, which celebrate the pleasure of smoking, suggest a song about the New Woman or "wild woman," another signifier of whom is sexual licence:

Blow rings, rings
    Delicate rings in the air;
And drift, drift
    —something—away from despair

Anna tries "[l]egions" and "[o]ceans" in place of "something," and then associatively settles on the "Caribbean Sea" (90–91). When Ethel confronts Anna with a long list of complaints (failure to live up to her expectations, disloyalty, going on about the dark and cold), working up to "'Why don't you clear out?,'" Anna responds, "'I can't swim well enough, that's one reason'" (124). At the novel's close, Anna, delirious after a botched abortion, imagines herself crossing a racial boundary by dancing to the tune of "There's a Brown Girl in a Ring" during Dominica Carnival. In the original version of the ending Rhys revised at the request of her publisher, Anna waits for "blackness" to come (*Voyage* IV 389). The publisher interpreted blackness as death. Rhys revised the ending to imply a repetition of the cycle. In the first and the published versions of the novel blackness acquires metaphorical and primitivist resonances, manichean possibilities for Anna, and catches up the negativity of her black nurse, Meta's, hostility and of English prejudice. Froude interpreted white Creole drift as symptomatic of the demoralizing influence of the power of the elective members; Rhys pointedly links Anna's drift to dispossession; lack of marketable skills, credit to borrow money, and emotional support; youthful romantic naivety in her affair with Walter; and the demoralizing pressures of economic circumstance and English xenophobia, sexism and class prejudice.

Rochester provides his patronym to readers when (assuming an Adamic prerogative) he names Antoinette "Bertha." The garden at Granbois contains a tree of life, but any regenerative possibilities in the relationship for both of them are closed off by Rochester's contempt. The novel's title implies on one level that this contempt is the wide Sargasso Sea that separates them and Antoinette from the place that sustains her and represses the treasure Rochester has discovered and its narratability in an English world of cardboard walls and a grey wrapper. Rochester interprets Antoinette's state as they prepare to leave Granbois as "blank indifference" (*WSS* 137) and acknowledges a hatred of the "indifference" of the landscape, but "[a]bove all" a hatred of Antoinette: "For she belonged to the magic and the loveliness. She had left me thirsty" (141). The Sargasso Sea is a barren sea covered with floating, entrapping seaweed, a place, Rhys thought, where "wrecks drifted" (letter to Peggy Kirkaldy, 30 July [1957]). Drift is conceptualized as a product in Rochester and Antoinette's relationship of English xenophobia, compounded by class, and racial and sexual anxieties. Rochester's mind projects barbarism and promiscuity on to place and people. Rhys diagnoses the "unprosperous condition" of Coulibri Estate in Jamaica before it is recapitalized by Mr. Mason's fortune as a product of difficult relations of labor and property under the transitionary apprenticeship system, demoralization by the wait for English monies to compensate for loss of slave labor, xenophobia, and the hostilities attendant on social change and a racialized social hierarchy.

Rhys writes in her autobiographical narratives of growing up in Dominica of a sublime desire to sustain an oceanic identification with "a very beautiful" land (*SP* 81). She reconfigures her drift and indifference motifs on a more personal level in representing the blockages to realization of her desire for transcendence of the pain of rejection and of the real world. In the autobiographical narrative in the Black Exercise Book (1938), she figures the desire as a frustrated sublime heterosexual romance: "To me it behind the bright colours the softness grace was something very wild austere sad entirely male I wanted to identify with it to lose myself in it. [B]ut it turned its head away indifferent. & It broke my heart."[25]

The representation inverts central topoi of European imperialism: by comparison with the usual feminization of exotic landscapes, for her the land is "entirely male"; and whereas European male travelers often write of these places using an erotics of sexual ravishment, Rhys implies an unreciprocated romantic ravishment. She "work[s] off the worst" of her romantic malady "by writing poems"; her aesthetic is one in which the words "most often" used were "pain, shame, sleep, sea & silence" (BEB). She edited out the gendering of the land in "Love," fragmented memories of landscape drawn from this narrative and dated 6–12-38 (David Plante Papers). The land's gesture of rejection and the romantic malady are rewritten as part of a fraught mother-daughter relationship in Smile Please (1979), her unfinished autobiography. "Yes, she drifted away from me and when I tried to interest her she was indifferent," Rhys writes of Minna Rees Williams (43). Rhys suggests that as a child she then sought oceanic identification with black surrogate maternal figures—servants Ann Tewitt, Francine, and Victoria—the landscape,[26] and finally the alternate world of the English book. Looking back, Rhys interprets the desire to lose herself "in the immense world of books" as an effort "to blot out the real world which was so puzzling" to her with its complexities of sex, religion, racial politics and tension, and class, inflected by gender, as the "business about ladies and gentlemen" (SP 62).

Late nineteenth- and early twentieth-century Dominican autoethnographic discourses of nature and place are integral to Rhys's worlding as a Dominican. For her the materiality of gender, race, ethnicity, class, nation, and desire was always already written or articulated in these discourses and the historical narratives embedded in them, and she engages and rewrites them, even as she transculturates from the position of the white Creole expatriate European literary and historical narratives, tropes, and motifs. Dominican journalism and the autoethnographic textual strategies of particular journalists and authors are crucial intertexts of and models for Rhys's writing.

NOTES

1. He compiled and published the Leeward Islands Almanac during this period, and his editorships of newspapers also included an earlier stint with the Dominican and the Echo (Trinidad) and later the Leeward Islands Free Press (1905–1908) and subeditorship of the Chronicle newspapers in Trinidad (before 1872).

2. [Lockhart], editorial introduction, "Dominica & Its Boiling Lake" [2]–[3].

3. Bringing to notice and making known are stock postures of Dominican autoethnographers and publishers towards their overseas audiences in the period.

4. The 1914 edition of A Text-book of Tropical Agriculture lists the following distinctions: F.L.S., C.M.Z.S., Corresponding Member of the New York Academy of

Sciences and of the Chamber of Agriculture of Basseterre, Guadelope, and Honorary Member of the Royal Agricultural and Commercial Society of British Guiana, and of the Central Agricultural Board of Trinidad. The book won a prize offered by the Jamaican government in 1890 for the best text-book of tropical agriculture. Nicholls was knighted in 1926 for his services to tropical medicine and agriculture. He is the historical original of "Old Master" in Phyllis Shand Allfrey's *The Orchid House* (1953).

5. Evidence of W. Marie, *Dominica Guardian* (Special Edition) 22 December 1893: [3].

6. *British Parliamentary Papers: West India Royal Commission* 123, 126. Davies's evidence is reported on 127–29, Lockhart's on 135–36.

7. "Indian Country" is usually termed the Carib Quarter.

8. The evidence of W. Marie, H. Le Blanc, and F. Pinard is reported in special editions of the *Dominica Guardian* 22 December 1893: [3]; 22 December 1893: [2]; 11 December 1893: [3].

9. [Righton], obituary of Joseph Fadelle. See also A. R. Lockhart's untitled reply to European racist remarks in the *Dominican* 1 December 1877: [3].

10. Reported in the "Local" column, *Dominica Dial* 24 March 1888: [2]; 14 April 1888: [3].

11. Steber, "Obeah Legislation"; "Dominica" [pseudonym]; and Steber, "What Is Obeah?"

12. Other examples of this mapping include "A Public Nuisance" and "Juvenile Lawlessness and the Compulsory Education Act."

13. "The Special Inquiry," *Dominica Guardian* (Special Edition), 29 November 1893, [2].

14. The author's name given here, Earnest H. Crosby, may be a pun. A slightly revised version of the poem was published in Crosby's *Swords and Ploughshares* (1903).

15. See, for example, A. R. Lockhart in the *Dominican* 1 December 1877: [3].

16. Chamberlain was secretary for the colonies in the British government.

17. Subscriptions from Trinidad, Grenada, and Dominica helped subsidize T. Fisher Unwin's publication of *Froudacity*. D. Wood, "Biographical Note," *Froudacity* 20–21.

18. Anna would help him sex his nutmeg trees when they first flowered (*Voyage* 62). Nicholls explains in *A Text-book of Tropical Agriculture* that "[o]ne male to every eight or ten females is quite enough; and those male trees should be, if possible, on the windward side of the plantation, so that the pollen may be carried by the wind to the pistils" (181).

19. See, for example, Sir W. Molesworth's speech in the House of Commons on 25 July 1848. Davies cites the speech in his evidence to the 1897 West India Royal Commission 127.

20. The mace is currently housed in the Dominica Museum.

21. The story seems to date from the late 1930s or early 1940s.

22. On the Dreads see also Honychurch 245–51 and 277–80.

23. In a letter to Diana Athill dated 28 April 1964, Rochester, Rhys says, "becomes as fierce as Heathcliff and as jealous as Othello" (*Letters* 269).

24. promiscuous: "characterised by or involving indiscriminate mingling" (*Macquarie Dictionary* 1379).

25. The Black Exercise Book is unpaginated. I have deposited in the Department of Special Collections at the University of Tulsa a copy of parts of my manuscript annotated with my page referencing for my quotations from the Black Exercise Book.

26. The land had "turned its head away, indifferent, and that broke my heart' (*SP* 81)

Chapter 2

"Grilled Sole" and an Experience of "Mental" Seduction

By Jean Rhys's own account in her Black Exercise Book, now held among her papers at the University of Tulsa, "lately," while she was writing the "last adventure love adventure of a woman who is growing old"—*Good Morning, Midnight*, another autobiographical reference establishes the year as 1938—she had been "drunk mostly all the time." One day she woke up to find her novel "wiped clean out" of her mind, and she compulsively wrote an autobiographical narrative of having been "mentally" seduced as a fourteen-year-old in Dominica by an English gentleman, "Mr. Howard," aged seventy-two or seventy-three, one of her mother's friends. The absentee owner of an estate on another Caribbean island, he had visited Dominica on his way back to England after inspecting his property. The year would have been 1905. The prose of Rhys's narrative is not polished. For Rhys the writing offered an opportunity of "just for once writing as I wished without being forced to torture the thing into the form of a novel."

Rhys's narrative recalls a series of incidents constituting a sexual rite of passage from naive girlhood to "doomed" womanhood, which had gone out of her "memory like a stone": an unreported indecent assault of her by "Mr. Howard"; her imaginary participation in a sadistic, pornographic "serial story" he tells her on subsequent outings, a story that interpellates her Creole sexual subjectivity,[1] in conjunction with a pattern of domestic violence and teasing, to give her a permanent "kink"; and his distressing second touch of her (a possibly violent sexual act, equivocally a rape), about which Rhys leaves disconnected textual fragments after the main account has apparently been brought to a close. The main account is a narrative of "terrible" self-recognition: "Yes, that is true. Pain humiliation submission that is for me." The experience is, she insists, "[t]he thing that formed me made me as I am—the thing I want to write about" (BEB).

Rhys contextualizes her vulnerability to and complicity with Mr. Howard's sexual advances, mainly in her relations with her parents and conflicted feelings about her great-grandfather and black Dominican people. She postponed the move from the contextualization to the account of actual assault and "mental" seduction several times; it is the very difficulty for her of writing beyond the ending of the account of these incidents that establishes its "textual authority" (Davies 113). The most traumatic aspects of her sexual experience with Mr. Howard are narrated in the extant manuscript through the perceptual splitting of disembodiment and through catachresis. The narrative moments of disembodiment and catachresis in Rhys's account of her corporeal memory of "seduction" highlight some of the complexities, crises of figuration, and blind spots of her gendered Creole subjectivity. I work to read the narrative in what Joan W. Scott has described as "the operations of the complex and changing discursive processes by which identities are ascribed, resisted, or embraced" (Scott 33).

The uncanny moment of Rhys's recuperation of the memory of having been seduced is one of temporal and spatial estrangement: she represents it as a movement over an "edge," a "border," but not to the "Madness," "Death" or "Paralysis" that might put the "finishing touch" to the alcoholic "wreck" she has made herself; she is sure she would "find" herself in Mr. Howard's house, ambiguously either the imaginary flower-bedecked house of his serial story to which she is to be abducted and in which she is seldom to wear clothes, to wait on his table, and to be punished for the "slightest mistake," or his temporary residence in Dominica (BEB). Explicitly the narrative is energized by two moments in which Rhys's gendered Creole experience is estranged by generalizations in European books: Richard Hughes's representation of Margaret Fernandez in *A High Wind in Jamaica* (1929, titled *The Innocent Voyage* for U.S. publication) and an unnamed book on psychoanalysis by a "gent" (BEB), which she skimmed in Sylvia Beach's avant-garde Parisian bookstore, Shakespeare and Company. The author may be confidently identified, for Rhys summarizes part of Sigmund Freud's account of his renunciation of his seduction theory of hysteria in "On the History of the Psychoanalytic Movement," which appeared in translation in his *Collected Papers. Volume I* (1924). Rhys says no, "honey," to Freud (BEB): she is not seduced by what Luce Irigaray terms the "seduction function" of Freud's reduction of "the little girl's seduced . . . desire" to "fantasy" (*Speculum* 38), to "fictitious" discourse (Freud 300). In her summary Rhys fixes on the word "fictitious."[2] The details of Rhys's "case" of having been seduced are produced as lived experience to counter Freud's overgeneralization. Rhys's attention to early childhood memories and relationships with her parents and nurse conforms broadly with a popularized understanding of the protocols of the psychoanalytic session.

Gendered colonial reading of European stories is described gothically near the beginning of Rhys's narrative. Her black nurse, Meta, tells her that the eyes of girls who read books "drop out" and they see "their own eyes looking at them from the page" (BEB). Without taking up the issues of gender, the historical specificity of the reader or reading practices, and positioning the colonial reader/consumer of stories as essentially passive, Diana Brydon and Helen Tiffin argue of Rhys's repetition of Meta's view in *Smile Please* that it is a "precise evocation of colonial textual interpellation. To the European and his book belongs [sic] the power of gaze and the right of perspective. And the result of that authoritative gaze is colonial self-perception as deviant from the European norm. The colonial does not read the text, the text reads/constructs her" (106). In the Black Exercise Book, Rhys challenges Meta, and Meta responds:

> If my eyes dropped out I would'nt [sic] be able to see them They drop out except the black part you see with that stays right there in your head
> I half believed it I imagined the black sockets of my eyes the horrible black pupil like a black headed pin[.]

Meta's is but one of a number of disciplinary gazes at Rhys: Rhys is the object, too, of the disciplinary gazes of her mother, her family, the nuns at the convent she attended, the local nonwhite people, and Mr. and Mrs. Howard, with all of whom she interacts verbally. Meta's image of perceptual splitting uncannily prefigures moments of disembodiment when Rhys's autobiographical protagonist (a voracious reader turned writer) becomes the observer or potential observer of her own traumatized sexual body.

"HE DID NT [SIC] TOUCH ME AGAIN ONLY ONCE"

Rhys explicitly represents Mr. Howard's "seduction" of her as a "mental" rather than a "physical" one (BEB). On the general question of complicity in seduction, Jane Gallop notes that "[t]he dichotomy active/passive is always equivocal in seduction, that is what distinguishes it from rape" (*The Daughter's Seduction* 56). This ambivalence is apparent in Rhys's representation of her experience. The descriptor "sexual abuse," which significantly shifts moral responsibility, was not available to her: sexual abuse emerged publicly in the West as a category of child abuse in 1975, child abuse as a medicalized category of cruelty to children in the early 1960s (Hacking 275, 269). Certainly for Rhys the events of her relationship with Mr. Howard were traumatic. I cite recent discussion of narrativizing sexual abuse to highlight aspects of Rhys's recovery and recounting of repressed traumatic experience.

Rhys was first "captivated" by Mr. Howard's "elegant" speech and treatment of her as if she were a "grown up" on his visit to her family home. While Mr. Howard and Rhys are sitting together on a secluded bench in the Botanical Gardens during an outing, Mr. Howard asks Rhys her age, and when she tells him she is fourteen he responds that she is "quite old enough to have a lover" and touches her breasts. She thinks the action is a mistake, which can be denied seemingly by both of them if she sits "quite still." Her response is somatized: "my breasts cold & dead" (BEB). Fearing her story will not be believed over any denial by Mr. Howard and not even thinking of telling her mother, Rhys does not report the incident to her parents from whom she is already alienated—from her mother by repeated beatings of her, from her father by his domestic and emotional aloofness. The effect of her silence may have been the appearance of consent. Rhys's resistance to a second excursion with Mr. Howard—she says she would prefer to read—is interpreted as rudeness by her mother and she is forced to accompany him. On the same park bench on a subsequent outing Mr. Howard initiates the telling of his pornographic serial story by asking whether she would like to belong to him. Rhys then "lived in this dream" of his, interrupting his narrative only once to ask whether they could have "grilled sole," "that English fish," for dinner sometimes (BEB). Rhys's adult humiliation at the memory of her entanglement emerges at several points in the narrative.

Mr. Howard seems to have known the limits of the English law concerning indecent assault and carnal knowledge and to have been a turn-of-the-century sex tourist, exploiting differences in age of consent legislation. The vigorous debate from 1912 to 1914 over raising the age of consent in Britain, which became caught up with the moral crusade of the Women's Social and Political Union and the panic over the "White Slave Traffic," could well have made Rhys aware of the English law. Rhys's awareness of aspects of English law informs her narrative, and the intertextual relation of the law and the representation of seduction works to imply at least an ambivalence about the criminality of the assault and to construct the effect of Mr. Howard's storytelling in terms of a rape/enforced prostitution scenario. In 1905 under English law the age of consent for indecent assault was thirteen; for carnal knowledge, sixteen. These ages had been set in 1885 under the Criminal Law Amendment Act as a means of dealing with child prostitution and the "white slave traffic," which were seen largely as working-class problems. The choice of the ages was highly contested in England in the early 1880s. In the House of Lords the choice was framed as a weighing of the question of a generalized chronological age of responsibility by which girls had acquired "faculties of discretion, will-force, and knowledge of the world, required to appreciate the dangers to which they were exposed, and the way of escape" (Lord Mount Temple 404) against the dangers to men of sexually precocious girls, constructed as both wily temptresses and potential blackmailers.[3] The age of consent in the Leeward Islands Federation was eleven ("Cases"). Under Leeward Islands law, Rhys was "quite old enough to have a lover." Mr. Howard seems to have partly internalized the prohibition of English law. Chronologically Rhys is for him over the English age of consent for indecent assault and he says in the fantasy scenario he "should'nt [sic] force" Rhys to "submit" to him.

Retrospectively, Rhys insists that even though she was fourteen, her worldly development was that of a twelve-year-old, having been held back by a "religious fit" and a "writing fit" (BEB). This may be one line of implicit query of her technically legal capacity to give sexual consent under English law; the second is Rhys's consistent metaphorical construction of her consent to seduction by the story as having been procured by the "intoxicating" effects of Mr. Howard's attentions to her and her ambitions, and the installments functioning as "doses" of a "drug because thats [sic] what it was" (BEB). In the 1885 British Criminal Law Amendment Bill "connection" with a "woman or girl" who had been administered sufficient "stupefying or overpowering" liquor or drug to produce a "state of insensibility" or want of "the power to express her will in regard to the act" was made a misdemeanor; sexual intercourse with a person taken "possession" of in this state could well constitute rape (Hopwood, Webster 710–11). The letter of the English law acknowledged physical rather than imaginative insensibility. Under English law at fourteen Rhys would have been in the "custody," "control" and "possession" of her father (Simpson 112, 115).

Mr. Howard proposes that Rhys will belong to him after he has abducted her, having lured her with a story, and removed her abroad to another Caribbean island where she will enter his sexual service. This part of Rhys's reconstruction of Mr. Howard's serial story conforms to a stock European "white slave" abduction scenario, which often involved drugging. The frequency and typicality of such scenarios were highly contested in Britain before the First World War, even by a women's rights activist like Teresa Billington-Greig. The two punishments Rhys mentions—waiting naked on Mr. Howard's table in front of guests, having her hands tied with a rope covered in flowers—are, for the day, brothel fantasies. The first also entails a loss of gendered racialized class prestige. "The British Empire," David Dabydeen writes, "was as much a pornographic as an economic project," energized by the "perverse eroticism of black labour and the fantasy of domination, bondage and sado-masochism" (61).

In a Caribbean colonial context Rhys is blackened in Mr. Howard's story. In relation to Mr. Howard, Rhys is "the little saleté" (BEB)—filth, dirtiness. Abduction, ownership, punishment, naked female bodies, tied hands, a woman serving at an Englishman's table dressed down to reveal her "body for consumption" by white eyes (Low 83)[4] are motifs drawn from the cultural archive of slavery. Mr. Howard sees within the naive white Creole girl a sexualized black slave/servant. This accords with a nineteenth-century and early twentieth-century stereotype of the white Creole: that white Creoles were often merely passing for white, covering up a family history of "miscegenation." Sander Gilman also suggests that in nineteenth-century European codes of representation promiscuous women and prostitutes held within their bodies the stigmata of the black slave/servant (*Difference* 102). Mr. Howard's "I should nt [sic] force you to submit to me [. . .] I shall punish you & force you to" (BEB) recalls historical scenes of cross-racial, cross-class, heterosexual rape. In fantasy dressed down, dressed in jewelry associated with black women (an earring long enough to touch her shoulder and many bracelets), Rhys bares white skin. Their fantasy relationship is structured by fetish rituals, which are part of a pathology of empire: master/slave, discipline/bondage, English/colonial, male/female, a hand fetish—"He said—How white your hands are against the grass [. . .] a whiter hue than white" (BEB), her hands tied with a flower-covered rope. Mr. Howard seems to derive pleasure from the fantasy spectacle of a white-skinned girl performing racialized, gendered, sexualized menial labor, and being mastered. The relationship eroticizes Rhys's transformations from girl to sexualized woman, from white woman to black slave/servant, and from black slave/servant to white mistress (in sexual and socioeconomic senses), yet nonetheless owned by a white man. The *fantasy*, the "mental" seduction, offers Rhys "the ritual exercise of social risk and social transformation" (McClintock 143); implicit consensual boundaries are constantly negotiated during Mr. Howard's telling of his story.

Rhys listens to the "will" of her "lover"—"Cruelty submission utter submission"—and his representation of her meets her commonsense expectations: "It fitted in with all I knew of life with all Id [sic] ever felt. It fitted like a hook fits an eye" (BEB). Her vulnerability to this kind of self-recognition is contextualized in patterns of punishment or anticipated punishment and dread abandonment in her life, patterns structured by a normative moralizing of middle-class white Creole domestic and religious purity. In a turn-of-the-century sexual context, "submission" was synonymous with consent; in the House of Commons in 1885 carnal knowledge was described as submission "to be ravished" (Mr. West 691). In 1905 Dominican society was rigidly stratified on ethnic and racial lines, to a lesser extent on religious lines. As Rhys makes clear in the Black Exercise Book, the middle-class Rees Williams family occupied a position beneath the solidly English middle class. Colored middle-class journalists and politicians advocated revised standards of social value, replacing an ethnic/racial hierarchy with a hierarchy based on earned "position," "intelligence," and "social merit" ("The Colour Question" 24 Sept. 1902 [2]) measured by a respectability entailing "soberness, honesty, industry and integrity" ("Moralizing" [1]). During the nineteenth century, too, the white Creole became the object of a European ethnographic discourse about tropical degeneration: white Creoles were seen to risk in "the physical and social climate of the tropics" and proximity to racial others, a degeneration apparent in disease, sickliness, and excessive appetites (Stepan 103). In popularized form the discourse was adapted in Dominica by the colored middle class from the mid-1880s to naturalize the inevitability of the decay of white authority and to moralize the racial injustice of the "forced conditions" that artificially guaranteed its continuity ("Rubbish on the West Indies" [3]).

As I have shown in chapter 1, racial adaptation/indigenization was figured in vegetative and horticultural tropes that distinguished between native and exotic species. Mary Douglas has popularized academically the idea that "societies define themselves in part by their relationship to pollution" (Hacking 279). Pollution beliefs, expressed in a language of "exhortation," are inextricably linked with the "moral values" and "social rules" that guarantee "good citizenship" (Douglas 3). Rhys's contextualizing narrative instances a range of moralizations of her as threat to the gendered purity of the family home or a gendered domestic role: Meta moralizes her reading and her dirty nails; her mother singles her out to moralize her failure to "be like other people," which Rhys glosses as being "alien" to her mother's standards; Mother St. Anthony, one of the "heretic" Rhys's teachers at the convent she attended (the Rees Williams family was Anglican), moralizes the class's sewing as redemption for "the souls in Purgatory"—and Rhys realises that her work, "so grimy & crumpled that it was nearly black," wouldn't "help them much" (BEB). Meta's projected punishments would abandon her to looking at her own pupil-less eyes and weeping tears of blood (for the dirty nails and other offences against domestic order). Mother St. Anthony gives "[l]ong" and "terrifying" descriptions of the souls of sinners in Purgatory.

Her mother would beat her; Rhys says she seldom knew why: "~~I was an irritating child I suppose~~" (words crossed out by Rhys). Rhys says no to Freud; at about twelve she said no to her mother's beatings, in place of her "usual stubborn silence": "God curse you if you touch me I ll [sic] kill you. Something that was no." The word "whipping" is heavily scored out in a way that suggests the visual evidence of marks on her body. Using a language of demonic possession and attempted exorcism, Rhys thinks her mother must have seen "something alien" in her "which would make" her "unhappy"; the beatings are efforts to "root it out at all costs," to "~~drive out something~~ she saw in me that was alien that would devour me. She was trying to drive it out at all costs" (BEB). Rhys implies that her possession violates her mother's acculturated boundaries of other/self, outside/inside, impurity/purity, corruption/innocence. Cannibalism, too, is an aspect of racial stereotypes of the Carib Indian and of the black African. (Dominica has one of the two surviving Carib communities on Caribbean islands.)[5] Rhys represents her naughtiness by her mother's standards as a self-cannibalizing othered appetite, marked as a racial atavism.

In Rhys's narrative her "race," "ethnicity," and cultural identifications are interpellated in many everyday contexts and through the sexual desire produced by Mr. Howard's story. She has a "drawling" Caribbean accent marked as "colonial" by English people. Her identification as white produces abjection when local black people call whites "white cockroaches," a name that summons up her utter terror of the large flying cockroaches of Dominica. "One could hardly blame them," she concedes, "I would feel sick with shame at some of the stories I heard of the slave days told casually even jokingly" (BEB). The name-calling, the stories disrupt the putative link between whiteness and purity in racial and moral discourses, which mark boundaries between high and low, cleanliness and filth, the civilized and the bestial, white and black, light and dark, reason and emotion. Her "sick revolt" at her family's implication in slavery and its colonial aftermath makes her desire "to be indentified [sic] once & for all with the other side which of course was impossible I could nt [sic] change the colour of my skin" (BEB). Helen Tiffin observes that in narratives from former European colonies, "the texts of Europe" are often represented as having "entered the minds and the bodies of the colonized to infect and dis/ease them" ("Metaphor" 52). Rhys links her somatic distress at her embodiment in white skin—sickening shame, "sick revolt"—to the legacies of slavery circulating in an oral discursive economy. The gazes of African Dominican people, her mother, and Mr. Howard are penetrative, seeing within her, and punitive; they break her bodily schema into the "thousand details, anecdotes, stories" (Fanon 111) that fabricate her "hysterical" identity across signifiers of gender, race, class, and sexuality.[6] The abjection produces in Rhys cross-racial and, in the racialized labor economy of Dominica, cross-class identifications, which cut across her awareness that her whiteness enables her to see herself "powerful & perhaps lightly for a women [sic]" (BEB).

Rhys can identify with Spanish Creole Margaret Fernandez in Richard Hughes's *A High Wind in Jamaica*; she implies a causal and fatalistic connection between what she reads as Margaret having been "beaten in the thoroughgoing West Indian fashion" as a child, sexual "use" of her by the sailors, and her being thrown overboard: the moment of estrangement in her reading is brought about by her sense that Hughes represents Margaret, and by extension other white Creoles, as "idiotic" (BEB). Margaret's governess, "whose blood was possibly not pure," was wont to beat her charges "ferociously with a hair-brush" (Hughes 15). (In thinking about her great-grandfather, James Potter Lockhart, and his many sexual liaisons with enslaved women, Rhys mentions her nagging sense of the racial indeterminacy of her supposedly Spanish great-grandmother.) On board ship Margaret tells the other children a "story about a princess who had lots and lots of clothes and was always beating her servant for making mistakes and shutting him up in a dark cupboard" (141); the story, which Emily thinks "very stupid," is interrupted by a drunken Captain Jonsen, whose voice evinces "suppressed excitement." Margaret is terrified, turning "yellow as cheese"; Jonsen proceeds to put "one hand" under Emily's chin and begins "to stroke her hair with the other" (142–43).

In response to this sexual advance, Emily, an English child, bites Jonsen's thumb; Margaret, having lost like all Creoles, Hughes says, "some of the traditional mental mechanism of Europe" (15), is first seemingly "exaggeratedly frightened of all the men," but then begins to follow them "about the deck like a dog," attaching herself, it is implied sexually, to Otto (144). By the time Emily kills the Dutch captain, Margaret's appearance has been transformed, her "dulled eyes standing out from her small, skull-like face" (176) and the sailors feel towards her a "contempt" and "complete lack of pity in her obvious illness and misery . . . in direct proportion to the childhood she had belied" (179). Believing she had killed the Dutch captain, the sailors have no compunction in throwing her overboard. She is picked up by a second boat and, realizing her abandonment, returns to the other children rather than to Otto.

The details of her physiognomy pathologize the "degeneracy" of a perceived other (Gilman, "Sexology" 85); their invocation of a late nineteenth- and early twentieth-century iconography of active female sexuality raises the spectre of venereal disease (Gilman, *Difference* 105). In early twentieth-century Britain "idiocy" had popular, legal, and medical currency. Legally and medically, idiocy was a category of mental defectiveness. The Protection of Mentally Defective Persons Bill of 1920 defined idiots as "persons so deeply defective in mind from birth or from an early age as to be unable to guard themselves against common physical dangers."[7] Women classed as mentally defective (especially as feeble-minded, a less severe category than idiots) were represented as highly vulnerable sexually in evidence given to the Royal Commission on the Care and Control of the Feeble-Minded (1908). Mr. Bagenal, a general inspector of the Local Government Board for the Yorkshire District, articulated a common sentiment: "Feeble-minded women are particularly open to the seductions of men. They seem to be deficient in will power and the power of resistance to attacks upon their virtue. In some the moral sense is altogether absent" (Report 25).

Rhys construes what her mother and what Mr. Howard see in her in several ways: she thinks her mother sees "something alien" in her character; in relation to Mr. Howard she is a "little saleté"[8] with the capacity to "go from bad to worse" after the experience, and not healthy enough. The suspicious Mrs. Howard tells her she is "a wicked girl" who will be punished (BEB). Judith Lewis Herman notes that

[p]articipation in forbidden sexual activity . . . confirms the abused child's sense of badness. Any gratification that the child is able to glean from the exploitative situation becomes proof in her mind that she instigated and bears full responsibility for the abuse. If she ever experienced sexual pleasure, enjoyed the abuser's special attention, bargained for favors, or used the sexual relationship to gain privileges, these sins are adduced as evidence of her innate wickedness. (104)

Rhys's mapping of her "bad," "dirty" character across a health/ill-health dichotomy may be read in two discursive contexts: the ethnographic discourse of the white Creole and the early twentieth-century British sexual discourse that distinguished between the healthy mother and the promiscuous woman or amateur (prostitute), the sexual activity of the latter being constructed as "subhuman" (Bland 376), her character as "ignorant" and "very dirty" (Marie Stopes, qtd. in Bland 384). In this second discourse "the categories "health/ill health" overlaid those of virtue/vice" (Bland 377), the healthy mother being entrusted with the responsibility of being the "guardian of the race" (Bland 374) and white imperial nationhood. In the "Facts of Life" chapter of *Smile Please: An Unfinished Autobiography* Rhys does not mention explicitly the "Mr. Howard" episode; she refers merely to "sexual experiences, for of course some occurred," which she tried to "shut away" at the "back" of her mind "not knowing that this would cause me to remember them in detail all the rest of my life" (62). These experiences, however, produce Rhys's transformation from disgusted reader of the childbirth section of one of her father's medical books to avid reader of books about prostitutes in the Carnegie Library in Roseau.

Did Mr. Howard touch Rhys once or twice? Her statement, "He did nt [sic] touch me again only once," is ambiguous: "only once" may affirm or contradict the first part of the sentence. Rhys says she has "often wondered" at the attitude of people close to her: "surely" she must have "betrayed" herself to them (BEB). At this stage in the narrative she uses what Michele J. Davies calls "perspectival language" ("I believe") to evoke the "possibility" of her mother having suspected "that something was up," but at a time when Rhys was well under his "spell" and "lied fluently." This is how she interprets a new coldness in her mother's manner to Mr. Howard, a questioning of her and a discouraging of her from "going out with him."

> He did nt [sic] touch me again only once
> > That day when I came home my mother said Why have you been crying?
> > I have nt [sic]
> > Now dont [sic] lie to me

The time at which her mother questions her strongly suggests that he touched her "again only once" (BEB).

"I LIE WITH MY FACE AGAINST THE EARTH CRINGING WAITING—SICK MAD WITH TERROR UNABLE TO MOVE CRINGING WAITING"

This sentence is from a remembered nightmare, placed after a fragmented series of memories of childhood. Herman writes of the "traumatic dreams" of trauma survivors that "[t]hey often include fragments of the traumatic event in exact form with little or no imaginative elaboration. . . . They are often experienced with terrifying immediacy, as if occurring in the present" (39). Rhys's nightmare has the "terrifying immediacy" of present-tense narration; it plays out at least Rhys's anxieties in her relationship with Mr. Howard and her desire for maternal solicitude and moves to articulate what may be covered by her lie to her mother.[9] Rhys first reworked the nightmare fictionally in an abandoned, fragmentary story dated 4 December 1938 and titled "Mr. Howard's House./ CREOLE." Mr. Howard does not explicitly figure in the fragments. It is a story of two sisters, Elsa and Audrey. Elsa has focused her romantic desire on a Captain Grieg. He had once taken her for walks. She fears she has been "wicked"; the earlier history of their relationship is not developed. Later Rhys revised parts of the nightmare as Antoinette Cosway Mason's second premonitionary dream of sexual menace in *Wide Sargasso Sea*.

In the nightmare the first person narrator leaves a house in the company of a man and is taken through a forest to a large room with an earth floor surrounded by a stone wall. She is wearing a beautiful dress, which she tries to hold up out of the dirt, but sick with fear at the inevitable that is about to happen, she stumbles over the dress and continues to follow him, crawling on her hands and knees, and is eventually reduced to immobility "cringing waiting": "It is here." In the top margin Rhys adds: "I am the earth & the core of the earth" (BEB). Within the normative hierarchies that interpellate a gendered white middle-class subjectivity, her progress is one of "degradation," of "regression" to a motility associated with female servants, stereotyped racial others,[10] and infants, a spectre of the primitivized. She progresses, too, to a kind of loss of self-boundary—"I am the earth & the core of the earth"—which can be a key symptom of child sexual trauma (Williamson 135). The desired loss of self-boundary promises disembodied invisibility at the point of "it" happening. Probably still part of the dream, she wakes screaming at this point to be comforted by her mother and scolded for frightening her young sister.[11] She tells her mother that she dreamt she was "in hell."

For Rhys to acknowledge sexual fear and to take the fragmentary narrative of the second touch to the point of "it" happening, the man's face has to become "black," "like a devil," "sly," with a "look of hate and loathing" (BEB). The cringing fear is linked with her earlier cringing at black Dominican hatred and loathing of white people in spite of a personal sympathy with local black people that makes her something of an outsider in her social circles. The contempt is epitomized for Rhys in their term "cockroaches," an instance of the kind of "metaphysical condensation" that Toni Morrison argues in another context "transform[s] social and historical differences into universal differences" and "prevents human contact and exchange" (68). (Morrison is describing the othering of blackness in the white imagination; Rhys calls this othering of whiteness in the black imagination "behaving badly.") Rhys can articulate "it" and dread fear of "it" to a point within the metonymic chain of a colonial interracial rape mythology. The "mad" female Creole figure crawling on all fours recalls the brutalized and desouled Bertha Mason in *Jane Eyre*.

"STRANGE WAILS THEY MAKE SUCH AN ECHO IN MY HEAD"

There is a limit in Mr. Howard's pornographic story—"I should nt [sic] force you to submit to me" (BEB)—but the context in which he articulates it opens it to two interpretive possibilities. Understood as a "normative statement, a *law*" of conduct, an etiquette of a particular kind of touch (consonant with English legislation governing the age of consent for sexual intercourse), it may function and indeed I would suggest has functioned to "cover up" (Irigaray, *Speculum* 37) the extent of the "seduction." For Carole Angier, Teresa O'Connor, and Coral Ann Howells, the touching of Rhys's breasts and the pornographic objectification of Rhys in and by Mr. Howard's story are the extent of the "seduction." Read differently, Mr. Howard articulates the limit at the moment of his transgression of it. In Mr. Howard's fantasy Rhys is to be punished for the "slightest mistake," and for Rhys, who represents herself consistently as an always and unwillfully transgressing child, the mistake happens

inevitably fatefully
Oh well I should nt [sic] force you to submit to me
strange wails they make such an echo in my head—of words I'd never heard them
spoken aloud only the thig [sic] never the words
I shall punish you & force you to (BEB)

The words Rhys has never heard spoken aloud may be identified as Mr. Howard's. If some of the wails are her own, they are in her only partially sensate

perception of the event overwhelmed by or lost in Mr. Howard's verbal accompaniment to his "force." Tactile and visual perception are notably missing. The
memory is void of any embodied desiring subjectivity on Rhys's part. Today
analysts treating trauma patients work to draw out all of the "bodily sensations"
of the "traumatic imagery" (Herman 177). In an analysis of Harriet Jacobs' *Incidents in the Life of a Slave Girl* (1861), Anne B. Dalton argues that the image of
a would-be seducer whispering "'foul words'" in the ear "also suggests greater
sexual abuse than the narrator literally reports. . . . In parables and folklore, the
ear has traditionally been one site of the virginal woman's molestation and im-
pregnation" (42).

"THE FRANGIPANI FLOWERS MUST BE CAREFULLY PICKED"

Vegetative tropes, as I have argued in chapter 1, were used by William Davies
to represent white settlers and settlement in Dominica. In her fiction Rhys
shifts between figuring European settlers and white Creoles as exotics or natives,
often with white, possibly white, or partly white flowers. There is a species of
frangipani native to the Caribbean. In *Child-Loving: The Erotic Child and Victorian Culture*, James R. Kincaid notes, too, the "widespread connection of children with plants, a connection so pervasive that the same word, nursery, can be
used for the place where both are brought up and managed" (90). A short fragment is placed after the nightmare and the glossing of it to the mother as hell:

The frangipani flowers must be carefully picked for if the branch is broken the tree
bleeds huge drops of thick white blood drip from it.
  I am still young enough to know that everything is alive & I turn my eyes away
not to see the tree bleed (BEB)

Rhys adjusted the first part of the last sentence to "I know quite well everything is alive." This fragment, I suggest, may effect the representation of Rhys's
embodied experience of a second touch—my reading and her inscription made
plausible with reference both to a Dominican metaphorical discourse of ra-
cial/ethnic "nativeness" and the English tradition of figuring male seduction of
women as the picking of flowers. Violence, excessive force, wounds/tears the
tree/Creole, the white blood figuring catechrestically both semen and a fetishized
"pure" European genealogy. The drops and Rhys's tears, which prompt her
mother's questioning, are reminiscent of Meta's warning that the "unclean" Rhys
will weep "tears of blood." The representation of a second touch may be effected
by a tropological objectification of Rhys's sexual body that removes agency and
desiring subjectivity. Rhys's witness of the bleeding tree shifts to the immediacy
of present tense. In a reading of *Don't: A Woman's Word*, Janice Williamson
argues that Elly Danica's "dislodgement of the self from the body" in her perception of having been multiply raped as an eleven-year-old by men including her
father—"I" becomes "A body . . . The body," an "it" "no longer capable of re-

sponse," losing her voice in the present-tensed process—is the "psychological splitting" that "initiates" Danica's amnesia and yet ultimately "provides her with the narrative distance" to recount the event (139).[12] Rhys's inscription of a probable second touch may evince a similar psychological splitting, reenacting a dislodgement of the self from the troped Creole body, not, however, in the telling consciously acknowledged to be hers. In *Smile Please*, Rhys reports having told a Frenchman in Paris, "'I can abstract myself from my body.' He looked so shocked that I asked if I was speaking bad French. He said, '*oh non, mais . . . c'est horrible.*' And yet for so long that was what I did" (118).

A tree figures crucially, too, in Rhys's revision of the nightmare as one of Antoinette Cosway Mason's premonitionary dreams in *Wide Sargasso Sea*. Here the nightmare emblematizes her fear of a gendered colonial sexual life outside the safety of the convent. The prospect, raised by her stepfather, Mr. Mason, and largely through innuendo, "almost" chokes her: "It was like that morning when I found the dead horse. Say nothing and it may not be true" (49). The poisoned horse had been lying under the frangipani tree; its death marked for the Cosway family a loss of racialized caste. In Jamaican terms the Cosways have become walking backra (white people), in a society in which ownership of a horse conferred class prestige. Annette, Antoinette's mother, understands the death of the horse as a marooning, a reduction of them to the level of the isolated black communities that resisted the plantation system and its forced and coercive racial hierarchies. Antoinette wakes from the nightmare and is comforted by Sister Marie Augustine, to whom she says,

"I dreamed I was in Hell."
   "That dream is evil. Put it from your mind—never think of it again," and she rubbed my cold hands to warm them. (51)

The earthen floored large room surrounded by a stone wall becomes an enclosed garden, a religious symbol of the Virgin. The trees in it are unfamiliar, different from those in the forest. She realizes that the inevitable that is about to happen will occur at the top of a set of stairs leading upwards from the garden:

I stumble over my dress and cannot get up. I touch a tree and my arms hold on to it. "Here, here." But I think I will not go any further. The tree sways and jerks as if it is trying to throw me off. Still I cling and the seconds pass and each one is a thousand years. "Here, in here," a strange voice said, and the tree stopped swaying and jerking. (51)

The "Here, here," a homonym for "hear, hear," seem to be the words of the man, whom she is following, whose face is metonymically "black with hatred," and who has said in the forest, "Not here, not yet" (51). "Here, in here" seem to be the words of the tree as it ceases to resist or discard her hold. "I will not go any further" marks a point of sexual resistance to the man, and it is at this point that the action of the tree, swaying, jerking, as if trying to throw her off, inscribes her experience of this resistance. Her "cold hands," like Rhys's cold breasts when Mr. Howard touches them, signal an absence of sexual responsiveness, indeed sexual terror. To throw off is to write with ease. The action of the tree is in one sense the action of writing; it may also be read as sexualized motion, masculine or feminine. The tree as a woman's refuge in a scenario of sexual terror reworks a motif from the classical myth of Daphne. Pursued by Apollo (Phoebus), Daphne calls upon her father, Peneus, for help. She is metamorphosed into a tree, but "[e]ven as a tree, Phoebus loved her. He placed his hand against the trunk, and felt her heart beating under the new bark. Embracing the branches as if they were limbs he kissed the wood: but, even as a tree, she shrank from his kisses" (Ovid 43). In Dante's *Inferno* suicides and depressive people have metamorphosed into trees.

"COULD WE HAVE SOLE SOMETIMES [. . .] THAT ENGLISH FISH"

Rhys's interruption of Mr. Howard's story with the request that they have sole, grilled sole, to eat sometimes is spoken in her "drawling" West Indian voice (BEB) that separates her from the local English settler children. She interrupts him as he is in fantasy about to tie her hands with a rope covered in flowers. The request is represented as one of several instances of Rhys having been sidetracked while Mr. Howard is telling his story. The other fantasy sidetracks—to the dresses she would be wearing and a "young & dark & splendid" lover (BEB)—belong to a conventional narrative economy of romance rather than pornography. In the context of Rhys's anxieties about the souls of sinners in Purgatory, the pathetic redemptive hope her dirty sewing might offer them, and her confidence that she is in or is going to hell, I read her request for sole as a slip of the tongue, a desire to be *souled* in his story and to have the fate of the "sinner" (by the standards of her religious upbringing) articulated in it. In 'Three Women's Texts and a Critique of Imperialism" Gayatri Spivak assumes that:

what is at stake, for feminist [later "female"] individualism in the age of imperialism, is precisely the making of human beings, the constitution and "interpellation" of the subject not only as individual but as "individualist." This stake is represented on two registers: childbearing and soul making. The first is domestic-society-through-sexual- reproduction cathected as "companionate" love; the second is the imperialist project cathected as civil-society-through-social-mission. (244)

In the Black Exercise Book Rhys's desire to be souled—marked as consumption of exotic English sustenance—implies the stakes of Mr. Howard's pornographic objectification and commodification of her: her lapse/being lapsed from the norms of middle-class English culture and the metaphorical "hell" to which the failure of the "English" colonizing mission in her case has consigned her. In the disconnected childbearing register Rhys writes mordantly: "No one can say of me

that I ve [sic] spoiled my children" (BEB). (Her first pregnancy was aborted; her
son, William Owen Lenglet, died of pneumonia in the hospital at the age of
three weeks, his death having occurred, Rhys realized to her lasting mortifica-
tion, while her husband, Jean Lenglet, was trying to cheer her up with cham-
pagne and the company of a friend, Colette; and she did not have custody of her
only surviving child, Maryvonne Lenglet, of whom she was very proud.) More
twistedly, and Rhys would claim very late in life that "everything gets twisted in
the West Indies" (*SP* 85), Rhys prays she will still love Mr. Howard when she
goes to hell.

The registers of the production of human beings are played out differently in
two of Rhys's reworkings of the Mr. Howard narrative within the generic protocols of fiction: "The Birthday," an unpublished short story now in the McFarlin
Library, which probably dates from the late 1930s/early 1940s, and "Good-bye
Marcus, Good-bye Rose," a short story written during the 1970s and published
in 1976 in the *New Yorker* and *Sleep It Off Lady: Stories*. In "The Birthday,"
Phoebe is indecently assaulted by Mr. Howard on her thirteenth birthday. The
implications of her white Creole heritage, measured in relation to religiosity and
"blood" passed through generations, are developed through representations of her
relations with her unnamed English auntie; Joseph, an elderly liberated slave of
her great-grandfather, who tells her stories of his former master's depravities
when she is out walking one day; Tite Francine, a "brown" girl of sixteen from
Martinique, who then chaperones Phoebe on her walks; and Mr. Howard, who
replaces Tite Francine on the birthday walk. There are no Meta or Mrs Howard
figures; Phoebe's parents are very minor characters. A turn-of-the-century temporal setting is indicated in "The Birthday" by the history of slavery in Dominica,
and in "Good-bye Marcus, Good-bye Rose" by the history of Western medicine.
In "Good-bye Marcus, Good-bye Rose," Phoebe is "twelve [. . .] and a bit"
when Captain Cardew clamps a hand "around one very small breast" (GM,GR
26). The grace of the feminine soul is measured, according to the nuns who teach
her, by the girl's "Chastity, in Thought, Word and Deed," her "most precious
possession" (29); the childbearing register is focalized through Phoebe's sense
that her fate is no longer determined by the marriage/sexual reproduction plot
that engages the fantasy lives of her peers. In this almost complete reworking
there is also no Meta figure, and the English auntie, Tite Francine, and Phoebe's
father are dropped. A servant, Joseph, is mentioned very briefly. The mother and
Phoebe are not identified as Creoles, merely as colonials.

In "The Birthday," Phoebe is in admiring awe and fears the disapproval of her
English auntie, who projects for Phoebe a "proper" model of graceful, feminine
Anglican religious observance and responds xenophobically to her brother's marriage into a white Creole family. The grace of her auntie's reverential manner in
church, extending to physical gesture, feminine costume, attentiveness to the
litany, and tone of voice, implies a larger religious grace, evident even in her
everyday "clear decided voice" (2). It is a grace of the English soul from which
Phoebe is excluded: she finds the litany "interminable" and, it is implied, yawns,

feels sleepy from the heat, and forgets to respond, concentrating on the auntie rather than the service (2). She habitually prays "to be delivered from what she imagined to be excessive and abnormal plainness" ([1]). (The plainness reminded me of Jane Eyre, the key function of reverence in the story of the meaning of Dominica's name, Sabbath Day Island.) Joseph calls her great-grandfather, Mas Edward, a "debbil of a man" and relates in a "primitive" English (French patois being his first language) "God knew what scenes of lust and cruelty" to the "frightened" Phoebe (3), scenes that sicken and terrify her into silence and then as night thoughts make her start "to scream and sob—hysterically" (4). The historical Canefield Estate on which the fictional Joseph was a slave was notorious in antislavery circles for the "fewness of the births as well as the fearful number of deaths" between 1817 and 1834 (Sturge and Harvey xvii).

In "The Birthday," the auntie locates a taint in her sister-in-law Evelina's family not in scenes like those Joseph remembers, but in the Spanish blood of Evelina's grandmother. For her that taint is apparent in Phoebe's wearing of a rose behind her ear, a Creole custom on birthdays Phoebe hopes will confer "loveliness" ([1]). The rose is called an English flower by Phoebe in "The Cardboard Dolls'-House," another of the Phoebe stories written at around the same time as "The Birthday." Made to feel "uncomfortable and self conscious" by the acidity of her auntie's reference to the "call of the blood," Phoebe removes the rose. The acidity is directed at the "very un-English" Evelina (2). Phoebe's "kindly" English father has a "vague tolerant" attitude to Creoleness, indulging signs of it in his daughter, and to ethnically mixed marriages and the children of them ([1]).

The moral burden of knowledge of the "lust and cruelty" of the slaveowning ancestor (3), a "return" of the socially and historically "repressed" to adapt a Freudian formulation, makes Phoebe "so frightened and so sad," and produces "long solitary broodings and puzzlings" (4); it robs her, the narrator says, of the "unquestioning animal happiness that ought to have been her normal state" (3). Running from Joseph, an agent of historical retribution, Phoebe had fallen, cutting her knee and putting a hole in her stocking. The kind of Romantic innocence evoked by "unquestioning animal happiness" is restored only on her walks with the nearly always happily grinning Tite Francine during which a rapprochement with a vivid corporeally apprehended spirit of Dominica occurs:

Dimly Phoebe realised that the little dark girl was a part of all the beauty which she had begun to perceive so acutely: the blue of the sky and the crimson of a hibiscus against the blue—the rustle of palm leaves in the evening and the mystery of a tom tom beating very far off, the heavy scent of certain flowers.

All these things which often seemed to be unbearable because unseizable, far away, almost alien, became warm and soft and close, a part of oneself as they were a part of Francine. (5)

The rapprochement is for Phoebe also with the racialized otherness of Tite Francine and an African Caribbean presence indigenized in the sounds of drumming and of Tite Francine's romantic patois songs. An aspect of the racialization that subtends the rapprochement may be elucidated with reference to Frantz Fanon. He quotes Bernard Wolfe: "It pleases us to portray the Negro showing us all his teeth in a smile made for us. And his smile as we see it—as we make it—always means a *gift*" (49n). In "The Birthday" familiar Romantic dichotomies—animal happiness/self-consciousness, grace/fall, nature/culture, child/adult— become entwined with a modernist primitivist yearning for an oceanic wholeness. Mr. Howard, whose ethnicity is unremarked here, takes Tite Francine's place as Phoebe's companion on her birthday walk (so he knows her age). When he places his hand down her blouse (her breasts are not mentioned, perhaps unmentionable for public consumption at the time of writing) Phoebe stays "as still as a little rabbit is supposed to when a snake is staring at it" (7). Phoebe is "dreadfully attracted, dreadfully repelled" by him; his "Greek profile" is "clear cut, benevolent and relentless as that of some aged—and ageless—god" (8). She steals glances at his otherness, spellbound as she had been by her auntie in church. The glances, the godlike profile bring the story to an abrupt close. The image of the Mr. Howard figure as "some aged but ageless god" (GM,GR 27) is used at a similar point after the indecent assault in "Good-bye Marcus, Good-bye Rose," but about a third of the way through the story, to evoke "childish admiration with a new inarticulate sexual awareness" (Howells 137).

Several of the pairings of characters in "The Birthday" are not worked through by its close. Had the narrative been taken as far as Mr. Howard's pornographic interpellation of Phoebe in his serial story juxtapositions of Joseph's and Mr. Howard's stories and the English auntie's and Phoebe's feminine reverence towards and spiritual dependency on god figures, a sexualized slave motif, playing off of constructions of gendered Creole subjectivity beyond a eugenic one (undeniably topical during the late 1930s), and a theme of retribution might have been developed.

In "Good-bye Marcus, Good-bye Rose," Captain Cardew is English, a colonial war hero. He and his wife find the Caribbean island on which Phoebe lives "so attractive and unspoilt that they decided to stay." The story charts Captain Cardew's despoiling of Phoebe. His model of love, far from being companionate, transposes his gendered investment in or interpellation as agent of colonial warfare and pacification to male-female relations: "He'd explain that love was not kind and gentle, as she had imagined, but violent. Violence, even cruelty, was an essential part of it. He would expand on this, it seemed to be his favourite subject" (GM,GR 28). The sexual self-consciousness produced by his stories of love, the penny a liners (cheap and superficial hack stories) of which he angrily suggests he is now captain, displaces Phoebe from the imperial "domestic-society-through-sexual-reproduction" plotting of gendered colonial subjectivity. She senses through her "bewilderment" (Howells 136) that she will no longer be "one of the chosen" in this plot (GM,GR [30]), the secularized religious language implying both its veneration as feminine social mission sanctioned by orthodox religion and a future of social and religious damnation.

Beneath a veneer of very formal manners and respectability structuring Captain and Mrs. Cardew's relationship with Phoebe's family (Howells 136), Phoebe is for Captain Cardew a sexual temptress, an embodiment of colonial attractiveness and innocence yielding to his worldly knowingness. Middle-class women, cultivators of an appearance of delicacy, are for him creatures of an appetite secreted from the masculine gaze with the complicity of servants: "He'd watch in wonder as the ethereal creatures pecked daintily, then sent away almost untouched plates. One day he had seen a maid taking a tray laden with food up to the bedrooms and the mystery was explained" (GM,GR 28). The secret appetite for food is metonymic of a secret appetite for sex. In the healthy imperial mother/promiscuous woman dichotomy that structured turn-of-the-century British sexual consciousness (Bland), Phoebe is relegated to the part of the promiscuous woman. This simple moralized dichotomy, hinted at in the suspicions of Mrs. Cardew and Phoebe's "puzzled, incredulous" mother (GM,GR 28), made explicit in the feminine religiosity of convent teaching, provides the "familiar frame of reference" (Howells 138) that produces in Phoebe a sense of her fundamental wickedness, which acts to exculpate Captain Cardew from moral blame.

Phoebe's efforts to consider the implications of her relationship with Captain Cardew after he and his wife return to England take place in the context of a sense of abandonment projected on to her relation to place: the stars, once so familiar, like the heterosexual romance narrative that dominates the fantasy lives of local Anglicized girls, are now "cold, infinitely far away, quite indifferent" (GM,GR 29). The language here, too, recalls Rhys's representation in the Black Exercise Book of her somatic response to Mr. Howard's touching of her breasts. As Howells argues, the story is "rinsed of the pains of future knowledge" (138) by Phoebe's childishly innocent relishing of the less protected, riskier and "far more exciting" territory (GM,GR 30) beyond the direction of sexual desire "to the needs of race and nation in the pursuit of healthy breeding" (Bland 376) within monogamous romance and marriage, beyond, too, the self-control entailed in the "Chastity, in Thought, Word and Deed" enjoined by Mother Sacred Heart in "her lovely English voice:

'So dear to Heaven is saintly chastity . . . '
How did it go on? Something about 'a thousand liveried angels lackey her . . . '"
(GM,GR 29–30)

Phoebe intuits the dimensions of a "vague irreparable loss": ironically, given Captain Cardew's comment about the collusion of servants in the secreting of middle-class women's appetite, loss of the grace implied by the "thousand liveried angels"; a marriage partner; a trousseau; and two of her three fantasy children—Marcus and Rose. (In the Black Exercise Book, Rhys lists a trousseau and six fantasy children.) The only child to remain part of Phoebe's life scenario and whose name is not part of (repressed from?) the story's title, is Jack, perhaps a colloquial, mordant authorial allusion to the venereal disease popularly associated with the promiscuous woman. The colloquial usage derives from rhyming slang (Jack in the box: pox). Bland points out that venereal diseases were construed in the nineteenth century as "God's retribution for sinful impropriety," in the twentieth century "more as incumbent on the "unnaturalness" of human promiscuity" (378). The ironic allusion would point to a gap in Captain Cardew's "enlightening" stories of love. A jack, too, is an ill-bred fellow, the pun implying the early twentieth-century eugenic construction of the amateur as an unhealthy breeder.

"I HAVE A GREAT WISH TO BE AS TRUTHFUL AS POSSIBLE NOT TO EXAGERATE [SIC]"

Wanting a book on "pchyco-analysis" [sic], Rhys visited Sylvia Beach's bookshop. She remembers having "read something like this": "'Women of this type will invariably say that they were seduced when very young by an elderly man. [. . .] They will relate a detailed story which in every case is entirely ficticious [sic]" (BEB). "If hysterics trace back their symptoms to fictitious traumas," writes Freud (300), the "gent" with the penchant for "laying down" the "law about the female attitude & reactions to sex" (BEB), "this . . . signifies that they create such scenes in phantasy, and psychical reality requires to be taken into account alongside actual reality. . . . [T]hese phantasies were intended to cover up the auto-erotic activity of early childhood, to gloss it over and raise it to a higher level; and then from behind the phantasies, the whole range of the child's sexual life came to light" (Freud 300). He now reads their stories of "passive sexual experiences in early childhood," "broadly speaking . . . seduction," as screen memories of "infantile sexuality" (299–300). Rhys responds to the gent, "No honey I thought it is not ficticious [sic] in every case. By no means, & anyhow how do you know. [. . .] No dear no: you dont [sic] play fair" (BEB).

In the short term Rhys's relationship with Mr. Howard "went out" of her "memory like a stone"; in the longer term it "formed" her, she writes at this time, "made her" as she was—a white Creole woman who believed that "[p]ain humiliation submission" were for her; an alcoholic "wreck," who has "spoiled" the body she "used to be so proud of." "I m [sic] too fat," she confesses, "& my face is flabby. I never see anyone & no longer wish to. I never go out. It seems as if every spark of vanity has been burnt out of me. Not only by whisky" (BEB). The metaphor of a stone passing out of memory links ingestion of the story and lived experience with urinary tract calculus (kidney, ureter or bladder stone). The symptoms of kidney stones are renal colic, characterized by "severe" spasmic pain that extends from "one side of the back" to the groin as the stones pass into and through the ureter. The intermittent spasms are experienced against "a background of continuous dull pain. There may be nausea, vomiting, sweating, and blood in the urine" (Smith, Robinson and Arnold 867). Bladder stones cause "difficulty in passing urine." Stones are normally caused by poor dissolution of the salt that oxalate, "an end-product of body *metabolism*," "forms with calcium," or in the case of infective stones "by the action of bacteria on urea" (Smith, Robinson and Arnold 225). The somatic metaphor graphically suggests the pain attendant on repressing the memory, attendant on her silence.

Much of the current controversy over repressed memory syndrome is focused on the role of the psychoanalyst in the recovery of memories of sexual or satanic abuse. Rhys's recovery of the repressed traumatic memories was not produced while she was under psychoanalysis. No analyst helped implant or shape the detailed production of the memories. In 1938 sexual assault as a concept-metaphor for imperialism was not historically available to Rhys as an implicit reference point. In thinking about the "mental" seduction, Rhys has, she writes, "a great wish to be as truthful as possible not to exagerate [sic]" (BEB).

NOTES

1. The concept of interpellation is central to Louis Althusser's influential theory of the ideological formation of the individual. Bill Ashcroft, Gareth Griffiths and Helen Tiffin explain this concept:

> subjects are 'born into' ideology, they find subjectivity within the expectations of their parents and their society, and they endorse it because it provides a sense of identity and security through structures such as language, social codes and conventions. . . . Ideology is perpetuated according to Althusser, by ideological state apparatuses such as church, education, police, which **interpellate** subjects, that is, apparatuses that 'call people forth' as subjects, and which provide the conditions by which, and the contexts in which, they obtain subjectivity. Interpellation has been explained in the following way: when a policeman hails you with the call 'Hey you!,' the moment you turn around to acknowledge that you are the object of his attention, you have been interpellated in a particular way, as a particular kind of subject. (221)

The process of interpellation entails the individual being an object of ideological address, internalizing the discipline integral to the address and identifying the self in and through it.

2. It is her fixing on the word "fictitious" that suggests she read Freud's account of his renunciation of his seduction theory of hysteria in "On the History of the Psychoanalytic Movement" rather than in "Femininity," the source nominated by Coral Ann Howells (17).

3. See, for example, the Earl of Milltown 1390.

4. Low, who concentrates on male cross-cultural dressing, notes that "it is the white man who dresses up and the native who reveals his body for consumption by dressing down." The same might be said of white and native women in some colonial contexts.

5. Hulme discusses the cannibal stereotype of Carib Indians in *Colonial Encounters*.

6. In *Black Skin, White Masks*, Fanon describes himself, the "black man," object of the frightened gaze of a white boy, being "battered down" by the "details, anecdotes, stories" that fabricate racial difference: the effect is complete dislocation, alienation, making himself an object, "an amputation, an excision, a hemorrhage that

spattered my whole body with black blood," metaphorically castration (111–12).

7. Protection of Mentally Defective Persons Bill: 5–6.

8. In *Quartet*, Stephan Zelli says of his wife Marya, after he learns of her affair with H.J. Heidler, "'*Quelle saleté!*'" (141).

9. Howells argues that the Mr. Howard narrative "curiously gathers to itself the dream of sexual fascination and dread that appears as Antoinette's in *Wide Sargasso Sea*, which Rhys tells as belonging to her adolescence" (16). She does not analyze the dream, or the fragment that follows it.

10. Stallybrass and White relate exhortations against kneeling on all fours, one of the "postures of servants and savages" to the regulation of the "lower bodily stratum" of the bourgeois child (144–45).

11. On the opposite page of the Black Exercise Book, Rhys begins to elaborate the scene of the mother's arrival as part of "Mr Howard's House./CREOLE." The sister is first named Audrey.

12. Sylvia Fraser, too, experienced amnesia concerning incestuous abuse by her father. In *My Father's House: A Memoir of Incest and of Healing* she represents herself as having coped with the abuse by splitting her personality in two to create a "secret accomplice" for her father: "I acquired another self with memories and experiences separate from mine, whose existence was unknown to me" (15).

Chapter 3 ————————————————————————

An Antillean Voice

In the preface to *The Left Bank and Other Stories* (1927), Jean Rhys's first book of fiction, Ford Madox Ford praises "the singular instinct for form possessed by this young lady," a quality "possessed by singularly few writers of English and by almost no English women writers" (25). He represents her origins as Antillean and her aesthetic tastes as French, rather than Anglo-Saxon, having been formed by "the almost exclusive reading of French writers of a recent, but not the most recent, date" (24–25). Ford measures the sketches against the "neatness of form" he admires in these French writers. His ambivalence about her "terrifying" Antillean "insight and . . . terrific — . . . almost lurid! — passion for stating the case of the underdog" is apparent in his construction of her having "let her pen loose on the Left Banks of the Old World—on its gaols, its studios, its salons, its cafés, its criminals, its midinettes—with a bias of admiration for its midinettes [Parisian working women] and of sympathy for its law-breakers" (24). On the one hand he thinks it a note "that badly needs sounding" (24); on the other he links it with the shortcomings of French youth who reject neatness of form, "determined violently not to be coldly critical, or critical at all" (25).

He tells an anecdote with a sexual subtext about Rhys's rejection of his advice to work more local color into her European sketches. Ford pressed Rhys, his ex-lover, to work the local color of Europe into the sketches

in the cunning way in which it would have been done by Flaubert or Maupassant, or by Mr. Conrad "getting in" the East in innumerable short stories from *Almayer* to the *Rescue*. . . . But would she do it? No! With cold deliberation, once her attention was drawn to the matter, she eliminated even such two or three words of descriptive matter as had crept into her work. Her business was with passion, hardship, emotions: the locality in which these things are endured is immaterial. So she hands you the Antilles with its sea and sky—"the loveliest, deepest sea in the world—the Caribbean!"—the effect of landscape on the emotions and passions of a child being so penetrative, but lets Montparnasse, or London, or Vienna go. She is probably right. Something human should, indeed, be dearer to one than all the topographies of the world. (26)

On the excuse of his knowledge of the publishing business, Ford "butted in" his preface (26), "Rive Gauche," the title piece, providing some of the topography and atmosphere he desired by writing sixteen pages of it in a twenty-page preface; Rhys's sketches are, as Coral Ann Howells notes, the *Other Stories* (31).[1]

My first point of departure from this sexual/textual imbroglio is Ford's invocation of "descriptive matter." The French realists recommended by Ford—Flaubert and Maupassant—aestheticized local color as "the essence of realism, the details and motifs characteristic of and appropriate to a particular setting" (Taylor 17). In *Bodies That Matter*, Judith Butler argues that materiality is a "site at which a certain drama of sexual difference plays itself out" and suggests that "to invoke matter is to invoke a sedimented history of sexual hierarchy and sexual erasures" (49). The narrative voice of three linked sketches among the *Other Stories*—"Trio," "Mixing Cocktails," and "Again the Antilles"—identifies herself as Antillean, soon Dominican. Each of the sketches materializes Dominican sexual, racial, and class difference for a predominantly European and English-speaking audience. Capitalizing on the success of *Wide Sargasso Sea* (1966) in generating interest in her earlier fiction, Rhys chose to recirculate "Mixing Cocktails" and "Again the Antilles" virtually unchanged in *Tigers Are Better-Looking: With a Selection from* The Left Bank (1968).

I disturb some of the sedimented history of sexual, racial, and class hierarchy and sexual, racial, and class erasures mediated, and in some cases, effected in the stories by analyzing some of the ways in which Rhys's "local knowledge" of Dominica "is grounded in virtue of its material location, its source of production . . . its sphere of reception" (Rothfield, summarizing Rouse 58) and the generic form—local color—through which it is "realized." Diana Brydon and Helen Tiffin argue of Rhys's fiction that she adopts a counterdiscursive textual strategy in relation to a European literary canon, and Tiffin has located an early example of it in "Again the Antilles" ("Rite of Reply" 72–77). My methodology, rather, relativizes Rhys's "local knowledge" to the textual and material "forms of practice which produce it" (Rothfield 58) and the "adaptation of locally situated practices to new local contexts" (Rouse, qtd. in Rothfield 59). I place Rhys's self-consciously Antillean narrative voice in *The Left Bank and Other Stories* in relation to nineteenth- and early twentieth-century travel writing about Dominica and examine the ambivalences and complexities of Rhys's gendered negotiations of Dominican autoethnographic expression in articulating a white Creole speaking/writing position.

My second point of departure is Ford's causal linking of Rhys's colonial origin and her "terrifying insight and a terrific—an almost lurid!—passion for stating the case of the underdog . . . with a bias of admiration for" the "midinettes" of "the Left Banks of the Old World" and "of sympathy for its law-breakers"

(Preface 24). Ford implies that the insight and passion are part of Rhys's baggage as an Antillean; he conflates her colonial difference with particular sensitiv-
ity to class injustice and with disrespect for law. Carole Angier says that Ford
"felt there was black blood in her" (656). Ford's "feeling" conforms with a
stereotype of the white Creole—that white Creoles are often passing for white;
Angier uses Ford's "feeling" to support her speculation that "black blood . . .
was part of her [Rhys's] mystery and her difference, both as a woman and as a
writer" (656). Stella Bowen's account of Rhys in *Drawn from Life* is unremit-
ting in its invocation of a unrespectable working-class stereotype: the impoverished Rhys, unnamed, has in Bowen's eyes a "complete absence of any desire for
independence," and is "violent," lacking respect for "patience or honesty or for-
titude," weak, part of an "underworld of darkness and disorder" (166–67). If one
of the unspokens of Bowen's portrait is that she shares Ford's "feeling," what I
have read as class stereotype is conflated with racial stereotype. Rereading Ford's
comments on Rhys's bias and sympathy, I note his representation of the effects
of her insight and passion on her writing and her reader: release of her writing
from captivity or constraint of aesthetic law; violent rejection of objectivity;
terror in the reader at a menacing democratization of viewpoint in art.

Ford's comments on Rhys's bias and compassion, and his attribution of their
origin, shaped the reception of Rhys's *"Other Stories"* in 1927. Gender, class,
ethnic, and racial stereotypes circulate, especially in critical assessment of her
partiality and sympathy. Rhys was advised in *Nation and Athenaeum* that she
would need to "chasten her emotionalism" to achieve "universal values" (424).
Promiscuity and emotionalism are sterotypical attributes of women, the working
class, white Creoles, and black people. The "universal" is implicitly identified
by the reviewer with hegemonic masculine, white, English, and middle-class
"values." In the *Saturday Review of Literature*, Rhys's stories were said to be
"tinged with a slightly hysterical sentiment" (287). Here the excessive emotion
("sentiment") is being implicitly racialized with the choice of the word "tinged."
Spirit possession is a reference point for the *Spectator* reviewer, who suggests
that Rhys was "temporarily possessed by the souls of those she writes about"
(772). A perceived want of control, "slightly" hystericized in the *Saturday Review of Literature* and by D. B. Wyndham-Lewis in the *Saturday Review*, who
described the stories as "vivid, nervous sketches" (637), is being referred in the
Spectator either to African-derived racial difference from a Christian European
norm, or to a white Creole stereotype: susceptibility to contamination by
"debasing" "superstition" (Rees). The *New Statesman* reviewer summed up the
worldviews in Rhys's stories: "Love, fame, life itself—they turn, one and all,
upon the question of paying for drinks" (90). The formulation has a number of
reference points: an ethnocentric British construction of "the Left Banks of the
Old World" as degenerate and the alcoholic disposition stereotypically attributed
to the working class, black people, and the white Creole.

In the second part of this chapter I analyze the 1927 version of "Vienne,"[2] a
story in which the narrator, Frances, expresses some sympathy for impoverished

women and those thought to be compromised by their want of sexual virtue and
criticizes the "huge machine of law, order, respectability" (V 241). Her husband,
Pierre, employed as "secretary and confidential adviser" (210) to a Japanese
member of the Inter-Allied Commission that was supervising the disarmament
of Austria, becomes a law-breaker. Concentrating in particular on the interplay
of narrative and ironizing authorial voices, I examine Rhys's representations of
the cross-articulation of gender, class, and race on the "fringe of international-
isms" (Ford, Preface 12) in post-armistice Vienna, Budapest, and Prague, cities
that had all been part of the Hapsburg Empire in 1914. Austria then "had ruled
over fifteen races and given the law to central Europe" (Fisher 1267). H.A.L.
Fisher writes that Austria's "[d]ynasty, army, empire disappeared in the whirl-
wind" of the First World War and the peace settlement. "The Hungarians declared
themselves independent and were invaded by the Roumans. The Czechs and Slo-
vaks broke away. The Serbs exploited their victory in the south" (1267). Austria
lost territory to Italy, Yugoslavia, Hungary, Romania, Czechoslovakia, and Po-
land.

"I REMEMBERED THE ANTILLES"[3]

"Mixing Cocktails" and "Again the Antilles" are memories of a Dominican
childhood, prompted by the homesickness which "descend[s] over" the narrator of
"Trio" as she witnesses the spectacle three nonwhite compatriots make of their
"pleasures" in a Montparnasse restaurant (83–84). Spectacle, as Mary Russo
notes, is in the judgment of the beholder; it implies inadvertancy (213) and a
transgression of the boundaries of the beholder's standards of propriety—
physical, social, and moral. The stereotypically sensuous physicality of the narrator's compatriots and stereotypical suggestion of sexual precociousness in the
girl in the group ("apparently about fifteen, but probably much younger" ["Trio"
83])—apprehended visually and aurally—activates through familiarity corporeal
memories of Dominica. The physicality includes a mature man giving the girl
"long lingering kisses" (84) and the apparent precociousness of the girl sitting
"very close to the man and every now and then [. . .] lay[ing] her head on his
shoulder for a second" (83) and dancing to show her nakedness beneath her red
dress. Judith L. Raiskin reads the relation between the two as sexual
"exploitation of the young girl" (154), appropriately asking, "What is the economic relationship between the man with the 'thick silver ring' and the frumpy
woman, and are the girl's sexual favors to the man part of the 'family' econom-
ics? What looks like a family is likely the bartering of the daughter; at the heart
of the gaiety is weariness and a plea for help" (153–54).

That neither the narrative nor an ironizing authorial voice poses the question
about the structural relations among the three suggests that the narrative and
authorial voices "naturalize" them by referring them to racial stereotypes of
sexuality. Dominica is remembered by the narrator of the three stories as sights,
colors, sensations, sounds, voices, ritualized performances of her classed,

gendered, racialized embodiment, and huge delight at the "undignified" spectacle of a dispute between a Papa Dom and a white English planter, Mr. Hugh Musgrave, conducted in the letters column of the *Dominica Herald and Leeward Islands Gazette* ("Again the Antilles" 95). The racial backgrounds of the nonwhite characters are epidermalized as shade and physiognomy: in "Trio" as "very black—coal black" (83), "coffee-coloured" (83), the "charming" face of a "fuzzy"-haired girl revealing "much white blood in her veins" (83–84) and in "Again the Antilles" as a "beautiful shade of coffee-colour" (93). The narrator's whiteness is indicated in "Mixing Cocktails" by nagging voices telling her "to come in out of the sun. ... One would one day regret freckles" (89) and by the Englishness of a visiting aunt; in "Again the Antilles," by the social familiarity with Mr. Musgrave, which allows her to know him to be "a dear, but peppery" (94). The discursive field within which whiteness is articulated in the stories is the nineteenth- and early twentieth-century ethnographic discourse of white degeneracy in the tropics.

The Creoleness of the narrator is articulated through allusion to Stradanus's allegorical painting of America discovered by Amerigo Vespucci as a naked woman in a hammock strung between two trees; the hammock, cannibalism, and the canoe paddle in the painting suggest stereotypically the Carib Indian. America's indolence is suggested by the proximity of the sloth in the shade she enjoys. Dominica was by the late nineteenth century home to the last group of "yellow" Carib Indians in the Caribbean islands. The (implicitly clothed) narrator remembers herself having spent most of the days at the rural retreat of her family in a hammock on the verandah, swinging "cautiously" and dreaming. She is the foregrounded figure, who looks out at the sea and the landscape in the background. Rhys alludes to the European construct of Carib resistance to European settlement and domination of Dominica: "A wild place, Dominica. Savage and lost" ("Mixing Cocktails" 88). The white colonial presence is marked by technology: steamers (which carry, among other cargo, the *Times Weekly Edition* for her father), a telescope, and "unloaded shotgun" (88).

The white person in a hammock on the verandah of an estate house also resonates within a Dominican discursive context. In an 1877 editorial in the *Dominica*, A. R. Lockhart critiques the "most silly" and "most fallacious" essentialist stereotype of the lazy "Negro" circulating in supposedly "enlightened Europe." He attributes low valuation of physical labor by African Caribbean people to the racial division of labor in the period of slavery and its "deep-rooted" cultural signifiers:

To the Negro under the old slave system the conception of respectability and honour was inseparable from that of idleness and a luxurious life. To his limited vision, bounded by the narrow surroundings of his plantation home, where

    Massa 'neath the shade would lay,

    While we poor niggers toiled all day," [sic]

the personification of all earthly happiness was "Massa" swinging in his hammock and sipping sangaree, while the spectacle of the field gang, toiling wearily beneath

the ardent rays of the West Indian sun, typified the beast of burden, the acme of degradation. ([3])

His usage of the term "nigger" to cite racism is typical of the strategy of elective
members of the assembly. In "Mixing Cocktails" the continuing racialized class
division of labor on the estate in the post-emancipation period is visible only in
the figure of Ann Twist, the cook, "the old 'Obeah' woman" (91). Linked with
the blackness of night, she embodies stereotypically the superstition of evil that
haunts the narrator's identifications with the othernesses of place.

The ethnographic discourses of white Creole degeneracy and the degeneracy of
the English abroad attributed a racial decay to the effects of tropical acclimatiza-
tion. Standard reference books as early as the 1810s cite the "enervating influence
of the sultry climate" (Rees); the signifiers of this lack of robustness were disease; sickliness; excessive appetites, especially for alcohol, sex (Stepan 103),
and spicy food; idleness; and luxurious life. The supposedly biological effects on
gait, complexion, eyes, intelligence, and fibers were documented minutely
(Edwards, vol. 2: 7–16). The vulnerability was both physical and moral; the fear
that white people would "go native" in an "alien . . . cultural environment" produced the idea, argues Nancy Stepan, "that the Anglo-Saxons' very refinement
required the greatest possible physical, social, and sexual distance from the peoples they increasingly governed abroad. It was a theory of social control and
separation that harmonized well with the British and German colonial policy of
maintaining sharp boundaries, socially, between themselves and 'natives'" (102,
104). Native, in Stepan's account, means nonwhite.

The discourse of tropical degeneracy was mobilized in turn-of-the-century
tourist discourse about Dominica and, as I suggested in chapter 1, by William
Davies in his refutation of James Anthony Froude's representations of race relations on the island. Fannie D. Ward's 1894 travel account is titled "In Drowsy
Dominica"—she draws no distinctions among the racial groups in describing the
people as "a trifle lazy" ([3]). In 1895 the Canadian journalist Kathleen Blake
Watkins comments on the exotic roses in the Botanical Gardens in Roseau:
"They lack the perfume our roses have, and looked indeed poor fragile blossoms
out of all place here in this sun-burnt spot." ([3]). Her account emphasizes decay
and neglect in colonial Roseau, and she praises highly the enterprise and refinement of the colored owner of Wall House estate, J. Cox Fillan. Watkins uses the
Dominican horticultural troping of Englishness.

The discourse of white tropical degeneracy is invoked ambivalently in the
performance of the narrator of "Mixing Cocktails"; more straightforwardly, the
narrator of "Again the Antilles" attributes Mr. Musgrave's "peppery" temperament to "much indulgence in spices and cocktails" during his "[t]wenty years in
the tropics" (94). Two signifiers of degeneracy circulate uncritically in "Mixing
Cocktails": the "comfort" of the father is bound up with the chess problem in
the *Times Weekly Edition* and the cocktails his narrator-daughter prepares ritu-
ally for him each evening, and the narrator luxuriates in "languid" indolence (89)

for a large part of the day. In "Mixing Cocktails" the English aunt will try to indulge the father by flattering his horticultural efforts, a syncretic blending of roses and hibiscuses. It is the aunt, unaccustomed to the heat, who drowses. The story's title puns on "cocktails." A cocktail is a "person assuming the position of a gentleman, but deficient in thorough gentlemanly breeding." The *Oxford English Dictionary* definition of a "cocktailed horse" refers to "a known stain in his parentage." The narrator's mother is never individualized in the story. Rather, Rhys quotes a nagging voice that "spoiled" the narrator's pleasure: "One was not to sit in the sun. One had been told not to be in sun. . . . One would one day regret freckles" (89); "I am speaking to you; do you not hear? You must break yourself of your habit of never listening. You have such an absent-minded expression. Try not to look vague. . . . So rude!" (89).

The narrator reworks the voice's invocation of "Other People" (90) one is supposed to be like. The nagging voice is recognizably that of a middle-class mother anxious to regulate the desires, manners, and respectability of a recalcitrant daughter. Her efforts at regulation are represented as a "passionate" levelling up (89), and what is desired is a maintaining of position in a racialized and classed social hierarchy. The negative attributes she fixes her attention on are some of those stereotypically attributed to the white Creole: a "want of proper objects for exercising the faculties" and "aversion to serious thought and deep reflection" (Edwards, vol. 2: 14, 15). The racial and class anxiety of the family is reflected in its mobility within Dominica. The "very new" "house in the hills" is "an hour's journey by boat and another hour and a half on horseback, climbing slowly up": it proffers a "sensation of relief and coolness" ("Mixing Cocktails" 87). The movement from town to estate marks a claim to social prestige, the classed labor economy of the estate preserving social distance from subjected nonwhite races.

The narrator's perceptions of the sea work intertextually to destabilize the color constancy vision of tourist discourse about Dominican waters. The superlative blueness of the sea around Dominica is a staple of tourist discourse. Froude, for instance, notes its "deeper azure" hue by comparison with the sea surrounding other Caribbean islands (142); Watkins observes a "sea of such deep and exquisite azure as we had never seen yet—blue with violet depths in it, violet with blue depths" ([3]). In "Mixing Cocktails" the sea is one of the objects of the narrator's dreaming; her descriptions of it discount "natural" or "local" color. These are terms from art criticism. "Colour constancy," the *Oxford Companion to Art* explains,

seems to combine a tendency to see things the colours they are remembered to be and a tendency to compensate for changes in illumination and viewing conditions. Colour constancy is favoured by the "object attitude" of perception when colours are noticed incidentally to the perception of objects rather than by the aesthetic attitude when they are attended to for themselves. . . .

In the language of painting the term *local colour* is used for the "natural" colours of objects towards which colour constancy vision tends to approximate. . . . [The

Impressionists] have striven to discount colour constancy and to see and depict each area of the visual field in accordance with the constitution of the light actually reflected from it upon the eye. This is a way of looking at the environment which requires considerable effort to counteract ingrained habits of practical "object-recognition" seeing. (Osborne 261)

In the morning the sea in "Mixing Cocktails" is "a very tender blue, like the dress of the Virgin Mary"; at midday "[t]he light made it so flash and glitter: it was necessary to screw the eyes up tight before looking. Everything was still and languid, worshipping the sun." The sky becomes "hard, blue, blue" (89). The narrator is projecting maternal attributes on to the blues—"very tender," "hard" (88, 89)—in a good mother/bad mother dichotomy. The descriptions of the blues attest, too, to intimate awareness, local knowledge, and an aesthetics of color different from the "practical 'object-recognition' seeing" of travel writers. In "Giotto's Joy," Julia Kristeva argues that

centered vision—identification of objects—comes into play after color perceptions. The earliest appear to be those with short wavelengths, and therefore the color blue. Thus all colors, but blue in particular, would have a noncentered or decentering effect, lessening both object identification and phenomenal fixation. They thereby return the subject to the archaic moment of its dialectic, that is, before the fixed, specular "I," but while in the process of becoming this "I" by breaking away from instinctual, biological (and also maternal) dependence. . . . chromatic experience can then be interpreted as a repetition of the specular subject's emergence in the already constructed space of the understanding (speaking) subject. (225)

Rhys's charting of the narrator's day through her local perception of the color of the sea performs in general terms a repetition of the fashioning of the gendered, classed, heterosexed, white Creole subject in the already constructed space of the speaking subject. Interestingly this remembered process of subject-formation entails a verbal cue from her aunt about the "exquisite" color of the sea and the narrator's contextualization of it in a recitation of tourist discourse. The recitation—"It is purple sea with a sky to match it. The Caribbean. The deepest, the loveliest in the world. . . . " ("Mixing Cocktails" 90)—is represented as part of the leveling up. Misquoting the recitation as "'the loveliest, deepest sea in the world—the Caribbean!'" (Preface 26), Ford cites it approvingly as Rhys's closest approximation to local color, understood in a literary critical sense.

In "Again the Antilles," set in Roseau, the narrator gazes back at Papa Dom from her family's garden. He has a habit of looking "solemnly out of his windows" (93). In women's writing a woman's look from a window is often used to figure her desire to transcend the materiality of her gendered social position. Nancy Armstrong describes this materiality as the "knowledge housed, as it were, in the body of the woman" (245). Rhys's positioning of the colored Papa Dom at his windows suggests his desire to transcend the materiality of his racialized social position and the solemnity of the knowledge housed, as it were, in the racial othering of his body by white settlers, and his own racial, class, moral, and religious othering of "the Mob" and "negroes" ("Again the Antilles" 94). Nineteenth- and early twentieth-century tourists often describe the scenery of Dominica as awe-inspiring; the narrator finds Papa Dom, the middle-class editor of the *Dominica Herald and Leeward Islands Gazette,* "awe-inspiring" (93). As Raiskin observes: "Rather than a subject deep in thought, he becomes an object of her gaze and later of amused memory of island life" (119).

The narrator's performance of her racialized class in relation to both Papa Dom and Mr. Hugh Musgrave is based on a highbrow knowledge of Chaucer's General Prologue to the *Canterbury Tales* in Middle English and relies on the knowingness of a similarly highbrow audience to achieve its full comic effect. Here I should confess my own unashamed vulgarity—I had to look up a Chaucer text in Middle English to discover the extent of the joke. I was compelled to study Chaucer (and Shakespeare and Milton) in my honors year at the University of Queensland in 1976, but my literary education in Australia has never included learning any of *The Canterbury Tales* by heart. Raiskin, Tiffin, and Jordan Stouck, who have written at some length about "Again the Antilles," assume, like Papa Dom, that the white man, Mr. Hugh Musgrave, quotes Chaucer accurately, which he does not.

My research on Dominican journalism poses questions about the motive for Rhys's misrepresentation of the historical Papa Dom, Augustus Theodore Righton, as a "born rebel . . . a firebrand" (93). The narrator of "Again the Antilles" lists a range of issues on which the fictional Papa Dom took a fiery stand. They do not match Righton's public record. Rhys's Papa Dom, for instance, opposes the imposition of Crown Colony rule in 1898. (Two of the not saids of Rhys's story are that Crown Colony rule disenfranchised at island level the propertied men of all racial groups who had enjoyed the vote and disempowered the elected opposition.) Righton took a compliant stand, although he did publish a letter from A. R. Lockhart, "No Crown Colony: Views of an Elective on the Question of the Hour." In the obituary of Righton in the *Leeward Islands Free Press,* A. R. Lockhart describes him as "a man of exceptional kindliness of temperament, absolutely free from malice or ill-will to his fellow creatures," but expressed reservation about the absolute value of this character attribute ("Death of Mr. Righton" [2]). There was a Mr. Christopher Musgrave living in Dominica during Rhys's childhood. A distant relative of Rhys's through his marriage, he was Dominica's registrar and provost marshal. Rhys's Mr. Hugh Musgrave is a planter.

A dispute involving Joseph Hilton Steber and the name of Christopher Musgrave may have supplied Rhys with a motif for "Again the Antilles": the narrator writing that she "used to think that being coloured embittered" Papa Dom (93). This characterization racializes and personalizes Papa Dom's political stands on matters of public concern. In October 1902, Steber remarked in a paragraph on government budget priorities in the *Dominica Guardian* on the increase in Christopher Musgrave's salary, when "[n]o greater efficiency is secured or promised thereby," at a time when "the proper administration of justice is seriously hampered by an unholy amalgamation of the Magisterial districts, and the poorer classes are denied free medical attendance, except in extreme cases" ("Up to Date" [3]). He suggested in another paragraph that Musgrave was rumored to be an applicant for the registrarship of Antigua, commented on his lack of professional qualifications in law, and stated that Musgrave's departure for Antigua would not "be the cause of any regret" in Dominica ("Up to Date" [3]). Steber's comments and an editorial on discrepancies in the increases in official salaries, "The Civil Service List," were interpreted by "A Dominican" in a letter to the *Dominican* as an example of Steber's "disgraceful habit of abusing and making unwholesome remarks" against "respectable persons in this community." Musgrave was defended as being "a hard-working official," "unblemished," and Steber's "Unmerited Attack" was attributed to a "*personal* antipathy" contingent on "the *colour* question" ("An Unmerited Attack"). Steber responded to "A Dominican" in a paragraph in the *Dominica Guardian*: "The letter is foolish and puerile in the extreme, and as we consider ourselves to be above any personal animus in what we chose to write in the discharge of our duty to the public, we do not think we are called upon to offer any explanation" (Paragraph [4]). "[T]he *colour* question" had been featured in the *Dominica Guardian* during September and October in editorial comment and letters to the editor concerning the establishment of a "White People's Club" in Queen's Lodge in Roseau, the racial exclusivism of which was an unwritten rule (Impartial, "Colour Question Dying Hard"). Steber essentialized racism as "the inherent curse of the white man" ("Colour Question"); his correspondent, "Impartial," who defended the establishment of the club, described "'racial hatred'" as the personality of colored people ("Colour Question Dying Hard").[4]

Righton, the historical Papa Dom, wrote in his first editorial in the *Dominican* that the "legitimate and only proper use to which a Journal professing to be an exponent of public opinion (and known to be such) can be put, is to make it strictly impartial." Discharging this function, he wrote, would "compel us to keep clear of faction" and to "maintain a conscience void of offence" (3 July 1880: [2]–[3]). The paper's motto was "Be Just and Fear Not." "All men are not supposed to have the same opinion," wrote "A Disgusted Dominican" in the *Dominica Guardian* in August 1893, "but unfortunately for Mr Righton he has none of his own, except that being the public printer, he is bound to cast his honour aside for fear of losing the contract printing" ("C'est Manicou"). The letter writer was complaining specifically about the coverage in the *Dominican* of the "Laplaine atrocities," the shooting of protestors against taxation levels. Papa masks were worn at Carnival in 1894. Even in Trinidad, the *Dominican* under Righton's editorship was renowned as "invariably" leaning "towards the Government and enjoy[ing] whatever loaves and fishes the Government had to give" ("An Editor's Complete Apology to Another").

Rhys may have tried to create a composite colored journalist figure, but to give him the nickname of a journalist reviled for dishonoring his public duty and the interests of the majority of the population is mischievous, or it could be a last (or first) twist in the story's thematic of knowingness. Living and publishing in Europe and under a pseudonym, Rhys is not accountable to the Dominican community for historical misrepresentation or mischief. How many of Rhys's audience outside Dominica, and the Caribbean, could fault her (white) narrator on historical detail, or, indeed, recognize that Papa Dom was an influential historical figure?[5] What authority and authenticity of detail do readers assume in the narrator? Is the mischief a joke on these readers? Rhys's pseudonym, and even her married name in 1927, Ella Lenglet, occlude the potential interestedness of her representation of the range of issues on which Papa Dom campaigned. Raiskin notes: "Papa Dom's political positions are rendered almost ridiculous by the way the narrator lists them[.] . . . Each of Papa Dom's objections is given the same weight, and his political positions become mere personal characteristics, part of his crankiness. He is a 'born rebel'; that is, his dissatisfactions are a product of his personality, not of specific political problems" (119). Two of the listed political stances are opposition to "the Island's being a Crown Colony" and to "the Town Board's new system of drainage" ("Again the Antilles" 93–94). Rhys's father, William Rees Williams, and uncle, Acton Don Lockhart, were leaders of the campaign in favor of Crown Colony rule, and her father was Crown-nominated chairman of the Town Board from the late 1890s until his death in 1910. The Roseau River was prone to flooding. Various methods of improving drainage were proposed and tried during Rees Williams's tenure as chairman ("The Roseau River Embankment").

The humor of "Again the Antilles" turns on exposure of the relative lacks of highbrow English cultural capital of Papa Dom and Mr. Hugh Musgrave. In admonishing Musgrave for an act he considered "tyrannical," Papa Dom bemoans the "degeneracy of a stock" in Musgrave and his removal "from the ideals of true gentility." He mistakenly attributes the line "He was a very gentle, perfect knight" to Shakespeare, misquotes the line from a modern translation of the General Prologue to the *Canterbury Tales*, and mistakenly places the second Marquis of Montrose as Shakespeare's contemporary. In rebuking Papa Dom for a perceived libel, Musgrave attributes the line from the General Prologue correctly, but in trying to upstage the editor by quoting it in context in Middle English, he mixes modern and Middle English. Uncrushed, not recalling a "correct" Middle English version, and not having works of reference, Papa Dom insists that "in the minds of the best authorities there are grave doubts, very grave doubts indeed, as to authorship of the lines, and indeed the other works of the immortal Swan of Avon" ("Again the Antilles" 97). He mistakenly assumes that Musgrave—and the implication is, that he being white—"certainly" has the necessary reference books. Papa Dom has censored Musgrave's letter, altering the last phrase of a sentence, so that it reads: "It is indeed a saddening and dismal thing that the names of great Englishmen should be thus taken in vain by the ignorant of another race and colour." Musgrave had written "by damn niggers." His letter is ambiguous—the "great Englishmen" could be Chaucer, Shakespeare, even himself—and the Biblical allusion unwittingly implies the godlike status he thinks is his right and English culture's right over the nonwhite population. Raiskin argues: "If Papa Dom exercises any control over the debate by his role as the paper's editor, the narrator, as 'editor' of this text, takes that power back. If Papa Dom edits out Musgrave's insult of 'damn niggers,' the narrator puts it back into the text" (119).

There is, as I have already noted, relatively radical Dominican textual authority for the practice of citing the offensive term to name white racism, but while this object of naming racism is achieved by Rhys, the genre of the sketch—local color—also produces humor from the citation for an implied cosmopolitan and urbane audience anticipating curiosities and strangeness to confirm their "normality" (Taylor 17). For Cheryl Alexander Malcolm and David Malcolm the story is "an affectionate reminiscence exposing a sense of loss" (6). Raiskin positions the narrator as an expatriate Dominican proferring "a bit of nostalgia, an ironic little snippet of the ridiculous and bizarre situations that are the legacy of British colonialism in the tropical islands" (118). Humor was the response of the narrator's social circle to the incidents, and one would be straining the argument to suggest that their delight is intended to expose their racism, or would have done in 1927. Even though, as Helen Tiffin argues, Papa Dom, and by extension Rhys, challenge the "deployment" of Shakespeare and Chaucer "as authorities in the service of racist superiority" ("Rite of Reply" 75), the textual strategy of calling on the knowingness of an audience to pick the errors in the allusions of two characters, objects of racism in markedly differing degrees, activates "a corporate subjectivity," those with the highbrow cultural competence in an English tradition to be "'in the know,'" or with reasonably ready access to a Middle English text of Chaucer's poem. The strategy is, as Peter Bailey notes with reference to popular knowingness in the music hall, "more in the nature of a transaction or co-production" (146). For some in an "English" Dominican audience of Rhys's generation or that of her parents the highbrow knowingness could well reflect ironically on the local discourses of black and colored "improvement" through education and competence in the dominant culture.

Musgrave and recent critical commentators on "Again the Antilles" do not pick up Papa Dom's error concerning the Marquis of Montrose. It is as if the historical allusion is a flat spot in Papa Dom's original comment on Musgrave, immaterial enough to pass over. I had never heard of the Marquis of Montrose. The racialized contest between Musgrave and Papa Dom is fought over Papa Dom's assumption of having acquired fluency in English *culture*. This suggests the centrality of English literary education in the production of the colonial subject, but also the anxieties that circulate in the white colonial subject about the closure through education of the social and class gap between the white and, in the instance of "Again the Antilles," the colored colonial subject. Musgrave's racist appellation of Papa Dom reasserts a social and racial distance.

Dominican autoethnography and the discourses of a politically dominant culture and travel writing ground Rhys's local knowledges of the Caribbean and

Creoleness in *The Left Bank and Other Stories*, and reveal the ambiguities, ambivalences, and complexities entailed in their sources of production, and their spheres of reception. In "Trio," "Mixing Cocktails," and "Again the Antilles," Rhys centralizes the gaze of the white Creole narrator. At the end of "Trio" the narrator acknowledges the party of three she observes to be her "compatriots" (85). That the story is titled "Trio" (and not "Quartet" or "Foursome") preserves her distance from the group, who remain objects of her disciplinary and stereotyping gaze. Rhys represents the racial, gender, and class dynamics of turn-of-the-century Dominican middle-class culture more minutely in "Mixing Cocktails" and "Again the Antilles."

"THE HUGE MACHINE OF LAW, ORDER, RESPECTABILITY"

In "Vienne" the English narrator, Frances, reconstructs episodically and anecdotally the period in which she lived in Vienna and visited Budapest and Prague in the early 1920s. The story opens:

> Funny how it's slipped away, Vienna. Nothing left but a few snapshots.
> Not a friend, not a pretty frock—nothing left of Vienna. (193)

Two things that have "slipped away" from her life, although their loss is not directly stated, are her husband and the child who must have been conceived in Vienna. Frances's narrative does mention marital tension. Rhys implies a causal link between the loss of husband and child and Frances's sense that she has left "respectability behind" (243) when Pierre breaks the law and they become fugitives from justice. Respectability, as it is lived and guarded among signs of international modernity and nostalgia for an imperial past, is a major thematic in Frances's narrative. Despite Frances's explicit contempt for the "hypocrisy" that sustains the cultural "fiction of the 'good' woman and the 'bad' one," what contemporary feminist critics term the virgin/whore dichotomy, she anxiously upholds it "against all [. . .] sense of fairness and logic" in order to keep up her own appearance of respectability (197). It is a fiction she links with an "old-fashioned" nostalgia (197) for the signs of imperial glory and patriotism, and one that Rhys's authorial voice judges in her punning choice of name for the "*jeune fille*" (young girl) whose "virtue" must be protected (197–98). Ironically the pregnant Frances comes to realize that respectability will be her surest protection from an unspeakable fate (240), although the "fate" is suggested in her comment about some of the women who frequent the "exciting and gay," and "[v]ery vulgar" Radetzsky Hotel: "All the pretty people with doubtful husbands or no husbands, or husbands in jail (lots of men went to jail—I don't wonder. Every day new laws about the exchange and smuggling gold)" (200–201). They are among the women "of the moment" for newly rich, philandering men (200), subject to the critical gaze of women like Frances. Frances fears a return to poverty and its weakening effects on her character. The limit of her sympathy for the "pretty people" is apparent when the prospect of her becoming like them is unspeakable.

The features of postwar modernity in "Vienne" are an international diplomacy in which its male agents and functionaries exploit demoralized and impoverished local women and measure cities in terms of the women's sexual availability; "amateur" prostitution or female participation in casual sex, a topic I discuss at length in chapter 4; "blanks" in communication between people because of language barriers (199); and a superficiality of relationship in which racial, gender, sexual, and class stereotypes circulate in the making of meaning in everyday encounters. Howells, indeed, reads *The Left Bank and Other Stories* as Rhys's "feminised version of [T.S. Eliot's] *The Waste Land*" (32). Rhys ironizes the ways in which characters, including Frances, denigrate other people as foils for their own self-regard and national or ethnic self-regard, and as objects of their sanctimony. Frances and Pierre, who come to represent conspicuous "new money" acquired through currency speculation, are apparently threatened with bankruptcy; Pierre faces charges of theft. Frances remembers telling Pierre that "somehow" she "would find the money to pay his debts" (239), probably by approaching friends, family, and acquaintances—a seemingly characteristic last resort (224–25). This personal financial history is allusively set alongside economic conditions in Austria. In October 1922 the League of Nations rescued Austria from bankruptcy (Fisher 1268).

The name Blanca von Marken, that of Frances's landlady's daughter, the "*jeune fille*," carries multiple resonances from French, German, and English. It suggests that she is blank(er), white(r), or shinier at core, free(r) of blemish, shinier because of the family's inheritance of wealth (in German, marks). In a later story, "Temps Perdi," Rhys uses the word "blank" to signify a tabooed epithet. The girl's Christian name could indeed, in a show of narrative "respectability" and observance of censorship law, carry this, among other significations. The blankness, linked with "blanc" as a racial signifier in French, suggests that the girl is empty, featureless, void of personal interest, lacking. Blanca von Marken meets Lysyl, a dancer with whom Frances and Pierre's flatmate, André, has had casual sex, on the stairs one morning, and Madame von Marken "protest[s]" to Frances (V 197). Lysyl has "a wonderfully graceful body" (196), but her face, according to Frances, shows the traces of her class origin. Frances speaks of "a brutal peasant's face," which makes André apprehensive that she is not "'chic' enough" (196). Blanca and, at second-hand, her mother have to have interpreted Lysyl's facial features, personal style, and presence on the stairs as signs of her being a "'bad'" woman (197), a contaminating and alien influence in the home of General von Marken.

Madame von Marken had already been "hurt" (198) by Frances's impiety towards the "old-fashioned" virtues (197) of the once dominant, now threatened social ideology observed in the sitting room of the flat in the display of a portrait of former emperor Franz Josef and portraits representing the family lineage. They suggest a conspicuous exhibition of conservative loyalties to empire, prewar social hierarchy, and pride in bloodline and upper-class whiteness, identified with purity. Madame von Marken expresses her outrage first to Frances, reminding her of her feminine role in preserving the innocence of children and domestic respectability and purity and castigating the laxness of the foreign housewife. Frances apologizes, though ashamed of her show of deference to a schematization of women she inwardly abhors; she rehangs the portraits, but feels out of place in the sitting room, retreating from its "gloomy and whiskery and antimacassary" atmosphere to spend her daytime leisure in her bedroom and enjoying the sensuous pleasure of lilacs in the Prater (198–99). Her characterization of the sitting room significantly highlights a "gloomy" foreignness, masculine bodily presence, and a feminine presence only in the "antimacassariness," a maintenance of a fastidious show of concern for domestic cleanliness. André, too, apologizes to Madame von Marken, relishing the show of piety to masculine chivalry and protection of young feminine innocence; he also dumps Lysyl, when another course that would have preserved a show of respectability would have been to keep their sex more private. His ethic of the "chic," though, does not rule out trying to seduce Frances.

Rhys juxtaposes the pieties of various characters, most of which rely on the production of woman as a moral or aesthetic sign. The von Markens, representing old money, worship empire, bloodline, patriarchy, and cleanliness, all of which are contingent on the family production of "good" women. The Japanese officials with whom Frances has social contact through Pierre venerate militarism, patriotism, and "good" women as wives. Colonel Ishima dehumanizes Viennese women (assumed to be sexually available) as "'war material'" (209). His ugly treatment of them makes Frances hate him, and to dehumanize him and Kashua as being like monkeys. Anne McClintock argues that monkeys in Victorian culture were allied with classes of people "collectively seen to inhabit the threshold of racial degeneration" (216). More closely to the 1920s, the hypermasculine "brutal Hun" of First World War anti-German propaganda was processed as ape-like. Frances notes the Japanese men's admiration for the German army and German control of women. André, a representative of the modern, idolizes the chic, seeking to acquire it through sexual attachments to beautiful women. Frances relishes the charming or pretty object, and herself as such. The inauthenticity of her experience of place and time is highlighted by the "dominance of looking" (and being gazed at as woman) "in modernity" (Rauch 85).

"Charming," "pretty," and "lovely" are Frances's favorite epithets, used variously to describe women as aesthetic objects, her bedroom, dresses, cities, and Hungarians. She reserves "graceful" for women's figures (V 196, 202). The reduction of Frances to the roles of looker and object of the gaze, to cite an argument of Walter Benjamin's, "compensates for the loss of experience and the debilitation of agency in an industrialized environment" (Rauch 85). The "pretty" takes on the quality of a fetish, a transcendental anchor in modernity. Rauch explains: "The individual's psychological adaptation to a fragmented world . . . proceeds by libidinally investing the various broken pieces of the past and treating them as souvenirs of a blissful experience of wholeness. Meaning in this modern world of fragments is now formed by the subject's conception of these fragmentary pieces as fetishes, as means for a substitute experience of bliss" (82). Frances reminds herself, "keep your eyes glued on the pretty face [. . .] so much better not to look" closely. Looking closely might take her into a moral domain in which she would have to confront the play of her own "prejudice[s]" in her judgments of what is ugly. Looking closely, she decides, is "[s]tupid" (V 201). When Frances recalls she and Pierre becoming rich she febrilely hails "great god money," which makes available

all that's nice in life. Youth and beauty, the envy of women, and the love of men.
    Even the luxury of a soul, a character and thoughts of one's own. (222)

Looking back, Frances realizes the fragility of her "joy of life" in 1921; her "joy of life" is "cracky" (202). It makes her largely oblivious before her change of fortune to the weaknesses of her marriage. At one point in her pregnancy she experiences "a calm sense of power," dreaming she might be "mysteriously irresistible, a magnet, a *Femme Sacrée*" (236). Rhys ironizes Frances's pieties, her investments in illusions. Frances, Rhys highlights, has a habit of abjectly turning away from the "ugly," particularly if it might attach itself to her. Her habit of not enquiring too closely into any possible dubiousness in her circumstances or herself means that she does not ask herself why André and other men who try to seduce her think she may be sexually available, "'bad'" for their sexual pleasure, and that she does not pursue closely the question of the origins of her and Pierre's new wealth. When she wants to escape her seeming fate of crossing beyond the boundary of respectability she denigrates Fate as an "old hag" (256).

In *Rhys, Stead, Lessing, and the Politics of Empathy*, Judith Kegan Gardiner misquotes Ford's description of Rhys's compassion as an "almost terrific sympathy with the underdog" and affirms this view (24). What makes it "almost terrific" in "Vienne" for Gardiner are the narrator's "contradictory" "moral pronouncements," based on "inconsistent" "attitudes to sexual roles and the double standard" (30). Gardiner's difficulties in distinguishing narrative and authorial voice in the story are apparent in the problem with pronouns in her summation: "Rhys pities victims of gender and class oppression, but she does not always enlist our sympathies, alienating us from the narrator's judgments by her misogyny, self-pity, self-hatred, and sporadic vindictiveness. Arbitrarily, she shifts between empathetic inclusions and angry rejections of herself, us readers and the people snapped in her fictional photographs, outbursts that she deleted in the later version" (31). In context the "misogyny, self-pity, self-hatred, and sporadic vindictiveness" could be the narrator's or Rhys's, although I think Gardiner means it to be the narrator's. Rhys certainly makes the deletions referred to in the last sentence. It is not clear whether in Gardiner's view the narrator or Rhys makes the shift between "empathetic inclusions and angry rejections."

I suggest that an ironizing authorial perspective in "Vienne" examines the

interestedness of Frances's narrative and the limits of Frances's sympathy and
gaze, including her gaze at herself. Ford's comments on Rhys's bias and sympathy are reductive, breezily passing over the complexities of her ironization of
point of view and of her moral investigations of narrative voice. "Vienne" is the
final story in *The Left Bank and Other Stories*. Placed at the collection's end, it
raises new questions about the earlier stories, particularly about what the narrators see, the values that structure their points of view, the limits of their sympathies, and the constitutive silences, blindnesses, or gaps in their storytelling.

NOTES

1. The anonymous reviewer of *The Left Bank and Other Stories* in the *New York Times Book Review* observed that "the book takes its title from Ford Madox Ford's preface" (28).

2. Rhys published three versions of "Vienne." An early, much shorter version of the 1927 story was published in *transatlantic review* in 1924. Rhys edited the 1927 version for inclusion in *Tigers Are Better-Looking: With a Selection from* The Left Bank (1968).

3. "Trio" 85.

4. I describe the furor over the club in more detail in "Jean Rhys, 'Human Ants,' and the Production of Expatriate Creole Identities."

5. My research on Dominican journalism was facilitated by the purchase from the British Library, a deposit library of the British empire, of microfilmed runs of Do-minican newspapers. The purchase was made from an Australian Research Council small grant, which also, among other things, financed some casual teaching relief for a semester, to enable me to read the runs.

Chapter 4 ———————————————

Telling of the "Amateur"

The protagonists of Jean Rhys's novels "Triple Sec" (1924), *Quartet* (originally published in the U.K. as *Postures* in 1928), *After Leaving Mr Mackenzie* (1931), and *Voyage in the Dark* (1934) are marked in various ways by other characters as engaging in forms of prostitution. In early twentieth-century Britain, Rhys's protagonists would have been classified as "amateur" prostitutes (called "straight girls" by prostitutes) or "sexual free-lance" women. As Lucy Bland and Frank Mort point out: "To many its meaning was unclear, but there was general agreement that the term [amateur] applied to a young woman engaging in promiscuous sex for 'free.' That she was referred to as an amateur *prostitute* indicated the continuing equation of active female sexuality with prostitution" (140). Between the amateur and her partner the sexual contract is implicitly negotiated, based on mutual understandings that sex may be available freely or in exchange for gifts (of money, clothes, jewelry, and the like), nights out, motor rides, and the like—"luxuries and amusements" (Haldane 157). The amateur was excoriated in two moral panics: the moral panic around the incidence of venereal disease during the First World War and the panic around the falling birthrate and changing attitudes toward motherhood during the 1920s. In each of these panics the amateur was, like the female vampire, constructed as a "monster in conflict with the family, the couple and the institutions of patriarchal capitalism" (Creed 61). Her monstrousness comprised sexual activity that was difficult to regulate, but also the consumption enabled by it.

I do not introduce the vampire figure lightly. Amateurs were in the first of those panics troped as vampires on the body politic: "at present they stalk through the land, vampires upon the nation's health, distributing and perpetuating among our young manhood diseases which constitute a national calamity," wrote M.D. in the *Times*. Rhys critically reworks the vampire and disease tropes in "Triple Sec," *Quartet, After Leaving Mr Mackenzie, Voyage in the Dark*, and

Good Morning, Midnight (1939). In both moral panics, which tapped eugenic fears, amateurs were represented as threatening a racial degeneration. In this chapter I argue that in "Triple Sec," *Quartet*, and *After Leaving Mr Mackenzie*, Rhys engages with, and often provides supplementary, at times transculturating, framings of the public discourses that circulated around the amateur.

"VAMPIRES UPON THE NATION'S HEALTH"

The amateur became the object of medical, legal, scientific, psychological, and moral discourses during the 1910s and 1920s. While the term amateur gained wide currency during the First World War, when 75 to 80 percent of venereal disease was attributed to her sexual activity (Bland and Mort 140), it "had been around for many years" (Bland and Mort 150). She was constructed as a national and racial threat *from within* (Bland and Mort 139). The discourses around her focused on her disease or dis/ease and racial health; the fitness of the mother body, her own or that of her partners' wives or future wives; and her lack of self-control, understood in moral or psychological terms, and the difficulties of regulating it. She was categorized in relation to "bourgeois female ideals," the good wife or the virginal unmarried daughter, as was the prostitute (Shannon Bell 40). To indicate briefly the discourses in which she circulated, I will concentrate on two representative accounts of her: "Venereal Disease: Sources of Infection," a letter to the *Times* by M.D., published on 14 December 1917, and Charlotte Haldane's account of her in *Motherhood and Its Enemies* (1927). M.D. addresses the problem of the fitness of the soldier-citizen in wartime; Haldane, the problem of the mother-citizen in peacetime. M.D. presents the amateur as a moral type, writing that she "prostitutes her body . . . because she wants to do so, and has not sufficient chastity or self-control to restrain her natural appetites." Comparing her with the prostitute, Haldane argues: "With her the lure to the streets is not essentially economic but psychological" (141). Haldane sketches the social formation of her psychology and its consequences, implicitly articulating a healthy, bourgeois, feminine, domestic, and maternal identity by producing the amateur prostitute as one of its others. Haldane numbers her among five "abnormal" types of women, which also include spinsters, prostitutes, the subnormal (in terms of her sex life), and the "intersexual," who deviates "towards the anatomical and psychological characteristics of the masculine sex" (158).

Both accounts pathologize an inner rottenness in the amateur. Using lurid metaphors, M.D. draws a distinction between prostitutes and "sexual free-lance young women." The figures of contagion totalize both groups of women as infection and disease, demonizing the female parties to "irregular," meaning non-marital, sex on the part of men. The prostitute, M.D. says, is a "persistent parasite on the body politic." At the time, gonorrhea was understood popularly to be spread by a vegetable parasite and syphilis by an animal parasite ("Venereal Diseases"). The vampire trope for the amateur produces blood as a site of transmission and abjection. Julia Kristeva suggests in *Powers of Horror* that "blood, as a vital element, also refers to women, fertility, and the assurance of fecundation. It thus becomes a fascinating semantic crossroads, the propitious place for abjection where *death* and *femininity, murder* and *procreation, cessation of life* and *vitality* all come together" (96). The trope evokes fear of the amateur as a vagina dentata figure and as transmitter of corrupt and corrupting blood, which destabilizes boundaries between human and animal, the living and the dead, health and disease. In a formulation with evolutionary connotations, M.D. places the soldier-citizen as the model of the Briton "at the height of his physical and mental vigour." The "sexual free-lance" is a "vampire of degeneration" (Dijkstra 346) whose insatiable appetite places at risk the regularity of the legitimate Briton family—man, wife, "future children" (M.D.)—and her own "birthright" to mother "future British children." "[I]t seems probable," M.D. insists, "that she is generally a young woman who is employed in a shop, munition factory, or domestic service." She is, then, characterized as generally a class other to the institution of the bourgeois family.

A dominant theme in M.D.'s letter is regulation: lacking necessary "chastity and self-control," the sexual free lance cannot "restrain her natural appetites"; the prostitute is "under a certain amount of supervision," but in any case has a vested monetary interest in maintaining a healthy body; and the infected soldier is "compelled to undergo appropriate and adequate treatment." By drawing attention to the fact that "the available evidence goes to show that as a class" the sexual free lances "are neither being treated nor controlled in their depredations," M.D. implicitly proposes that their activities be made subject to medical and legal regulation. M.D.'s desire was met "[t]owards the end of World War I" when "the 'amateur' as well as the professional prostitute was subjected to the regulatory powers of the Defence of the Realm Act (Dora 40d): 'no woman who is suffering from venereal disease . . . shall have sexual intercourse with any member of HM forces, or solicit/invite any member to have sexual intercourse with her.' A woman so charged would be required 'to be remanded for not less than a week for medical examination'" (Bland and Mort 140). The regulation "was revoked in November 1918" (Bland and Mort 140). Lucy Bland and Frank Mort also discuss feminist activism against clauses "criminalizing venereal disease's transmission" proposed, but not enacted, "within a reintroduced Criminal Law Amendment Bill and a Sexual Offences Bill" in 1918. "To many social purity feminists and moralists promiscuous intercourse was," they note, "by definition unhealthy and could never be otherwise; they wanted the state to act in its public health capacity as a *moralizing* agency—to discourage promiscuity and encourage responsible sexual relations through moral education" (141).

For Haldane, a "feminist journalist and popular science writer" (Squier 101),[1] the "amateur prostitute" is "of the masses" (139) and, if she marries, she brings "to home-life and matrimony her own [problems], very different from those of the ordinary housewife" (146), which threaten "the future of the race" (250). Haldane's public-school morality is apparent in her emphasis on the working-class girl's restricted access to team activities: "organized games and sports"

(140), because of their expense; after she leaves school, "dances which must be performed by several persons, each of whom has a part to play to complete the whole"; and hymn singing in congregation, because of the decline in church attendance (142). The "decay of the home" (141) is attributed to two flourishing new institutions, the cinema and the star system of the movie industry, and the deterioration of two institutions that had in the past acted as the young working-class girl's "great safeguards"—the church and domestic service (140).

While Haldane acknowledges that the "inhibitions" of service and religiosity "used to condemn young women to a rigorous and sometimes cruel 'self-control'" (142–43), she represents the amateur as unable to make proper use of her new freedom. This inability is apparent, for her, in both the quality of the amateur's amusements and the mind she brings to them. Her education is inferior to that of the "middle-class girl," Haldane's norm, and she lacks the discrimination and sophistication to resist the lures of "American-made" popular film narratives (142) and the institution of the female film star, which encourage consumerist individualism and escapist desire. Her fantasy life, Haldane insists, is determined by uncritical aspiration for the "setting of the film-star" and "fashions in clothes and furniture of the screen" and indiscriminate identification with the heroines of rags-to-riches stories who rise socially through their adventures in promiscuous sex. Haldane fears the rise of a culture of conspicuous consumption, marked as foreign, which was shaping "new forms of subjectivity for women, whose intimate needs, desires, and perceptions of self were mediated by public representations of commodities and the gratifications that they promised" (Felski 62).[2] As Andreas Huyssen notes, "[t]he lure of mass culture . . . has traditionally been described as the threat of losing oneself in dreams and delusions and of merely consuming rather than producing" (55).

Haldane suggests that the amateur who marries brings the dis/ease of her "moral body" (Shannon Bell 71), her desire for luxuries and amusements, to the marital home, individualistically allowing "her own interests to compete with those of husband and children" (158). Those interests are not "domestic" (144), and as her desires fail to materialize in marriage or children, if she has them, her "circumstances will hardly improve her happiness or her temper" (145). Her dis/ease pollutes familial relations. In her account of the amateur being irredeemably corrupted by the "fashions in clothes and furniture of the screen" (141), Haldane is updating and reworking an older discourse about the causes of prostitution. Mariana Valverde has discussed the adducing of love of finery as a cause of prostitution during the nineteenth century. The conspicuous display of "fine clothes" by "well-dressed women of the town" was cited as corrupting of the morals of working-class girls in 1871 (176). She observes the ways in which "'love of dress' is . . . linked to vanity and idleness, that is, to specifically female vices subversive of Victorian thrift" (178). Haldane's idealized working-class domesticity is analogous with Victorian thrift. Amateurs, Haldane states without offering evidence, are also uncritical consumers of the idea of feminists ("spinster groups") that "man is always the woman's enemy, seeking to exploit her" (158).

"SOMETHING BEASTLY ABOUT THIS"[3]

The original title of "Triple Sec," "Suzy Tells," promises revelation, exposé—a promise heightened by its form, a young woman, Suzy Gray, at times sexually active, at times exposed to sexual coercion, writing her diary as if talking to an intimate friend. The reader, then, is positioned as an eavesdropper. Suzy Gray, though, has more to tell about having been kissed, propositioned, and sexually insulted, than about sex. The narrative pattern follows formulae of the female gothic: seduction, abandonment by a lover, ruin, and rehabilitation through more "honest" work for which she is eventually rewarded with the prospect of marriage to a man, Michel, who does not desire to exploit her sexually. Rhys draws in particular on melodrama's capacity to highlight issues of gender, class, and exploitative power and to foreground the female protagonist, "however passive or suffering she might be" (Walkowitz 87). As Judith Walkowitz observes, while melodrama may offer "a powerful cultural resource for female political expression," "it set limitations on what could be said, particularly in relation to female agency and desire" (93). Its personalization of good and evil tends to individualize agency for change. Suzy's episodic narrative implicitly reworks the vampire and disease tropes of the amateur. It charts a growth from naivety through experience of the world and the flesh (my clichés are deliberate) to realization: "that the devil is ever so much more powerful than God and that he arranges most things" (TS 33); that she does not have "the nature to make a successful demi-mondaine" (140); that "the truth of life under the lies of social forms, and religion, and the protection of women" is that "things" are "ugly, menacing, horribly cruel" (176);[4] and that while "[l]ots of platitudes are lies, one isn't"—"To be happy one must work" (219).

Suzy tells a tale of beset womanhood, in which her own naivety, aversion to "beastly meanness" (150), and "something strong" in her character (33), "pluck" (127), protect her from the "fates" of three monitory figures: her friend Alison, a chorus girl and amateur so hardened that she colludes with a boyfriend in an attempt to procure Suzy for him; and two streetwalking prostitutes, "horribly painted, eyeing all the men who passed them—not young any longer" (155). Tony, implicitly a "nice Englishman" (47), and Lord Richard Blunt, who tries to kiss her at one of Tony's parties, eroticize Suzy's child quality. Tony has her display this at parties through his choice of her costume; Suzy, on the other hand, desires the confidence and sophistication she thinks looking "grown up and very smart" would give her (7). Tony's paternalism calls for her to play a part that infantilizes her sexually, emotionally, and intellectually. It exacerbates her shyness, increasing her dependency on Tony and on being part of the couple they form. Suzy's sexual inexperience is emphasized by a want of sexual knowingness apparent in her reference points for understanding her all-consuming love for Tony—what her sister chorus girls had told her and what she has read in books—and a gullibility and innocence that make her vulnerable to entrapment plots and shameable by sexual suggestions and practices unspeakable to her diary. Striking postures, Suzy does resolve to make use of men, who after all use her and sexually assault her, but she accepts "luxuries and amusements," usually stopping short of sex, and she also resolves to make quite a few fresh starts, through working, usually by returning to the stage. Her most concerted effort is made after a "common sensical [sic]" (212) man from Manchester, "who wanted his money's worth or he'd know the reason why" (213), loses his temper and starts "telling" Suzy "home truths" (212).

White Creole Suzy has not been trained in domestic skills, cooking or sewing, and her relations with her family or changes in her family's circumstances are seemingly such that she must make her way as an isolated modern individual within a metropolitan capitalist culture. Around 1918 or 1919 Suzy gets a job in the Pensions Office "surprisingly easily" (230). Meta Zimmeck points out that for clerical work women were paid wages "just sufficient to maintain them in decency though not in comfort" (163). The work available to Suzy before and during the First World War is on the border of respectability for women. As a chorus girl she is one of the "thousands of utterly obscure performers living with and like the working classes" (Davis 163). Tracy C. Davis has analyzed the ways in which Victorian and turn-of-the-century "female performers functioned at the centre of an erotically-bonded neighbourhood. . . . Theatrical impropriety was symptomatic of a complex network of Victorian attitudes and practices. The consequence for actresses was a social identity saturated with moral equivocacy. The work, not the individual, made this an inevitability. This marked their social identity in the culture" (163). Suzy's work as manicurist and (often nude) model for artists makes her particularly vulnerable to sexual "assault": kisses (a condition of payment for a manicurist she learns) and uninvited lewd propositions. In bohemian London, Suzy, sickeningly for her, circulates as a sexual and aesthetic object, part of a "common pool" (Sedgwick 251) of working-class women, the sexual use, exchange, and conspicuous consumption of whom secure upper middle-class English homosociality. In *Voyage in the Dark*, Germaine, Vincent Jeffries's French girlfriend, explicitly speaks of the "climate" of English misogyny (70) and hints at a concomitant "'homosexual panic'" (Sedgwick 251), played out in unsatisfying sexual relations with women.[5] Abortion is represented in both novels as an illicit service industry of middle-class and upper-middle-class English homosociality.[6]

Like other men Suzy meets, Tony eroticizes her neck, and Rhys uses the implicit vampire trope to allegorize, episodically rather than consistently, gender relations and relations of class and capital.[7] Suzy's metaphors of her subsequent illness emphasize her liminal condition between life and death—mundane versions of the "undead" status of the vampire. She feels herself to be a "ghost" (TS 29) or a "melancholy skeleton." Tony leaves "red marks" on her throat when he kisses her there. "I hope they'll never go—I love them," writes Suzy (25).[8] Her desire emphasizes her emotional investment in signs that seem to emblematize her loss of apparent virginity and affirm a sexual and reproductive maturity. The relationship makes her realize a tremendous physical and *emotional* hunger "for love." The physicality and paternalistic protection of Tony's embrace make her "feel utterly happy and satisfied"; apart from him she is "achey and lonely" (20).

Stephen D. Arata has argued that Bram Stoker's *Dracula* may be read as a "narrative of reverse colonization," playing on fear "that what has been represented as the 'civilized' world is on the point of being colonized by 'primitive' forces. These forces can originate outside the civilized world . . . or they can inhere in the civilized itself (as in Kurtz's emblematic heart of darkness)" (623). Vampiric episodes in "Triple Sec" may also be read as returns of the primitive. Suzy's hunger for love awakens what is represented as an archaic, indeed atavistic, desire in the modern woman not to work and to seek satisfaction in infantilized emotional, intellectual, and financial dependency and utter monopolization of her life, loyalty, and emotions. (Only later does Suzy's hunger for the upper-middle-class lifestyle of the rich man's mistress, which she no longer enjoys, threaten corruption.) Suzy is not really interested in the singing lessons that Tony hopes will help her future career on the stage. The lessons suggest that Tony sees his keeping of her as a temporary break in her career. It is surely significant that when Suzy must acknowledge the mutability of Tony's love after he has her dismissed by his cousin Guy she loses her singing voice.

Suzy's reckless hunger, though, is shadowed gothically by a "thought that spoils things," that gives her a "horrible twist just to write it" (TS 16): a fear of being abandoned by Tony, which makes her "so frightened" of herself and of her love for him (21). Her sense of the enormity of her risk fractures and explicitly hystericizes her feminine identity. When Tony announces he is making a trip to America, she becomes "suddenly deathly, horribly sick" and collapses, her "forehead [. . .] covered with perspiration." "I suppose it was hysteria, diary—extraordinary thing," writes Suzy. After losing Tony's "protection," Suzy's health deteriorates into passivity, indifference, a feeling of being "quite dead inside" (33) and "outside" of her bodied self and looking on (35)—depersonalization. "In depersonalization," Elizabeth Grosz explains, summarizing Paul Schilder's work, "subjects lose interest in the whole body. They refuse or are afraid to invest any narcissistic libido in the body image. They may feel a dramatic change in self-conception and in relations to the external world. Self-observations seem completely disinterested or disinvested, viewed from the point of a spectator or outsider. Not only is the subject's own body treated with disinterest, but the outside world is also experienced as flat and disinvested" (*Volatile Bodies* 76–77).[9]

While Suzy is in this condition, she is introduced to the life of the amateur by Alison. In a later stage of her "hysterical" decline (Rhys's popular understanding of a female body out of conscious control), Suzy will briefly lay claim to a Creole difference through *corporeal* memory of the landscape of her childhood. Her "very homesick" feelings (88) mark a return of embodied experience that cannot be assimilated into her usual passing as English. In the naturalistic register of Rhys's representation of Suzy's illness, comparative poverty and worry over money are among the causes of the severe depression that reduce Suzy to a "melancholy skeleton" (120).

If Tony epitomizes upper-middle-class English paternalism and homosociality, Carl Stahl (his German patronym means steel or sword) represents American monopoly capitalism and ethnic heterogeneity.[10] In *The English in the West Indies*, James Anthony Froude figures the relation between Dominica and the "hand" of the English (153) as a failed romance: Dominica is a beauty "conscious" of her "charms" "thrown aside" by the "enterprising youth of England"; she would "surrender herself to-morrow with a light heart to France, to America, to any country which would accept the charge of her destinies" (160). Froude feminizes the colony as a woman under threat of foreign domination (160) and "emancipated" "negro morals" (152). Carl's masculinity is more vigorous, fecund, and "primitive" than Tony's,[11] and is associated with the expansion of American commercial interests in Argentina,[12] and the so-called "American invasion," a reinvigoration of British commerce in decline in the late nineteenth and early twentieth century through U.S. capital investment (Reid 97).

Before Carl has sex with Suzy, he "overpowers" her (TS 70), not by kissing her, but by his impression "of being very strong and forceful" (69) and "often" looking at her "mouth and throat with such a queer look" (70). Suzy submits out of fear, and he "hurt[s]" her "frightfully and did not care," leaving a disfiguring mark where he bites her on the mouth (72). The last night she spends with him is "awful": she "learned what shame meant" (93). His "horrible hairy hands that always hurt" and "hot panting breadth" emphasize his beastliness. "Beastly" and "beast" are commonly used words of Suzy's,[13] occasionally functioning self-reflexively, usually moralizing the actions of exploitative men and "looser" women (the bad company into which she has fallen) in ways that emphasize her innocence or comparative innocence. In *Voyage in the Dark* the words are used more sparingly and pointedly and are interwoven with a metaphoricity of blackness, which more consistently engages with a colonial history. Carl Stahl's hairy hands are a sign of the ape, the werewolf, and indeed the hypermasculine evil "Hun" in First World War propaganda.[14] In the context of turn-of-the-century discourses about relations between South America and the U.S., Carl's hands recall through physical stereotype Uruguayan Enrique Rodó's well-known characterization of the United States as "the crude, materialistic Caliban" (Whitaker 361) of the Americas in *Ariel* (1900).

Arata suggests that "[v]ampires are generated by racial enervation and the decline of empire" (629). Carl's "victim" is enervated by the break-up of her relationship with Tony. Tony monopolizes Suzy through her atavizing "hunger for love"; Carl, through force, threats of violence, a spy, and a promise to take her to New York, where she thinks she may be able to start afresh. Suzy's relationship with Carl fills her with self-contempt. Carl insists, "'Now, Suzy, you belong to me, and I'll look after you, so you've not got to worry'" (TS 72).[15] He refuses to allow Suzy to work while she is in his "protection." Franco Moretti's comment on Dracula is apposite to Carl: "Like monopoly capital, his ambition is to subjugate the last vestiges of the liberal era and destroy all forms of economic independence" (74). Suzy's acknowledgment of her cheapness for Carl links his extension of monopoly capitalism into gender and class relations with a history of colonial slavery: "My great grandfather paid much more for a pretty slave" (TS 83). This historical allusion facilitates a reading of Carl and Suzy's great-grandfather and Carl and Suzy as doubles. If Suzy's great-grandfather's ownership of slaves represents the prosperous past of a vicious form of feudalistic monopoly relations in the "New World" and Suzy its dispossessed and deracinated vestige, Carl represents the present and future of a vigorous and cruel "New World" neocolonial capitalism.

Suzy has archaic and modern racial fears about the potential monstrousness of her baby by Carl, and these pressure her to have the fetus aborted. Only the short-lived fantasy that the fetus has been conceived with Tony reconciles her to her pregnancy. Suzy fears "the strength of the imagination" of the pregnant woman "on the foetus" (Boucé 88), thinking it might be "a little monster" because of the "thoughts" she has been "having" (TS 85–86). Paul-Gabriel Boucé has traced this kind of fear back through medical, paramedical, and popular ideas to the early eighteenth century (88–89). Suzy's other fear concerning the monstrousness of the baby is more modern and naturalistic. She has been drinking regularly to ameliorate one of the effects of her enervation—insomnia—and "was drunk" when the baby was conceived. In *Parenthood and Race-Culture: An Outline of Eugenics* (1909), Caleb Williams Saleeby describes alcohol as a racial poison and endorses the view "'that drunkenness of the parents at the time of conception may have a harmful effect on the nature of the offspring'" (208).[16] Suzy fears that she will "go mad" if she sees her drunkenness (and, I would suggest, the "shameful" sexual acts that she says she performed while she was under its influence) reflected in the "dreadful little deformed monster" she imagines will be born of them (TS 99).

Rhys represents Suzy's disease and illness in gothic and naturalistic registers, using "mirror" scenes to striking effect. After her abortion, Suzy writes that she has a "hysterical" sense that she is "surely getting perfectly *hideous*"; she then proceeds to document naturalistically from her reflection "in the glass" the physical and psychological symptoms of her decline from the relative picture of health she presented after her recuperative seaside holiday with her friend Jennie. The symptoms (unwilled excessive thinness, circles under the eyes, anxiety, loss of appetite for life, unsociability, low self-esteem, and compulsive walking) suggest severe depression. She concludes: "I'm appallingly, hideously lonely, but I wish to see no one" (121). The novel suggests that Suzy's assimilation to upper-middle-class English masculine self-restraint in her social manners is a major cause of her depression. Referring her anger to ethnic stereotypes, Suzy thinks of it as a product of a non-English heritage (Welsh and white Creole);[17] the effort to repress her anger or disgust at the way she is treated brings her several times to uncontrollable public tears, and exacerbates her depression. Suzy does visit a Chelsea doctor, and his diagnostic and medical mirror of her condition accords with the assumptions of the medical men involved in her abortion.[18]

The Chelsea doctor prescribes a "tonic." When she tells him her medical history, his diagnosis reflects his assumptions about sexually active women he considers promiscuous:

> "You're craving for love and denying yourself—isn't that so?
> It'll make a wreck of you, if you go on. Why if you gave your body what it wanted you'd be a different girl in a month." (123)

When Suzy resists the diagnosis, he "brutally" dismisses her credibility, patronizes her as "'little girl'" (123), and invokes the medical authority of his reference book by insisting on illustrating and proving his diagnosis with medical diagrams, which reduce her to voracious sexual organs. Suzy is disgusted and hastens to leave. To her diary she insists that it is not morality that constrains any sexual relations with men, but "simply the morbid feeling that as I'm not pretty any longer I won't be desirable" (124). Angelika Rauch summarizes Sigmund Freud's definition of melancholia: "the inability to mourn and 'work through' the loss of the object. Successful mourning would allow a reconstitution of the subject independent of the lost object. Melancholia introjects the image of the other, thus preventing separation from the object" (81). The picture of prettiness, vitality, health, pluck, innocence, and "honour" (TS 126) that aroused Tony's desire and allowed Suzy to trade on the aesthetic and sexual commodification of her body to earn a living is her nostalgic aesthetic ideal—her introjected lost object of desire and desirability.

In the sexual modernity represented by the life of the amateur and her relations to men, Suzy experiences her self as fragmented, a collocation of ruin and illness. Tony, Carl, and Tommie, an artist for whom she sits, fetishize her neck. Medical men totalize her as her sexual organs. Tony's cousin Guy's doctor, who attends her after the abortion, regards her with "a sort of Oh-ho-somebody's-bit-of-fun-ah-ha" expression (109) and euphemistically refers to her uncontrollable sexual appetite as "sweethearting" (109). Tony does not want her "figure spoilt" by her pregnancy, so he issues instructions that she wear "damned uncomfortable plaster things" after her abortion (109–110). Tommie will use her body for a subject painting illustrating Robert Browning's "Song" ("Nay but you, who do not love her,/Is she not pure gold, my mistress"), but he will hire another model for the mistress's hair.

The maternal Madame Poupèye, a Belgian refugee, exercises her domestic skills to make over a "hideous [. . .] place" as a comfortable home for her family in England. Contrasting herself with Madame Poupèye close to the end of the novel, Suzy feels "very small," one of the "haggard, nervous, hysterical, females who talk like blazes and can neither cook, sew, nor do anything else useful," a risky marriage partner (230). Her response to Madame Poupèye—"If I were a man I'd marry someone like that" (230)—suggests a continuing disidentification with her own femininity "that seems too saturated with injury or aggression" (Butler, *Bodies That Matter* 100). Her desire for a domestic and mothering presence in her life and the desirability of the mother are articulated from the perspective of a generic man.

Examining a European tradition of melancholy and psychoanalytic discourses about melancholia, Juliana Schiesari has argued that "melancholia as a *discursive and cultural practice* . . . has given men a cultural privilege in displaying and representing loss so as to convert it into a sign of privileged subjectivity" (68), of being "especially gifted" (7). Melancholy, especially during the Renaissance, had rhetorics and postures of despair. She suggests that "women who fall into the depths of sorrow are all too easily dismissed with the banal and unprestigious term 'depression'" (4), and tries to locate sites where women "might be able to articulate loss and lack in terms of a feminine symbolic that offers a counterdiscourse to the melancholic tradition" (77). Women's depression may be read, she proposes, "not as a failed expression of loss—as prosaic grief—but as an *incipit* to a mourning of both daughter and mother's devalued status in a symbolic governed by a masculine economy of self-recuperation" (77).

In "Triple Sec," Suzy herself is daughter and pregnant mother-to-be, and her depression is a locus of multivalent loss; writing, friendship, the discipline of work, and sharing critical gazes at the English are her means to recuperation. In her relationship with Tony, Suzy had resisted the word "mistress" and the stock narratives of the transitoriness of the rich man's affection for his mistress. Her dismissal forces her to accede to the power of the signifying economy that separates women into the respectable and disrespectable, virtuous and whore, marriage and mistress material. Seduced, she has lost caste and prospects. Abandoned, she has lost not just Tony, but sexual confidence, faith in her reckless streak and the risk of intimacy, and pride. Her dispossession is exacerbated and she is reexposed to the struggle of the unpropertied modern woman and individual to earn a living in a capitalist economy structured by profoundly unequal gender and class relations.

Moretti argues of *Dracula*: "The first-person account is a clear expression of the desire to keep hold of one's individuality, which the vampire threatens to subjugate. Yet so long as the conflict is one between human 'individualism' and vampirical 'totalization,' things do not go at all well for the humans" (77). Suzy's diary does help her to keep hold of and reflect on her individuality, with all its naivety, rationalizations, compromises, error, anger, and disgust. Walter Benjamin has generalized from a reading of Baudelaire to argue that in modernity the commodified sexuality of the prostitute has become the transcendental anchor of the male subject (Rauch 80). Suzy's diary (an intimate, uncritical friend) and her friendships with Jennie Kent, Pamela, and Raoul Poupèye are her transcendental anchors in modernity. Having spurned Tony's pension (which has paid her small rents) and committed herself to the discipline of dancing training, Suzy begins to recover her health in a seedy boarding-house community of European and South American expatriates and Belgian refugees. They are, like her, ethnic outsiders in English culture, and she enjoys their "mixture of dislike and contempt" for England and the English (TS 216) and their returns of a popular ethnographic gaze. "I could scarcely keep from giggling, I found it so funny," she writes (217).

THE MATTER WITH MARYA ZELLI

Marya Zelli's obsessive and adulterous love for H. J. Heidler in *Quartet* is represented as vampirizing. "When I think of you and Lois together I really feel as if I were going mad," writes Marya to H. J. "You don't believe me. I can see you smiling. But it's true. It's as if all the blood in my body is being drained, very slowly, all the time, all the blood in my heart" (121). Usually H. J. Heidler and Lois Heidler presumptuously tell Marya what is the matter with her, just as they assume the prerogative of defining her and her relationship with her husband, Stephan Zelli, and deciding her future, including severing her relationship with Stephan. At one point Marya imagines H. J. claiming God as "'a pal [. . .] I'm in His image or He's in mine'" (125). The publicly articulated word is certainly with H. J. and Lois, and they try to mold Marya in images that accord with a bourgeois signifying system that splits women into good women and bad women (more briskly, "[i]ntact or not intact") and people into those with "an income or not an income" (125). Their capital, they think, gives them the right to control Marya and her life, and to make her into an object that will reflect well on their patronage. Marya's account of her drained condition in her letter accords with a metaphorization of her love for H. J. as an open wound (95). A contemptuous comment of Stephan's after he is released from jail and Marya tells him of her affair links her metaphorical loss of blood with questions of character raised earlier in a summary of Marya's sense of the "haphazard" quality of her "existence" (10).

The narrative of *Quartet* is usually read as a roman à clef, with Marya being equated with Rhys herself; H. J. with Ford Madox Ford; Lois with Stella Bowen, Ford's partner; and Stephan with Jean Lenglet, Rhys's husband. It follows a pattern of abandonment by husband, seduction, abandonment by lover, ruin, abandonment by husband. While I do not read *Quartet* as a roman à clef I do suggest that Rhys draws on and reworks Ford Madox Ford's ideas about the emotional conduct of the English in *The Spirit of the People* (1907). Marya's sense that her love for H. J. is vampirizing her is integral to her awareness of ruin. Her growing awareness of the extent of the ruin is realized through a vision of virgin forest (which resonates in both a French modernist and a Dominican autoethnographic context) and a sense of her bed plunging "downwards with her— sickeningly—into blackness" (126). Rhys uses figurations of blackness in the novel to represent a major depressive episode and questions of demoralization, degeneration, and class hierarchy. These questions are linked occasionally and briefly with empire.

In her representations of Marya's establishment of relationships with Stephan and H. J. Rhys focuses on Marya's desire for protector/savior figures to provide her a transcendental anchor in modernity. What Marya eroticizes is protection/salvation. At nineteen, longing to play "a glittering part [. . .] against the sombre and wonderful background of London," Marya (of genteel poor background) had become a chorus girl in "Mr Albert Prance's No. 1 touring company." The decision was motivated by an individualistic "adventurousness," a desire to earn "her own living" "without expensive preliminaries" (15). The "hard and monotonous" life and part of the chorus girl had reduced her to a state of "drift," "a lack of solidity and of fixed backgrounds," experienced "very mechanically and listlessly" as a "vague procession of towns all exactly alike, a vague procession of men also exactly alike" (14–15). Benjamin suggests that in modernity "[t]he regimentation of the assembly line has come to be reflected in a new form of sexiness: the chorus line, with its display of women 'in strictly identical clothes'" (summarized in Buck-Morss 125). As a chorus girl Marya lived outside settled notions of home and of romantic courtship leading to marriage. In the touring company, which functions as an assimilative alternative family, men are renowned as being "'Swine, deary, swine'" (*Quartet* 14).

"Drift" is Marya's characterization of her depression, which includes the stock depressive symptoms of weight loss and an indecisiveness she terms "extraordinary muddle" (16). Peter Nicholls argues that Wyndham Lewis, James Joyce, Ezra Pound, and T. S. Eliot, in different ways, explore questions of "the relation of mimesis to sexuality" (182). Lewis, Joyce, and Pound, he suggests, use artist figures, Tarr, Stephen Daedalus, and Hugh Selwyn Mauberley, to develop visions of aesthetic transcendence of the narcissistic drift of sexual desire. Lewis's vision idealizes the artist as Enemy, denying "passive identification" in desire "by reviving the principle of active antagonism lost to modern social life." A vision of the capacity of art to "'impersonalize' personal emotion" saves Stephen Daedalus "from the 'drift' of desire" (189). Mauberley's "way out of his 'anaesthesis'" is to use aesthetic objectification as a "form of 'armour' against 'utter consternation' and the 'drift' towards sensual indulgence" (192). On tour, Marya's desire is locked into a cycle of seemingly endless and enervating imitation (towns and men all alike, assimilating as a chorus girl), and marriage to Stephan is her way out. Her desire for Stephan is essentially narcissistic. She is seduced by an image of herself as "Happy, petted, charming" (what Stephan promises her she will be), no longer "lonely" and "frightened of her loneliness" (*Quartet* 15) and as relieved of her "dread" (at twenty-four) of growing old—being "left 'on the shelf'" in Haldane's phraseology (144)—and from feeling life to be an "extraordinary muddle" (16). By contrast with the "vague procession of men [. . .] exactly alike," Stephan is "[d]efinite" and a "person" (16). Marya's marriage does not domesticate her to the "solidity" of her performing domestic labor and managing a house (she and Stephan live in hotels). Marya spends "hours alone in the bedroom" of their hotel room, reading unnamed books in a pastoral of solitude and leisure, acquiescing in Stephan's objection "with violence" to her "wanderings in sordid streets" (9) after she unknowingly enters a homosexual bar.

Polish Stephan tells Marya that she has a "Slav type and a pretty silhouette"

(16), but in Paris their relationship seems to be read as mixed race, euphemistically internationalist (27). Jewish artist Miss Esther de Solla wonders, on hearing that Stephan is Polish, whether the couple are indeed married (8); Lois, strongly identified as Anglo-Saxon, thinks Marya's marriage "extraordinary" (51).

Stephan and H. J. are doubled in several ways. Stephan is a "*commissionaire d'objets d'art*" (16), H. J. a picture dealer, specializing in modernist art—both find Marya a "beautiful" object (16). Marya finds H. J. "big and calm and comforting" ([86]). If Stephan stood between her and the horror of repetition and imitation in the life of the chorus girl and amateur, H. J. stands "between her and the horror" of the prison ([86]) and what it represents for her: loss of Stephan's protection (which she reads as abandonment), reexposure to "muddle" (25), contamination, and failed confidence in her deliberate blindness to the "dirty" side of Stephan's business. The experience of loss of individuality and contamination that brings her abject response to crisis is standing in a queue of women at the prison. Earlier this routine had produced a sense of "unreasoning shame" (45) at her presence among "prisons and drains and things, tucked away where nobody can see" (44); she feels "like a grey ghost walking in a vague, shadowy world" (46). Brought to crisis, she decides she has been "wasting" her life. The moment produces a "longing for joy, for any joy, for any pleasure," which possesses her, being embodied as "a mad thing in her heart. It was sharp like pain and she clenched her teeth. It was like some splendid caged animal roused and fighting to get out. It was an unborn child jumping, leaping, kicking at her side" (59). "I don't want anything black or miserable or complicated any more. I want to be happy, I want to play around and have good times like—like other people do," she tells H. J. The prospect of returning to misery in another depressive episode scares her: "'I don't want to be hurt any more[. . . .] If I'm hurt again I shall go mad,'" she confides in him (61).

The precise terms of Marya's abject response to the queue are revealing. She is revolted by the manner in which the women "would edge forward mechanically and uselessly, pushing her as they edged. So that she was always forced to stand touching their musty clothes and their unwashed bodies" (58). Marya's mind processes the queue through tropes of class difference inflected as an encounter with the primitive. The queue is for Marya "a faceless mass" (Torgovnick 18), repetitive, mechanical, and useless in its progress, threatening, dirty, low, intervening in Marya's case, as Torgovnick argues the primitive often does, "in anxieties about identity as something fragile, random, subject (in Bataille's terms) 'to a thousand accidents and chances'" (18). Marya's projection of her fears about her declining social status as a sense of being contaminated by class others and othering is integral to the production of her desire for H. J.

Adulterous Marya, marked out by others as a hussy (*Quartet* 69) or a prostitute (66), experiences her obsession with H. J. as disease; eventually she is totalized by it. Echoing M.D. on the amateur in the *Times*, Marya moralizes the matter with her as "[n]o self-control," and, echoing Haldane on the amateur, as

"[n]o training" (92). In her marriage she had conspicuously consumed being petted and protected and feminine leisure; in her relationship with H. J., individualistic pursuit of pleasure, but not just for its own sake. Marya starts drinking to
"deaden the hurt" of being thought "the villain of the piece" by the Heidlers'
circle and of having Lois make a spectacle of her as the "other woman" to her
"wronged woman" part. Lois's stifling of her anger towards H. J. and Marya
surfaces in vindictiveness towards Marya. "Loving" H. J. has, Marya thinks,
"made her ugly," consumed by a "perpetual aching longing" (95), "devouring
hope," and—"the worst"—fear of further dispossession (96), giving her a sense
that there is "[n]ot a kick left in her" (96). The symptoms are resolutely somatic:
"her obsession gripped her, arid, torturing, gigantic, possessing her as utterly as
the longing for water possesses someone who is dying of thirst" (113). Her
vampirizing illness debilitates her physical appearance, and her sense of the spectacle of her failing looks makes her feel sick and retreat to her bed "huddled with
her arm over her eyes" (97).

Ironically her pursuit of love, in large part to ward off depression, plunges her
into what would today be termed a "major depressive episode," characterized by
"loss of interest or pleasure in all or almost all normal activities or pastimes,"
"poor appetite," "insomnia," "psycho-motor agitation" (imaged on p. 97, for
instance, as "[l]ittle wheels in her head that turned perpetually"), "indecisiveness,"
"fatigue," "self-reproach," and "wishes to be dead" (Radden 241). Her illness becomes a metaphorical prison, prompting Marya to identify herself with the spectacle of a restless caged fox (124). Howells observes that "neither her pain nor
the fox's is allowed to signify within the codes of civilised social discourse"
(51). Howells herself reads Marya's pain as Rhys's "only" direct addressing of
"female sexuality" in her novels (50), as a "Gothic victim fantasy," which appeals to "male power fantasies" (46–47), and colludes "with the fantasy images
of much male pornography" (48). The signs of Marya's illness remain unread,
and her "total prostration to the man who is both lover and torturer" is intelligi-
ble only as "erotic fantasy" (48). Her condition is read as and moralized as aber-
rant sexuality, a critical move replicated in accounts of the essentially masochis-
tic "Rhys woman," even if the aberrance is explained as a sign of her social subordination in a patriarchal culture.

While living with the Heidlers, Marya had rejected the part of the *bonne*
(servant) "to be made love to every time the mistress's back is turned" (*Quartet*
78), but she learns to "live up" to, to imitate, the part of the *petite femme* kept
in a hotel "for the express purpose of being made love to" (92), which H. J.
wants her to play. The wallpaper—"Yellow-green and dullish mauve flowers
crawling over black walls" (93)—disturbs Marya. The black background recalls
the dark walls of the prison and the "stale scent" left by the procession of mistresses "who had lain" in the room, the musty smell of the clothes of the women
in the prison queue. The imagined action of the flowers ("crawling") is like that
of flies or cockroaches. Marya's disturbance compresses an abject response to her
eroticization as *petite femme*. She has a depersonalizing sensation of feeling

"giddy and curiously light, as if she were floating about bodiless in the scented dimness" (93), while H. J.'s heaviness leaves a physical and psychological impress. Marya steps outside H. J.'s sexual game when she takes Stephan back. She had begun to sentimentalize her relationship with "'chic'" Stephan (98) because of the capacity of her prison visits to soothe and comfort her, to make her pretty again, "'Not half so peaky,'" "once more desirable" for H. J. (97). Demanding (like Carl Stahl with Suzy Gray) absolute loyalty and exercising a sexual double standard, H. J. tells her, "I've never shared a woman in my life, not knowingly anyhow, and I'm not going to start now. [. . .] I have a horror of you. When I think of you I feel sick'" (115). Marya then allows herself to be picked up by a young man, going tiredly and "silently" back to his room "like a sleepwalker" (118). Significantly, they have sex by blue light.

The visibility of Marya's emotion on her body is diagnosed by other characters—and in ways that produce her as their moral other and diseased other and confirm their sense of superiority. Stephan, as I have noted, reads her disease as a lack of character. "'*Quelle saleté!*'" [What a piece of filth!] he says, commenting on Marya's affair (141), and he implies she is a prostitute, as he leaves her for dead after a violent confrontation. H. J. reads her disease in class-bound moral terms and in popular psychoanalytic terms as hysteria. H. J. tries to regulate Marya's show of feeling through cliche-ridden moral suasion: "'you can't let Lois down. [. . .] I can't let Lois down,' he kept saying, 'we must keep up appearances, we must play the game'" (90). Miss Anna Nicolson, a landscape painter and friend of Lois, notices Marya's nerves and want of poise (91). Monsieur Bernadette, a friend of Stephan, tells Marya that "'what's the matter'" with her is that she "'thinks too much,'" and thinks to himself that she is neurasthenic (135). Rhys criticizes, sometimes satirizes, the self-serving and vacuous bandying about of popular psychoanalytic ideas and the "mania for classification" (91). My favorite example has to be a sexually importuning H. J. telling Marya, who is hesitating over a sexual relationship, "'You've got a fear complex [. . .] that's what's the matter with you'" (61).

Aspects of H. J.'s behavior and language to Marya seem to engage with Ford's discussion of the Englishman's conduct in *The Spirit of the People*. H. J.'s willful blindness to Lois's psychological cruelty towards Marya recalls Ford's account of the Englishman's "official optimism" about the world, a scepticism in the face of "greed, poverty, hunger, lust or evil passions," of "the state of things on the Congo": "People, he will say, do not do such things." Ford attributes this "optimism" to the Englishman feeling "very deeply" and reasoning "very little." "He hides from himself the fact that there are in the world greed, poverty, hunger, lust or evil passions," Ford explains, "simply because he knows that if he comes to think of them at all they will move him beyond bearing. He prefers, therefore, to say—and to hypnotize himself into believing—that the world is a very good—an all-good place" (294).

Rhys implies in *Quartet* that H. J.'s blindness allows him to not confront Lois's anger and pain, and his responsibility for them, and that his class othering

of Marya against the institution of bourgeois marriage, his political and racialized othering of her as a "savage" ("'Bolshevist,'" 90, and "Kalmuck," 102), his
infantilization of her as a "'child'" (97), and his construction of her as a not-
intact woman lead him to dismiss as "nonsense" (101) her complaints about
Lois's treatment of her and his insistent exposure of her to it and unpleasant
gossip and looks from Lois's friends in the name of keeping up appearances.
Ford comments, too, in *The Spirit of the People* on the often implicit "saving
phrase" that "dominates" English social encounters: "'You will play the game'"
of repressing emotions (297). The Englishman is "able to go about the world in
the confidence that he can return to a restful place" in which the written law and
this "more vital law which is called Good Conduct" are "conscientiously" respected (297–98). H. J. accepts his "good" wife, Lois's, facade of "Good Conduct" towards Marya, and rationalizes his desire for bourgeois respectability as
"playing the game." It is a phrase that saves the consciences of H. J. and Lois.
     Humiliated by H. J.'s rejection and by Miss Nicholson, a cruel emissary
from H. J. and Lois, sensing that H. J. thinks she is a "prostitute," and feeling
that the couple have "stripped and laughed at" her in her torment, Marya has a
vision of "[v]irgin forest" (*Quartet* 125) and the sensation of plunging into
"blackness" (126). The vision and the sensation are experienced when Marya is
drunk and has taken "several cachets of veronal" to help her sleep (124). The
prospect of forest is caught up with Marya's feeling of having been abandoned,
that she is a woman scorned. She sees "[d]ark trees growing close together with
thick creepers which hung down from the branches like snakes. Virgin forest.
Intact. Never been touched" (125). Susan Buck-Morss cites Walter Benjamin's
finding that "[t]he popular literature of flanerie [male idling in public space characteristic of capitalist modernity] . . . referred to Paris as a 'virgin forest'" and
adds pointedly that "no woman found roaming there alone was expected to be
one." "[A]ll women who loitered risked being seen as whores" (119). Primeval
forest, figured as a prospective object of European capitalist invigoration and
masculine acquisitive desire, was in the late nineteenth and early twentieth century a canonical Dominican image of local place. Read in relation to Dominican
autoethnography and Froude's reworking of it, Marya's recondite image seems to
compress the implications of Marya's "not intact" condition for H. J. as generic
bourgeois European man—his gaze and wealth turned away from her scornfully.
Two days later Marya reads "indifferently" H. J.'s letter refusing her what he
calls "a large sum of money" (*Quartet* 127). This accords with Froude's account
of European scorn towards Dominica being returned as indifference to English
authority.
     Marya's demoralization (somatically, blood drained from the heart) is repre-
sented as the sensation of the bed "sinking under her in a sickening fashion" and
"into blackness": "She was trying to climb out of the blackness up an interminable ladder. She was very small, as small as a fly, yet so heavy, so weighted
down that it was impossible to hoist herself to the next rung. The weight on her
was terrible, the vastness of space round her was terrible. She was going to fall.

She was falling. The breath left her body." (126) The sensation is, in one reading, a reference to depression, imaged earlier in the novel as black. Suzy Gray also describes her depression as having "been in blackness" (126). The link between the negativity of depression and black affective moods is conventional. During the Renaissance melancholy was thought to be caused by black bile. Jennifer Radden points out, "no bile ever was or would be black. Black bile, several authors have argued, was a kind of metaphor for the dark mood of melancholy rather than a reference to any actual substance" (238). Melancholy, she writes, "suggested darkness, a purely psychological apprehension. But the weight and pressure upon the afflicted person conveyed by the term 'depression' (Latin *deprimere*—to press down) carries images of physical as much as psychological burden and oppression" (243).

Marya's sensation may also be read, however, as a very private reflexive comment by Rhys on herself, the model for Marya in a roman à clef. According to Hesketh Bell, the feeling that blood is being drained is for "any Quashie" (an offensive term for a black person) a sign that he or she "has been sucked by a loogaroo" (*Obeah* 167), loups-garoux in Rhys's spelling (*SP* 30). Rhys understands loups-garoux to be werewolves. Bell, who recounts 1880s Grenadian beliefs, notes that loogaroos are "generally old women," whose nonhuman form is "only visible as a ball of bluish fire" (*Obeah* 166) and who seldom threaten the person of white people. Souciants, Rhys's nurse, Meta, told her, "were always women [. . .] who came at night and sucked your blood. During the day they looked like ordinary women but you could tell them by their red eyes" (*SP* 30). Referred to Caribbean beliefs, Marya's sense of her illness as draining of her blood suggests that her illness is like a souciant she carries within her. Froude suggested that the English whites in Dominica had "lost heart" (a probable pun on Lockhart) and were under threat of racial degeneration into uncapitalized barbarism. In this context the ladder Marya is climbing may be read as a ladder of Darwinian racial hierarchy; in the context of Marya's response to the prison queue the ladder is more a class hierarchy. The weight could be interpreted as the obstacles to her individualist effort to improve herself, the physical and psychological burden of her illness, and the presence of H. J., and the fatness that effeminizes him.[19]

JULIA MARTIN'S INDIFFERENCE

In *After Leaving Mr Mackenzie*, Mr. Mackenzie thinks about Julia Martin, his former lover: "But it was obvious that she had been principally living on the money given to her by various men. Going from man to man had become a habit. One day she had said to him, 'It's a very easy habit to acquire'" (20). The anonymous *Times Literary Supplement* reviewer called Julia Martin a "prostitute"; Gerald Gould in the *Observer* referred to her as a "paid mistress to one man after another." In the *New Yorker* the more urbane R.M.C. described the novel's theme as "woman's inability successfully to emulate the amorous nomadism of a bachelor." Rhys, in *After Leaving Mr Mackenzie*, engages particularly with 1920s discourses of the amateur. Julia's liminal condition between life and death is marked by her ghostliness, not vampirism, and her depressive disease is represented as debilitating, rather than vampiric. Rhys repeatedly terms her depersonalized condition "indifference." It is a condition that composes Julia's identity and confers a limited capacity for coherent public voice-agency. The third-person narrative voice speaks of "an indifference which was after all a sort of hard-won courage" (37). Julia's condition is set in the context of a larger socioeconomic event, the Great Depression. In her reading of depressed women in Marguerite Duras's fiction, Julia Kristeva argues that "abandonment structures the remains of history in Duras' texts" (*Black Sun* 241). I argue that "indifference," often focused by Rhys through the motif of burial alive, structures the "remains of history" in *After Leaving Mr Mackenzie*. Rhys's Julia characteristically exhibits the *"exhaustion of erotic drives"* Kristeva discerns in Duras's depressed women (*Black Sun* 244, Kristeva's italics). Kristeva calls the language of "aching affects and devalued words" heard in these women *"reduplication*. It creates echoes, doubles, kindred beings who display a passion or a destruction such as the aching woman is not up to putting into words and suffers for being deprived of" (*Black Sun* 246). Reduplication is, I suggest, a stylistic feature of *After Leaving Mr Mackenzie*.

Sisters Julia Martin and Norah Griffiths were brought up "'Middle class, no money'" (*ALMM* 53) by their widowed, expatriate Brazilian mother in London; they and the surrogate paterfamilias, Uncle Griffiths, are locked into various kinds of indifference. The quality of their family life is compressed in a persistent motif of burial alive.

"[S]crupulously, fiercely clean" Norah, the unmarried sister left to nurse the mother paralyzed by two strokes, has been "trained to certain opinions which forbid her even the relief of rebellion against her lot" (53). Her disgust at Julia and her othering of her as not "even look[ing] like a lady now" (53) and "people like that" (74), excites "some spirit of rebellion to tear her to bits" (74). The ambiguity of the referent of "her" suggests that the violence is directed at both Julia and at Norah's own "'slave'" status within her mother's home. Norah identifies herself in a description of the characteristic "apathetic indifference" of the slave Taminah in Joseph Conrad's *Almayer's Folly* (Conrad 85). She thinks: "'My life's like death. It's like being buried alive. It isn't fair, it isn't fair'" (75). Rhys may be playing on "fair." While Norah refers explicitly to the injustice of her situation, a second meaning of "fair" as a racial signifier implies that she feels she has lost racial caste. Slavery, which undoubtedly structured class and race relations in her mother's childhood home, had been abolished in Brazil in 1888. Norah's tropological identification with the slave Taminah accords with a tradition of feminist orientalism in which "objectionable aspects of life in the West" are figured through "'Eastern'" analogies (Zonana 594).[20] Norah's anger is placated by the thought of legacies from her Aunt Sophie and mother: "she would have some money of her own and be able to do what she liked" (*ALMM* 76).

When Julia was nineteen her affair with Mr. James "ended quietly and decently, without fuss or scenes of hysteria" (78). After the First World War she married "to get away" from England in the spirit she imagines a "boy has when he wants to run away to sea," but in her "adventure" "men were mixed up, because of course they had to be" (40). On her return to London she visits her wealthy Uncle Griffiths, who looks down on her insistence "on going" her "own way," represented as her having "deserted" her "family" (61). His language implies his xenophobia about Julia's life outside the "family" of stolid middle-class Britishness. His social outlook is characterized by habitual parsimonious indifference to the perspectives and circumstances of others. Julia characterizes him, Norah, and, more generally, "good, respectable people" as "such beasts, such mean beasts," who will "let you die for want of a decent word" (98), implying that their humanity is dead and buried. The streetscape as Julia leaves Uncle Griffiths's home emblematizes her sense of London: it is a place in which she has no "clear idea of the direction she was taking": the houses are exactly the same, "a melancholy tune" is broken by "a startlingly powerful bellow, like an animal in pain," "complaining and mindless," and a "heavy darkness, greasy and compelling [. . .] made walls round you, and shut you in so that you felt you could not breathe. You wanted to beat at the darkness and shriek to be let out. And after a while you got used to it. Of course. And then you stopped believing there was anything else anywhere" (61–62). This physical sensation of being buried alive can be a preliminary to a major depressive episode. Julia's "calm" indifference "to anything that had ever happened or could possibly happen to her" is represented as a defense mechanism: "Just when in another moment your brain would burst, it was always like that. She sat placidly with her knees rather wide apart, and her eyes fixed calm" (99). In this state she is "without any pity at all" for poverty-stricken and starving people or horses "standing like statues of patient misery." She, too, has lost her humanity and social conscience: "It used to be as if someone had put out a hand and touched her heart when she saw things like that, but now she felt nothing. Now she felt indifferent and cold, like a stone" (136).

The Brazilian childhood of Mrs. Griffiths is an almost closed book, unstoried for her children, buried in her inarticulacy. As a child, Julia "had woven innumerable romances" about it (76). Julia thinks of her mother as "accepting transplantation as a plant might have done," as having been "[a]ustere, unconsciously thwarted perhaps, but not unhappy" (76). Bedridden by her strokes, she is an "inert mass" (71), "'a dead weight'" (72), reduced to uttering animal-like or child-like noises. Indifference is the sign of her nonrecognition of people around her. Significantly, when Julia thinks that her mother may have recognized her she thinks her mother has said "'orange-trees.' She must have been thinking of when she was in Brazil'" (72). And, it is implied, she wanted to redeem the silence or inadequate responses that used to greet Julia's questions about South America.

The motif of burial alive is echoed in Rhys's representations of Julia's upper-middle-class bachelor English lovers, Mr. James, Mr. Mackenzie, and Mr.

Horsfield, all of whom exhibit in their everyday lives an emotional reserve or indifference that borders on the sexual anaesthesia Eve Kosofsky Sedgwick argues is typical of the bachelor type that was developed in Victorian fiction (Sedgwick 247). Their burial alive is also linked to other attributes of this bachelor type: "a preference of atomized male individualism to the nuclear family (and a corresponding demonization of women . . .)"; "emphasis on the pleasures of . . . senses" other than "genital sexuality"; "and a well-defended social facility that freights with a good deal of magnetism its proneness to parody and to unpredictable sadism" (Sedgwick 251).

Julia realizes that for Mr. James she was "for sleeping with—not for talking to" (*Quartet* 125) and that money and his material pleasures were her rivals. He loves his art collection, but would need the approval of an art connoisseur before he could abandon himself to the pleasure his pictures give him. Without that highbrow approval of his object-choices, he is "in their presence modest, hesitating, unsure of his own opinion" (83). In his material presence Julia feels that she is assigned an abject position: she is "a kind of worm [. . .] because" she has "failed," has "no money," and is not "even sure if" she hates him (81).

Mr. Mackenzie thinks that "[t]he secret of life was never to go too far or too deep" (20). Sexually he finds himself "more than once" "morbidly attracted [. . .] to strangeness, to recklessness, even unhappiness" (18–19), qualities exhibited in himself in a "volume of youthful poems," but suppressed by "a tight and very tidy mind," committed to the "code of morals and manners," compressed in never going "too far or too deep," and having "enough nose to look important, enough stomach to look benevolent" (17). In Julia he found a lost object of desire: his own youthful "strangeness," "recklessness, even unhappiness." Even his purported abandon with her, remembered by him as "I would like to put my throat under your feet" (21), suggests a desire for a reckless posture, rather than for Julia. When he contemplates Julia's life as an amateur he projects on to her his anxieties about the perversion—"kink" (18)—which he expresses in their relationship, thinking her "irresponsible," subject to "fits of melancholy when she would lose the self-control necessary to keep up appearances," and anticipating her "inevitable" "descent in the social scale" (21).

Mr. Horsfield's familiar daily life is "quiet and not without dignity, part of a world of lowered voices, and of passions, like Japanese dwarf trees, suppressed for many generations" (127). His visit to Paris, where he meets Julia, is a "kick of the heels" (28), an escape from a "stuffy, snuffy life" (121). He is disgusted by the sight of an embracing couple: "You couldn't get away from that sort of thing for a moment in this place" (36). The lost object of desire he claims to find in Julia is his own youth, emblematized as sun and vitality (117, 121); he judges her to have rebelled in her youth "[n]ot intelligently, but violently and instinctively" (42). His claim to have had his youth returned to him is belied by Julia's scream on the staircase as they try to creep to her bedroom unnoticed in the dark. He feels a "strange pleasure in touching her [. . .] wordlessly, in the dark" (118); she screams because she senses "someone dead [. . .] catching hold of" her "hand" (120). More generally his own sexual anaesthesia towards her (his object of desire being his own youth) is mirrored in her demeanor towards him: "Her body looked abandoned when she danced, but not voluptuously so. It was the abandonment of fatigue. [. . .] It was like watching a clockwork toy that has nearly run down" (107).

Julia's indifference is represented as originating in the death of her baby and the consequent failure of parenthood to secure her marriage; the originary moment is scarcely comprehensible to others. Julia has told or tries to tell her lovers about the death of her baby. Mr. Mackenzie recalls it flatly in a recital of her path to becoming an amateur: "She had had a child. The child had died—in central Europe, somewhere—and then she had separated from her husband and had divorced him or been divorced by him, Mr Mackenzie could not gather which. Or perhaps she had never really been married at all. In any case she had come to Paris alone" (20). She mentions the child's death to Mr. Horsfield in recalling a reduplicative identification with a woman in a Modigliani painting that left her feeling "like a ghost," dislocated from her own history (41). Mr. Horsfield says: "'Now look here, I'm going to talk sense to you. Why don't you come back to London?'" (42). Julia thinks about the child's death during her visit to Mr. James, but realizes that in the atmosphere created by his effort "to be so kind" she cannot tell the story (81). He dismisses her desire to explain her life: "'My dear, don't harrow me. I don't want to hear. Let's talk about something else'" (82). Julia thinks about her relations with her husband and their baby in Mr. James's presence:

"It was just my luck, wasn't it, that when we needed it most we should have lost everything? When you've just had a baby, and it dies for the simple reason that you haven't enough money to keep it alive, it leaves you with a sort of hunger. Not sentimental— oh, no. Just a funny feeling, like hunger. And then, of course, you're indifferent— because the whole damned thing is too stupid to be anything else but indifferent about. . . . He's so little. And he dies and is put under the earth." (80–81)

The marriage did not survive the souring of adventure, severe financial setback, the death of the baby, the unresolved guilt and grief over the circumstances of its death, and the difference of response to this set of events—her husband "seemed" to Julia "fed up"; she was left "with a sort of hunger." "'I felt it natural to go away if he was like that,'" Julia explains to Mr. James (80).

The trajectory of her marriage begins in her being "fed up, fed up, fed up" in wartime England and desirous of adventure (39) and ends in this hunger, which defensively lapses into indifference. Her desire for adventure is similar to what Paul Fussell examines in the generally male travelers he discusses in *Abroad: British Literary Traveling between the Wars* (1980). He suggests that during the war there was "in England a loss of amplitude, a decay of imaginative and intellectual possibility[.] . . . The tone of England turned stuffy, complacent, cruel, bullying, and small-minded" (Fussell 10). This tone and the male experience of trench warfare, he argues, motivated postwar travel. Rhys implies, rather, that the repressive tone structures early twentieth-century English culture. Julia's characteristic response to it and to life crises is to go away or want money to go away. In childhood Julia would escape to an imaginary country, the Brazil she associates with orange trees.

Rhys's representation of the failure of the marriage engages with ideas about the amateur that circulate in Haldane's *Motherhood and Its Enemies*. Haldane insists, as I have suggested already, that the dis/ease of the amateur's moral body, her corrupting desire for conspicuous consumption of luxuries and amusements, pollutes her familial relations with husband and children. Children, she writes, are a "serious impediment from every point of view" when family resources have habitually been diverted to "keep[ing] the pace, in the matter of clothes and pleasures, expected by the young wife" (Haldane 145). In *After Leaving Mr Mackenzie*, it is Mr. Martin who gave Julia "lovely things" when "he had money" (60). Julia recalls the gifts when Uncle Griffiths criticizes their "gallivanting about" (59) and Julia's failure to demand a financial settlement from Mr. Martin. The word "gallivanting" suggests the foreignness and frivolity of their lifestyle in Uncle Griffiths's system of value. For Julia the gifts are emblematic of her husband's difference from Uncle Griffiths; they are signs of generosity, spontaneity, love, and pampering care, a warm core in the marriage. It is as if the gift-giving husband fills some of the emotional void in Julia's life left by her sense that her mother changed from being the sensuous, caressing, "warm centre of the world" to being "a dark, austere, rather plump woman, who, because she was worried, slapped you for no reason that you knew" (77). This shift was effected by her mother's absorption in the newly-born Norah, the death of Julia's father twelve months later, and the "sickening" effect of the "cold, grey country" of England and Englishness (76, 89).

Julia's narrativization of her life story tends to begin with her self-reinventive desire to escape England; her realization that the story is inconsequential to and outside the comprehension of Ruth, an artist for whom she sat in Paris, produces a reduplicative moment that makes her feel as though "all" her "life" and "all" of herself "were floating away from" her "like smoke and there was nothing to lay hold of—nothing." "'And it was a beastly feeling, a foul feeling, like looking over the edge of the world. It was more frightening than I can ever tell you. It made me feel sick in my stomach,'" Julia explains to Mr. Horsfield (41). Julia's double in the scene of storytelling is a female figure in a reproduction of a painting by Modigliani. Julia's description of a woman with an "utterly lovely" body and "a face like a mask" with "blank" eyes "lying on a couch" suggests Modigliani's "Reclining Nude" (1918) or "Reclining Nude (On a Cushion)." Douglas Hall's comment on the closed eyes of the model in Modigliani's "Nude with Necklace, Her Eyes Closed" is apposite to the blank gaze of the figures in the other paintings: it "damps down considerably the erotic aspect of the painting, and recalls the convention in nude photography that the model's eyes must not look at the camera" (comment on Plate 39). Julia feels that she is explaining herself "as if [. . .] before a judge" to herself (*ALMM* 40), Ruth, and "the woman in the picture." Julia's sense that Ruth "didn't believe a word" of the story makes her begin to doubt its authenticity and feel that Modigliani's woman is "laughing at" her "and saying: 'I am more real than you. But at the same time I *am* you. I'm all that matters of you'" (41). The words ascribed to the double imply that Julia is merely an aesthetic form for Ruth; that her value for others lies in her body and pose, which discreetly does not return the aestheticizing or sexual gaze at her or the primitivism she signifies to others. Julia's projection of the words through identification makes Modigliani's woman rather than herself the subject of this knowledge and self-recognition. Julia becomes the subject of visceral distress, not attaining "'the truth about'" herself "'and about the world and about everything that one puzzles and pains about all the time'" (41).

Julia's reduplicative identifications with the old woman who lives upstairs from her in the Hotel St. Raphael and with her imagination of "herself old, quite old, and forsaken" (55) spur her to make the effort to transcend the seeming fate condensed in the identifications. The "old, forsaken" woman upstairs (11) who "depresses" Julia (137) has the "humble, cringing manner" of someone with "neither money nor virtue"; "horribly malevolent eyes"; and is "a shadow, kept alive by a flame of hatred for somebody who had long ago forgotten all about her" (11–12). During the frenetic phases of Julia's depression in the Hotel St. Raphael she is "obliged to walk up and down the room consumed with hatred of the world and everybody in it—and especially of Mr. Mackenzie. Often she would talk to herself as she walked up and down" (9). This confuses and frightens her (9). Julia's continuity in the part of the amateur is grounded in a "founding repudiation" (Butler, *Bodies* 3) of becoming an "old, forsaken" woman with no money reduced to the single passion of hatred, and of the self-knowledge entailed in acknowledging that "[s]omething in her was cringing [at] and broken" by the masculine gaze at a woman who might be sexually available (*ALMM* 131). The "dreaded identification" integral to that repudiation rouses Julia's fight against entering what are for her "'unlivable' and 'uninhabitable' zones of social life" (Butler, *Bodies* 3). Her salvation will be the man who says to her "'My darling. . . . My lovely girl. . . . *Mon amour*. . . . *Mon petit amour* . . .'" (*ALMM* 131). The prospect of these kinds of address becomes her transcendental anchor in modernity.

VOICE-AGENCY AND THE AMATEUR

Rhys represents the amateur sympathetically in "Triple Sec" through Suzy Gray's first-person diary narrative; in *Quartet*, as Howells notes, through the displacement of the perspectives of H. J., Lois, and Stephan "to the margins" of Marya Zelli's story (44). "As readers," she continues, "we are forced into complicity with Marya's point of view, hearing snatches of the others' stories which can only be accommodated in relation to their effects on her" (45). Rhys uses the same strategy in *After Leaving Mr Mackenzie*. The amateur herself is unvoiced in the public discourses about her that circulated in the early twentieth century.

Through the first-person voice of Suzy and the centralization of Marya's and Julia's points of view, Rhys contests the vampire and disease tropes associated with the amateur. In "Triple Sec" sexually predatory men are the vampire figures, and in *Quartet* Marya's depression vampirizes her. In this shift one may also mark the shift from a melodramatic gothic to a modernist gothic mode (the latter elaborated well by Howells 44–52). The disease of the amateur in these novels is not syphilis or gonorrhea, but depression, represented naturalistically in "Triple Sec," surreally in *Quartet*, in part through reduplicative identification in *After Leaving Mr Mackenzie*, and not romanticized or eroticized. It is presented in all of its scarifying detail. The depression of Suzy Gray and Marya Zelli is produced by their sexual commodification and the difficulties of earning a living in European modernity; Marya's second and major depressive episode marks the illusoriness of seeking a transcendental anchor in male protector/savior figures. The repressive atmosphere of England, the death of a baby and failure of a marriage, subsequent abandonments by lovers, and reduplicative identification with an old woman depress Julia.

The voice-agency and points of view of Suzy Gray, Marya Zelli, and Julia Martin are grounded in splittings of femininity. Their assumption of subjectivity, in Judith Butler's terms, "requires the simultaneous production of a domain of abject beings, those who are not yet 'subjects,' but who form the constitutive outside to the domain of the subject." These beings "constitute that site of dreaded identification against which—and by virtue of which—the domain of the subject will circumscribe its own claim to autonomy and life" (*Bodies* 3). Suzy Gray defines herself against the hardened amateur, the prostitute, the male "beasts" she encounters, and eventually the English. Her frequent casting of herself in melodramatic scenarios of female gothic crucially allows her to claim comparative innocence and confidential voice to her diary in relation to "beastly" others. Marya Zelli anxiously produces the abject figure of her younger, depressed self to justify her claims to life with her male protector/savior figures. Her confidential point of view, rarely articulated to H. J., Lois, or Stephan, is grounded in fierce repudiations of the "vague procession of men [. . .] exactly alike," the women in the prison queue processed through tropes of class difference, and the bourgeois respectability of H. J. and Lois. Julia Martin disavows her identification with figures of old, abandoned women and acknowledgement of the psychological effects on her of the epistemic violence and devaluations of her words and subjectivity that structure the exchanges between the amateur and her partners.

NOTES

1. Sheila Jeffreys, by contrast, characterizes *Motherhood and Its Enemies* as an "antifeminist classic" (174).

2. Sally Alexander discusses these new subjectivities for working-class women in "Becoming a Woman in the 1920s and 1930s."

3. Rhys, TS 55.

4. In the period the proposition that male chivalry is a lie would have been endorsed by prosuffrage and antisuffrage activists. Susan Kingsley Kent points out that "[f]eminists and antisuffrage women . . . shared the goal of protecting women from men." Antisuffrage women urged that "women could only find security in the private sphere. Because that private sphere, for feminists, justified oppression and abuse, they sought the elimination of separate spheres and the extension of the positive qualities associated with women to society as a whole" (233–34).

5. "'They can't make women happy because they don't really like them,'" says Germaine (Rhys, *Voyage* 70).

6. The industry not only bonds men of the upper middle class through arranging of abortions and sharing of illicit knowledge; in "Triple Sec" it bonds men of the upper middle class and the doctors who perform the abortion on the working-class pregnant woman. Suzy Gray is subjected to sexual advances by these doctors. She is, in effect, introduced to the doctors as part of the "common pool" of sexually available working-class women.

7. Once the vampire trope is explicit. Suzy becomes engaged to Ronald in 1914, remembering to her diary that she had thought, "'How lovely to be taken care of— How good to belong somewhere, to trust somebody—to dare to trust somebody'" (177). Suzy finds it difficult to brazen out the 1917 break-up scene by behaving "like a first class vampire" (191). Given M.D.'s 1917 letter to the *Times*, the date is significant.

8. In *Smile Please*, Rhys nominates Filson Young's *The Sands of Pleasure* as one of the books about prostitutes she read while living in Dominica. Richard Grey, the novel's protagonist, is shown Paris, and especially Montmartre, by John Lauder. There he meets Toni, whose "little red mouth, alluring and repelling in its perversity, reminded him of a childish vampire—childishly greedy, childishly cruel" (161). She is kept by men. Engineer Richard's fascination with her draws him away from his "father's bequest of labour to him" (10), the completion of a lighthouse for the Brethren of the Trinity, but he eventually discovers that he should "enjoy" the relationship "while he could, that it was of its very nature transient and fleeting; that the abiding things of life were of greyer, sterner, more sombre fabric" (253–54).

9. Grosz comments further: "These symptoms may well result from severe sexual abuse, although Schilder does not discuss this" (*Volatile Bodies* 77).

10. My analysis of Carl Stahl draws on Franco Moretti's compelling analysis of Dracula as monopoly capitalist (74–75).

11. Arata comments on the vigor and fertility of Dracula and the undead in Stoker's *Dracula* (628, 631).

12. He normally lives in Buenos Ayres.

13. The frequency of the word "beastly" reminded me of the comment in the *Dominica Guardian* about William Rees Williams's overuse of the word ("The Saint; the Sawbones and the Speculator").

14. They are rewritten as a sign of the zombie in the first version of the ending of *Voyage in the Dark* in which images from Anna's sexual experiences in London are cross-cut with memories of Dominica Carnival. Carl Redman is not bestialized, does not have a German family heritage, and does not monopolize Anna.

15. In the Black Exercise Book, Mr. Howard asks Rhys, "Would you like to belong to me?" Rhys continues, "I don't know I gasp breathlessly heart beating looking into the eyes./It was then that it began the serial story."

16. Saleeby quotes August Weismann in *The Germ-Plasm, A Theory of Heredity*: "'It has often been supposed that drunkenness of the parents at the time of conception may have a harmful effect on the nature of the offspring. The child is said to be born in a weak bodily and mental condition, and inclined to idiocy, or even madness, etc., although the parents may be quite normal both physically and mentally'" (208). Saleeby dismisses Weismann's qualifications of and reservations about this position, pointing out that Weismann was writing "in 1892, before the accumulation of the modern evidence on the subject" (209, n. 1).

17. Richard Faber cites second-hand Hector Maclean's description of the "'dolichocephalous Celt.'" His quotation opens: "Quick in temper and very emotional, seldom speaking without being influenced by one feeling or another" (150). In the account of white Creole character that was most influential in the nineteenth century, Bryan Edwards states that the leading features are "an independent spirit, and a display of conscious equality, throughout all ranks and conditions" and "an impatience of subordination" (8–9). "Temper in the West Indies being hot and a certain tradition about these waters," writes Rhys in the Black Exercise Book.

18. Dr. Smith, the first abortionist Suzy approaches, and Dr. Barton, the chloroform doctor, sexually assault her, assuming an indiscriminate promiscuity and the prerogative of their power over her; and Tony's cousin Guy's doctor, who attends her after the operation in which she loses a lot of blood, looks at her with "a sort of Oh-ho-somebody's-bit-of-fun-ah-ha expression" and tells her that she will not be able to resist her sexual appetite (euphemistically termed "sweethearting"), although he recommends abstinence "for a good six months" (109). Dr. Richardson, who performs Suzy's abortion, tries to protect himself from prosecution by insisting that she write him a letter detailing symptoms legally admissible as grounds for abortion (because they pose a threat to the mother's life) and that he be paid in gold.

19. After sex with H. J., Marya's "body ached. He was so heavy. He crushed her. He bore her down" (93). The heaviness is both literal and metaphorical. At one point Marya thinks H. J. "'looks exactly like a picture of Queen Victoria'" (89). If H. J. is for Marya effeminized by his fat, Lois is masculinized by her public school voice.

20. In relation to the *Other Stories* in *The Left Bank and Other Stories*, Ford had recommended to Rhys the manner in which Conrad introduced local topography into his short fiction. In his preface he specifically mentions *Almayer's Folly* (26). Norah's response to *Almayer's Folly* brings into focus a previously inchoate aspect of her *emotional* and *structural* relation to her family and social position.

Chapter 5

The Equivoice of Caribbean Patois and Song

"I felt sad walking back to my house, it would all get twisted, as everything gets twisted in the West Indies," writes Jean Rhys in *Smile Please: An Unfinished Autobiography* (85). She has intended to do "good works" among African Dominican people during a childhood "religious fit," as she calls it. Her naively "innocent" efforts to teach John, her family's overseer at "Morgan's Rest," to sign his name have been curtailed as a result of his wife's threatened violence—and will soon be sexualized it is implied by his friend Émile, who offers Minna Rees Williams a large yam in exchange for her daughter's hand in marriage. Rhys represents the "twisted" real world of turn-of-the-century Dominica, demarcated on lines of ethnically-inflected religious, and class-inflected racial, racial shade and sexual differences, as labyrinthine in complexity. The autobiographical protagonist tries "to blot out the real world which was so puzzling" to her by losing herself "in the immense world of books" (62) or in the landscape (81), but as with her efforts to repress her awareness of sex, the effort to withdraw from the insistent realities of differences, produces "curiosity" about, "fascination" with them (62), "near obsession" with African Caribbean people states Teresa O'Connor (*Jean Rhys* 15). Rhys's representations of them are usually deemed complex and conflicted;[1] Phyllis Rose, however, makes damning comment on Rhys's autobiographical reflections on racial differences in Dominica, finding in them "thinness" of thought and "no complex historical vision" (103).

In *Voyage in the Dark* (1934) and the posthumous *Smile Please* (1979), Rhys reinscribes in modernist form two of the stock generic layers of colonial narrative based on the manichean allegory of racial stereotype, "a field of diverse yet interchangeable oppositions between white and black, good and evil, superiority and inferiority, civilization and savagery, intelligence and emotion, rationality and sensuality, self and Other, subject and object" (JanMohamed 63): a white Dominican woman, now resident in England, journeys into the maze of her colonial memories to discover her own identity or reaffirm her colonial difference and come to some appreciation of meanings of life and death; the ambivalences of her representations of African Dominican difference may be traced to doublings of two black female servants, one alluring, the other destructive,[2] and in *Voyage in the Dark* also to the colonial English interpellation of Caribbean women. The title of the novel draws on a motif from Joseph Conrad's *Heart of Darkness*—London as a place of darkness rather than colonial light—but also signifies the protagonist's discovery of the fortunes of a "darkened" lineage and origin. Caribbean patois and song occupy an ambivalent, an equivocal site in Rhys's representations of the possibility of cross-racial community among women and African Dominican and white creole difference. This site also fits Hélène Cixous's space of the maternal equivoice, her "privileged metaphor for 'femininity in writing'" (Stanton 167). Mary Lou Emery justly notes that "Rhys has remained a disturbing presence on the edges of current feminist criticism" (11); the mirroring of Cixous's theory in Rhys's representations of African Caribbean difference reflects the primitivisms of Cixous's rehabilitation of the pre-Oedipal mother/daughter bond.

My argument retraverses, in the Irigarayan sense, that is, goes back through historicized "social, intellectual, and linguistic practices" to "unravel" the labyrinthine turnings (Irigaray, *This Sex* 221) of Rhys's representations of African Dominican difference and Cixous's utopian speculation on the equivoice:

Text, my body: traversed by lilting flows; listen to me, it is not a captivating, clinging "mother"; it is the equivoice that, touching you, affects you, pushes you away from your breast to come to language, that summons *your* strength; it is the rhyth-me that laughs you; the one intimately addressed who makes all metaphors, all body (?) —bodies (?)—possible and desirable, who is no more describable than god, soul, or the Other; the part of you that puts space between yourself and pushes you to inscribe your woman's style in language. Voice: milk that could go on forever. Found again. The lost mother/bitter-lost. (93)

Cixous's ideal community entails a rehabilitation of the mother-daughter relationship from a time before the Law, the proper name—a time analogous to the pre-Oedipal phase in psychoanalytic thought and Julia Kristeva's semiotic chora. The Law is associated with death; the equivoice is *"rhythmos*, a respiration, an exhalation, a breath of life, *souffle"* (Conley, *Cixous: Writing* 61). I will be dispersing Cixous's words as italics, especially in my discussion of *Voyage in the Dark*, as "a way of marking what has always already been said[.] . . . Italics are also a form of intonation, 'the tunes,' McConnell-Ginet writes, 'to which we set the text of our talk'" (Nancy Miller 29). My italics are part of a jam with (improvization on) rhythm as a sexualized and racialized sign, and several meanings of twist besides to distort: a means of tracing one's way in a labyrinth, a mixed beverage, a dance in which the body is turned from side to side, a loose woman, and twine.

In "Sorties," Cixous declares women "the labyrinths," and in metaphoric pro-
gression, "the ladders, . . . the trampled spaces; the stolen and the flights—we
are 'black' *and* we are beautiful" (69): this declaration culminates a section of the
essay that reflects on woman as "Black to his white" (67) and some implications
of Freud's infamous representation of female psychosexuality as a "dark conti-
nent." Cixous, of colonial Algerian Jewish background, now resident in France,
journeys into the labyrinth of her colonial memories to begin a process of un-
raveling gendered meanings of life and death; those meanings are shaped by a
doubling of maternal figures—the equivoice of the "lost mother" (associated with
breath, life) and a "captivating, clinging 'mother'" (associated with the thetic,
death) who impedes female self-realization. Ann Twist, the Obeah woman in
Rhys's story "Mixing Cocktails" (1927), is based on a family cook Ann Tuitt
(fictionalized too as Ann Chewett in *Voyage in the Dark*). Rhys usually spells
her last name Tewitt. The language she is given in the story is not the English
patois or the far more widely spoken French patois of Dominica; rather it is the
all too familiar early American stage language of the black person that essentializes in linguistic caricature "the difference that separated white from black"
(Gates 6): "'You all must'n look too much at de moon . . .'" ("Mixing Cocktails" 91)—Rhys twists the Dominican vernacular into a language English
"subjects" of that period could understand.[3] In improvising on "twist," I address
briefly Rhys's narrative problems in rendering patois and song.

The opening vignette of *Smile Please*—in which an upwardly mobile
"yellow black" photographer takes a family portrait—is an edited version of the
beginning of Rhys's original ending for *Voyage in the Dark*, which she changed
reluctantly at her publisher's insistence. "'Smile please,' the man said. 'Not
quite so serious,'" unpunctuated in the first version, opens both vignettes (*SP*
19, *Voyage* IV 381). The mother urges the young girl dressed in white to keep
still for the photographic gaze, but she moves: her arm, hand in the earlier version, "shot up of its own accord." Smiles and the "proper" motility of the "pure"
white middle-class woman's body are key elements in Rhys's representations of
Caribbean racial differences, taking on distinct connotations in each text.

In *Smile Please*, Rhys's relationships with black female servants, her
mother, and the landscape are represented insistently in terms of the dualisms
smiles/indifference or smiles/menace and of oral communication. Smiles and
shared laughter come to signify an idealized intersubjective recognition characterized by long talks and a nonthreatening storytelling; they are set in opposition to
an indifference or hatred that refuses Rhys's childhood oceanic desire for an absolute identification with the dark (m)other, for the "boundaries of self and other,
subject and object" to "dissolve in a feeling of totality, oneness and unity"
(Torgovnick 165). This oceanic desire is based on immediate, face-to-face relations mediated by voice and gesture.[4] Rhys is "wary" of black people she does
not know well or know at all; they merge with the mob that "surrounded" her
(49). The desire represses any effort to understand the power structures inherent
in the relationships or the subjectivities of the women who are the objects of her

desire. There is no truly "shared feeling of belonging and merging" or shared "ecstatic sense of oneness" (Dorothy Allison, qtd. in Iris Young 309).

During her cross-racial talk or singing with Ann Tewitt and Francine, Rhys is welcomed across rigidly racially demarcated boundaries of domestic space and brought into intimate contact with African Dominican religious difference in the person of Ann Tewitt and in ritualized invocation of story. These women, though, have demonic doubles. The doubling replicates the good black person/bad black person dichotomy found in many colonial and American narratives. The demonization brings Rhys up "willy-nilly against the two sides" of racial questions in Dominica (*SP* 64). John's wife, with her skirts "girded up far above her knees," a cutlass in her hand, and a menacing laughter that made Rhys "more and more nervous" (84) is the double of Ann Tewitt, the cook at Bona Vista, an Obeah woman, with whom Rhys had "long talks [. . .] Or rather she would talk and I listened but what she talked about I haven't the faintest recollection." Rhys is sensuously fascinated with the comportment of Ann's "bare brown legs" as, "skirts girded up," she carries dishes from the kitchen to the house (22). The alliteration and long vowel sounds in "bare brown" slow the rhythm of the sentence in which this occurs, reenacting the lingering gaze. That Ann's actual words are not important and that the memory of Ann—who simply dropped out of Rhys's life after the sale of Bona Vista—is placed in a context of unforgettable sensuous delight suggests, too, that her voice is central to her fascination. In remembering the story of her teacher-pupil relationship with John, Rhys implies, in a play on words, a repressed awareness of an endangering transgression. Immediately before the memory of the laugh that alerts her to John's wife's arrival, she writes that she and John "got on like a house on fire and I looked forward to the lessons" (84); the burning house is Rhys's stock representation of slave rebellion against the master and his family.

The crucial doubling within Rhys's labyrinths, though, is Francine/Meta. Meta, her nurse, never smiles, seems to be always muttering curses, and frightens the young Rhys with her gothic stories of zombies, soucriants, and loupsgaroux; she is the bedeviled double of Francine, whose "stories were quite different, full of jokes and laughter, descriptions of beautiful dresses and good things to eat. But the start was always a ceremony" (31). Rhys acknowledges that she has written about Francine more extensively in her fiction. (In *Voyage in the Dark*, Francine's songs, stories, laughter, sensuous and ritual eating of mangoes, smell, shade, stature, rhythmic hand movements, "beads of sweat" [27]—Anna Morgan knows "ladies" perspire discreetly—are key parts of Anna's corporeal memory of Dominica, identified by cartographic coordinates.)

Rhys's affirmation of her adolescent religious consciousness resonates with the terror and violence of her relationship with Meta. Rhys was, she writes, an "unconscious Manichee" convinced that "the Devil was quite as powerful as God [. . .] the Devil was responsible for everything that had gone wrong" (*SP* 82). Rhys, who represents herself as having responded to Meta's violence with cries of "Black Devil, Black Devil, Black Devil!" (31), holds Meta responsible for showing her "a world of fear and distrust" (32), a consciousness of which she has never been able to transcend. This fearful world is metonymic of the realm of the Devil in the larger adolescent theological scheme. Rhys describes her nurse as seeming to be "always [. . .] brooding over some terrible, unforgettable wrong" (29). The phrasing is ambiguous: the unnameable wrong may be a trauma produced by the legacies of slavery or racist colonial law, or, in a different reading of brooding, the child Rhys and Meta's race- and class-inflected charge of her may be the "terrible, unforgettable wrong." Meta, Rhys wrote in a draft of *Smile Please*, "was the exact opposite of the sentimental idea of the dark, loving, faithful servant" (David Plante Papers). In *Voyage in the Dark* the Francine/Meta doubling is crucially linked to the meanings attached to being a white creole woman—a topic to which I return.

In *Smile Please*, Rhys's smiles/indifference duality is insistent. The "indifference" of Victoria, the housemaid, "sad and unsmiling" (80, 48) replicates the primary indifference of Rhys's mother. Carole Angier speculates that Rhys was the child the Rees Williamses "had to assuage their grief over the loss of her little sister," Brenda Gwenith:

When a baby dies doctors often say that the mother should have another child straight away, to staunch her grief. . . . Often, perhaps mostly, this works, and pulls the mother back into life. But sometimes it doesn't. Then there is a phenomenon which doctors also recognise: what can happen to a child with a mourning mother. It can be left with a lifelong sense of loss and emptiness, of being wanted by no one and belonging nowhere; of being nothing, not really existing at all. (11)

Having overheard her mother expressing a preference for black babies, Rhys anxiously—and with a repeated self-loathing of white racial embodiment—checks the mirror each morning to see whether the "miracle," a racial transformation to blackness, has occurred (42). Rhys's failure to sustain an oceanic identification with her "dark" complexioned and emotionally distant mother or black surrogate maternal figures pushes her to seek that identification with the Dominican landscape at Morgan's Rest, ascribed human sentience and figuratively replicating the gesture of maternal rejection: "It was alive, I was sure of it. Behind the bright colours the softness, the hills like clouds and the clouds like fantastic hills. There was something austere, sad, lost, all these things. I wanted to identify myself with it, to lose myself in it. (But it turned its head away, indifferent, and that broke my heart)" (81). Even the stars of the Southern Cross, associated with redemptive possibility, are at times "close and benevolent," at others "far, far away, quite indifferent" (87).[5]

The one secured place of transferred oceanic possibility for Rhys as an adolescent is the alternate world of the English book. The vernaculars of the moments of oceanic wholeness with Ann Tewitt or Francine are exchanged for written English words; as Rhys sits on the veranda of the Carnegie Library "lost," she writes, "in what I thought was the real world, no one could have been happier than I was. My one ambition was to plunge into it and forget everything else."

With hindsight she observes that "from books (fatally) I gradually got most of my ideas and beliefs" (63). Her interpellation as colonial subject produced by her immersion is linked with the racialized association in her fiction and autobiography of whiteness with the coldness and stillness of death, and blackness with life. This association of whiteness and death was made at Dominica Carnival in Rhys's childhood: "a number of ladies dressed in black and wearing high comical head gears (white) with kerchief of the same colour crossing the shoulders marched funereally about by way of burying the festival" ("Last Week's Carnival"). As an adult Rhys developed a persistent sense of the failure of English (and less often European) narratives to register plausibly her own experience and the experiences of her characters; this becomes a stock motif in her novels and short stories, and indeed, as her letters reveal, the impetus to write *Wide Sargasso Sea* in response to *Jane Eyre*.[6] The motif is twisted up with a disillusionment at the colonial, patriarchal English lexicon of ideas that pass for universal "truths" in the last refuge of oceanic desire; in her fiction she works to trace a way, to follow a twist in the labyrinths of a gendered colonial literary and cultural archive.[7]

In *Smile Please* the vitality of African Dominican people is signified in dance and what Kamau (formerly Edward Kamau) Brathwaite would term the "auriture" of drumming, carnival music, and song (*The Colonial Encounter*). Black dancing and auriture become marks of emerging indigenization: "Every night someone gave a dance, you could hear the drums. We had few dances. They were more alive, more a part of the place than we were" (*SP* 50). Racialized motilities of the body circulate in all Rhys's representations of Carnival and African Caribbean festivities. At Carnival "[w]e couldn't dress up or join in but we could watch from the open window and not through the jalousies. There were gaily masked crowds with a band. Listening, I would think that I would give anything, anything to be able to dance like that. The life surged up to us sitting stiff and well behaved, looking on. As usual my feelings were mixed, because I was very afraid of the masks" (*SP* 52). In the Carnival sequence in *Voyage in the Dark* the emphasis is on sensuous gratification, the vibrant sights and sounds of "turning and twisting and dancing," the distance between racial groups being marked by the domestic enclosure of the whites and in the first version a sense of the "done" thing socially and an aestheticized language of the picturesque (385). *Texts Rhys's, Anna's bodies: traversed by lilting flows*, by "vocal" and "kinetic rhythm."

In a 1946 letter to Peggy Kirkaldy, Rhys writes: "Adore negro music for instance. It's life according to my gospel" (*Letters* 45). Life, gaiety, the rhythms of black bodies dancing and singing contrast with the stiffness, propriety, and enclosure of the white onlookers within a middle-class family home. Her black/white dichotomy plays out standard modernist primitivist tropes, tropes caught up, too, in the autobiographer's ambivalent loathing of an inhibited white physicality in her wistful envy of what seem to her to be the "perfectly free" sexual mores of black women: "Children swarmed but negro marriages that

I knew of were comparatively rare. Marriage didn't seem a duty with them as it was with us" (*SP* 51). Rhys does not explicitly use a language of the primitive, but she represents African Dominican people through identifiably modernist primitivist tropes elaborated by Marianna Torgovnick: they are more "in tune with nature, part of its harmonies . . . free . . . live life whole, without fear of the body" by comparison with sexually repressed and physically inhibited European people. As such they are "implicated in forms of Western self-loathing." But like other groups "processed" through primitivist tropes they are also shadowed as "a threatening horde, a faceless mass, promiscuous, breeding" (8, 18)— in Rhys's text during a riot, Carnival, and in sexual and procreative customs.[8]

The more celebratory aspects of Rhys's primitivism are replicated in the African vitalist psychophysiological tenets of the négritude movement and in the influential Caribbean cultural theory of Kamau Brathwaite. The négritude movement developed in the "jazz age" Paris of the 1930s, which Rhys visited on several occasions—"When I say I write for love I mean that there are two places for me. Paris (or what it was to me) and Dominica[. . . .] Both these places or the thought of them make me want to write."[9] Léopold Senghor asserts: "By the very fact of his physiology the Negro has reactions which are more *lived*, in the sense that they are more direct and concrete expressions of the sensation and of the stimulus, and so of the object itself, with all its original qualities and powers." "Rhythm," he writes, "is the architecture of [African] being, the internal dynamics which gives it form, the system of waves which it sends out towards *Others*. It expresses itself through the most material, the most sensuous means: lines, surfaces, colours, volumes in architecture, sculpture and painting; accents in poetry and music, movements in dance" (qtd. in Irele 74, 76).

Caribbean critic Kenneth Ramchand has called *Voyage in the Dark* "our first Negritude novel" (qtd. in Emery 12), noting briefly in his introduction to *Tales of the Wide Caribbean* "the negritude qualities Anna Morgan contrasts with whiteness" (n.p.). The attribution of those qualities, as in the négritude movement, is based on a "reaction to bourgeois rationalism" (Irele 81), and, as Wole Soyinka has observed in *Myth, Literature and the African World*, does not escape the manichean logic of the racial stereotype (134); it is a "revalorization that is a 'simple reversal,' a displacement of positive/negative value from one term to another in binary structures" (Stanton 172),[10] rather than a dismantling of those structures.

Kamau Brathwaite has developed an aesthetic of postcolonial Caribbean nation performance based on "music and rhythm" ("riddim") and "kinesis and possession" as a groundation—indigenization—of the African diaspora in the region (*Colonial Encounter* 71). His aesthetic is a celebration of survival of African traditions in the creole englishes and cultural forms—dance, oral storytellings, and histories, religion—of the "folk." The influence of négritude, reinflected, too, on an African Caribbean class axis, is readily apparent, even in his argument that "nation language"—creole english—is a "coming to the surface" of "submerged surrealist experience and sensibility" (*Colonial Encounter* 71). His suggestion that the kinetic energy of cultural forms in the African Caribbean is an aspect of, or an "analogue of religious experience" is a valuable reminder that Rhys's and Anna's sensuous apprehensions of Carnival music and dance do not encompass an appreciation of the functions of that music and dance in African Caribbean spiritualities or conceptions of the relations among body, words, and subjectivity.

In reviewing *The (M)other Tongue* (1985), the "first anthology of psychoanalytic feminist criticism," Jane Gallop addresses a contemporary fascination with the pre-Oedipal dyad of mother and child, a "realm of fusion and indifferentiation": "The pre-Oedipal attracts us irresistibly and holds us motionless, and in place of the phallic amulet, we are bewitched by the figure of the mother. The maternal having replaced the phallic, the early seventies' opposition between psychoanalysis and feminism can give way to a charmed union" (57, 61). Domna Stanton situates Cixous's celebration of the equivoice as one of many hypostatizations of "pre-oedipal unboundedness, relatedness, plurality, fluidity, tenderness, and nurturance in the name of the difference of female identity" from the mid-1970s onwards—linking it with the maternal metaphor in the work not only of Irigaray and Kristeva, but also of Adrienne Rich, Nancy Chodorow, and Sara Ruddick (176). Cixous's "Sorties" rehabilitates the pre-Oedipal as an "elsewhere," a site outside and with the potential to transform patriarchal culture and open a space for women to write the "natural" rhythms of their bodies from the memory of the mother tongue: "The mother touches the daughter with her voice. The bodily touch, through voice and musical vibrations, give [sic] the daughter her rhythm; they make her breathe and write." (Conley, *Cixous* 55). The celebration of the space of the equivoice is implicated in forms of Western women's loathing of a physicality and language acquisition inhibited and degraded by patriarchal culture and psychoanalysis. Gallop points to the illusoriness of the mother tongue: "The early mother may seem to be outside patriarchy, but that very idea of the mother as outside of culture, society, and politics is an essential ideological component of patriarchy" (61).

I frame my references to Cixous's concept of the equivoice in language that highlights the modernist primitivism of the dualisms that structure her theorization of it: life/death, body/no-body, freedom/inhibition, "black"/"white," wholeness/fragmentation, natural rhythms/patriarchal civilization, prehistory/history. The utopian desire for a surfacing of the memory traces of the pre-Oedipal mother is integral to an eschewing of bourgeois rationalism and individuation and foreshadows a libidinal economy of the gift, aptly summarized by Toril Moi as a "deconstructive space of pleasure and orgasmic interchange with the other" as opposed to a masculine realm of the proper (or empire of the selfsame) (113). Cixous's valorization of the gift is based on the mediation in the French intellectual tradition of Marcel Mauss's anthropological work on "primitive" forms of exchange.[11] Torgovnick demonstrates "the way gender issues always inhabit Western versions of the primitive," "familiar tropes for primitives become the tropes conventionally used for women" (17). She discusses in some depth

Freud's representations of the pre-Oedipal phase and the oceanic (both linked with the mother) as primitive, needing to be transcended because they are "at odds with the modern city-state and the sense of consummate individualism upon which it depends" (205). Efforts to rewrite the pre-Oedipal "to eliminate its pejorations in Freudian texts" may not free themselves of "old metaphors," but rather reinscribe an overdetermined "stereotypology," not just of "woman as mother" (Stanton 164–65), but also of the gendered primitive—"Sorties" is a prime and stark instance. Stanton asks what "exigencies" are fulfilled by current hypostatizations of the pre-Oedipal maternal (176). One might speculate that part of its "charm" lies in the appeal and the consuming satisfactions of its modernist primitivisms.

In *Voyage in the Dark*, Rhys's representation of Carnival is integral to the text's somatic aesthetic of the Caribbean. For Anna Morgan, a Dominican expatriate in pre–First World War London, the Caribbean is a site of a nurturant corporeal memory activated by a mnemonics of pain and loss, which acts as her transcendental anchor in modernity. Her expatriation is experienced as disjunction: "It was as if a curtain had fallen, hiding everything I had ever known. It was almost like being born again. The colours were different, the smells different, the feeling things gave you deep down inside yourself was different. Not just the difference between heat, cold; light, darkness; purple, grey. But a difference in the way I was frightened and the way I was happy" (7). The sounds, voices, smells, colors, sights, climate, topography, tastes of Anna's Dominica are relived through a poetic sensation-memory, for example:

(When the black women sell fishcakes on the savannah they carry them in trays on their heads. They call out, "Salt fishcakes, all sweet an' charmin', all sweet an' charmin'.") It was funny, but that was what I thought about more than anything else—the smell of the streets and the smells of frangipanni and lime juice and cinnamon and cloves, and sweets made of ginger and syrup, and incense after funerals or Corpus Christi processions, and the patients standing outside the surgery next door, and the smell of the sea-breeze and the different smell of the land-breeze. (7)

Text, Anna's body: traversed by lilting flows.

These memories, described by Emery simply as "'creative consolation' in 'inward dialogue and space'" (75), surface usually as a defense against the English cold, both physical and emotional, and feelings of extreme isolation. For instance, Anna recalls Francine as nurse and her own desire to be black after her landlady wants to evict her and she feels ill (27) and Francine's smell among memories of sunshine, bats at sunset, a local store, a hibiscus, and tropical rain after she leaves her lover, Walter's, home in the early morning. The memories intensify her sense of her own sadness in England. To adapt Elizabeth Grosz summarizing the work of Alphonso Lingis: "The intensity and flux of sensations traversing the [white Dominican woman's] body [have] become fixed into consumable, gratifiable form, [have] become needs, requirements and desires

which can now be attributed to an underlying psyche or consciousness"
("Inscriptions" 70). As O'Connor notes, but not in relation to Rhys's doubling
of black women, Dominica starts to "become a malevolent aspect" of Anna's life
with the return of a repressed memory of Meta immediately after Anna has left
the premises of the abortionist (*Jean Rhys* 121). Anna feels vulnerable and
acutely ill—"the slanting houses might fall on me or the pavement rise up and
hit me," passers-by might knock her down "just because" she is "dying." She
associatively links their potential contempt in putting "their tongues out as far
as they would go" with Meta returning at Masquerade to "put out her tongue at
me through the slit in her mask" (*Voyage* 151).

The Carnival masks, as Emery points out, "imitate to excess, to the point of
ridicule, the faces of pink, mildly blue-eyed, straight-nosed, and painted-mouthed
white men and women"; further, in the wire covering of the face "the black
women confront the white 'ladies' with their own subordinant [sic] and silenced
condition" (77). In an early 1930s typescript, "Lost Island. A Childhood. Fragments of Autobiography," Rhys writes that the masks at Masquerade were
"probably" shouting "defiance" of "white people."[12] In the first version of Part
IV, the nightmarish photographer-Carnival-fall sequence of memories,[13] Francine's place as nurse is taken by Meta.

When *Voyage in the Dark* opens Anna is caught up in a cycle of repetition in
her life as a chorus girl—"You were perpetually moving to another place which
was perpetually the same" (8)—and at the novel's end the doctor who treats her
suggests that she will enter into a repetitive cycle of promiscuity. The first section of the novel introduces several motors of linearity: Anna as "Hottentot" (the
implications of which I discussed in chapter 1) and reader of Emile Zola's *Nana*,
and Walter Jeffries's purchase of stockings "with clocks up the side" for Anna. In
Actresses as Working Women: Their Social Identity in Victorian Culture, Davis
argues that the actress' tights were "fetishized garments," "sensual referents" by
turn of the century: "the symbol of her profession," "the icon of her sexual appeal," and "the indexical sign of her skin" (138). Anna "let[s]" Walter pay for her
stockings (*Voyage* 10), and this action sets in progress her move from virgin to
amateur, who, in the fever that closes the novel, relives her sexual performances
in London to the tune of "There's a Brown Girl in a Ring."

Anna's glimpse of herself and Walter in his bedroom mirror on the night
their relationship is consummated graphically suggests the implications for her
identity of her becoming an amateur. She had crawled up the stairs to his bedroom—this is stereotypically a motility associated with animals, servants, children, and nonwhite people. Anna resists Walter's first effort to seduce her. Looking at herself in the mirror of the bedroom in which that seduction was to occur,
Anna feels "as if" she "were looking at somebody else" (21). The next day she
remembers "the shop-windows sneering and smiling" at her because of the taw-
driness of her clothes. "People laugh at girls who are badly dressed," producing
in them a desire "to be beautiful." "You look at your hideous underclothes and
you think, 'All right, I'll do anything for good clothes. Anything—anything for

clothes'" (22).

Rhys is confirming the "love of finery" explanation for female promiscuity, but implying that social and class attitudes to clothes rather than simply decadent consumerism lead impoverished women to invest so much in their appearance. Walter sends Anna twenty-five pounds to buy clothes. When she looks at herself in the mirror of Walter's bedroom she is dressing in the clothes his money purchased. She sees him surreptitiously putting more money into her handbag. The earlier reflections of herself show her as an isolated, modern, dispossessed individual; this image shows a doubling of bodies. It reflects the hidden sexual economy necessary to sustain her new, improved look and the "warmth" of physical intimacy (32). If Anna's look into the glass "not thinking of anything," for it is as if "everything" in her "head had stopped," suggests a vacuous vanity, Walter's turn away from the mirror indicates public concealment of an aspect of his masculinity and the inequalities of his class relation to Anna. Anna acquiesces in Walter's construction of her by accepting the money.

Zola's Nana at one point reads a sensational novel about a prostitute, railing against it, "declaring that it was all untrue, and expressing an indignant revulsion against the sort of filthy literature which claimed to show life as it was," and expressing a preference for "tender, high-minded works which would set her dreaming and uplift her soul" (qtd. in Felski 79). Maudie saying of Nana, "I bet you a man writing a book about a tart tells lots of lies one way and another" (9), suggests a narrative motor of Rhys's novel: a woman writing a book about an "amateur" with higher claims to truth than a man's, and with Zola's "commitment to an unflinching exploration of the grim realities of modern urban life" (Felski 79). By contrast with "Triple Sec," the discourse of beastliness is turned on Anna, and there are several figures of disease and illness in the sexual plot.

Hester, Anna's English stepmother, suggests that Anna's maternal genealogy—fifth generation West Indian—is tainted by colored blood and miscegenation. In the published 1934 text Anna's biological mother is only present in references to her Caribbean genealogy. Hester's suggestion accords with influential late nineteenth-century racial ideas; Paul Rich cites as a key example Grant Allen's assertion in In All Shades (1886) that the "visibly white Anglo-Saxon colonists in the West Indies" frequently have "coloured ancestry" (52). Anna links the "myth" of having colored blood with "Maillotte Boyd, aged 18, mulatto, house servant" (Voyage 46), an entry she found in an old family slave-list; she takes on this name during a postcoital moment with Walter Jeffries when she commits herself pleasurably in her mind to the life of the mistress. The repetition of the name and age, her own age, may imply "white slavery" after her passage to England[14] or a drunken affirmation of suspected black blood within. But the incantation of the name also makes possible the acknowledgement of her desiring body. "Being black is warm and gay, being white is cold and sad," thinks the adolescent Anna (27). Gay: "disposed to joy and mirth"; of "loose or immoral life"; "Hence, in slang use, of a woman: Leading an immoral life, living by prostitution" (*Oxford English Dictionary*).

This last connotation is crucial to Rhys's story "Till September Petronella," written by the mid-1940s and set in pre–First World War London. "'*Look gay*,' they say" to Petronella Grey. "'Gay—do you know the meaning of the word? Think about it, it's very important'" (*Tigers* 16). As Gregg notes of Anna's memory of Maillotte Boyd, "[t]he presence of 'history' during an apparently intimate moment collapses the past into the present even as it exposes the fiction of private, individual subjects connected to each other through unmediated desire or romantic love." Gregg does not, however, consider the primitivism that structures Anna's writing of her Self "as sharing an identity with its Other" (119).

Anna details Hester's contempt for her relationship with Francine. Hester's voice represents a repressive English colonial law, especially in her maxims concerning the proper behavior of white ladies and gentlemen and menstruation and her unabashed racism, most marked in her persistent use of the word "nigger"—used by whites in the turn-of-the-century West Indies "in cases of ignorance or of ungovernable temper" attests Hesketh Bell (*Glimpses* 91). For Hester the key sign that Anna is "growing up more like a nigger every day" (*Voyage* 54) is her degenerative speech. African Dominican intonations, speech rhythms, patois are for Hester a mark of submerging (and sub-merging) of Englishness: this complements a late nineteenth- and early twentieth-century repertoire of racialist ideas of "social *devolution*," rather than racial progress, in the West Indies usefully elaborated by Paul Rich (52). White people in the tropics were thought to risk, "in the absence of continual cultural contacts with their temperate northern culture, being reduced to the level of those black races with whom they had made their 'unnatural home'" (Rich 19). Back in England Hester bemoans her failure with her stepdaughter, attributing it to an inability to segregate Anna from the "contaminations" of the local environment and a "submerging" of social class: "I tried to teach you to talk like a lady and behave like a lady and not like a nigger and of course I couldn't do it. Impossible to get you away from the servants. That awful sing-song voice you had! Exactly like a nigger you talked—and still do. Exactly like that dreadful girl Francine. When you were jabbering away together in the pantry I never could tell which of you was speaking" (56).[15] The language is unintelligible—jabber—to the ladylike English subject.

This representation of black speech is stereotypical: "It is said," writes Frantz Fanon, "that the Negro loves to jabber" (26). Rhys or her editor may have felt the language would be unintelligible to her prospective audience: in the published version some words of Francine's single English song are recalled; there are only three nontranslated phrases associated with ritual drumming accompaniment with the hand and fingers or with invocation of story. Hester is totalized as "jawing" voice; Francine's voice is experienced by Anna as sensuous fascination—it merges with the sensuousness of origin. Anna's accent is distinctive. The landlady who evicts Anna after accusing her of "[c]rawling up the stairs at three o'clock in the morning" conflates her Caribbean accent, "lip" (perhaps subconsciously linked with the fetishization of lips as stereotypical markers of blackness), and assumed promiscuity: "'I won't 'ave you calling me a liar[. . . .] You and your drawly voice. And if you give me any of your lip I'll 'ave my 'usband up to you.' [. . .] 'I don't want no tarts in my house, so now you know'" (26).

In the nurturant physical presence of Francine—established by voice, the *rhyth-me* (respiration, exhalation, breath of life) that *laughs Anna into being*, making her feel comfortable with her menstruating body—Anna thinks, "Being black is warm and gay, being white is cold and sad." This racialized coldness and stillness is linked associatively with the coffin- or shroud-like rooms in which Anna lives in England (for example, 22, 26) and, in the first version of the pho-tographer-Carnival-fall sequence of memories with a sickbed scene, ambiguously the early death of the mother or a second memory of Anna's induced illness after the onset of menstruation and realization that the bitter racial history of Domin-ica will separate her from Francine. *The lost mother/bitter-lost.* Loss of the *strength*, the *body (?)—bodies (?) possible and desirable* Francine summons.

After her painful acceptance of the inevitability of separation from Francine and exposure to Hester's maxims about menarche, which interpellate her sexual and reproductive body in a way that makes her feel "awfully miserable, as if eve-rything were shutting up around me and I couldn't breathe" (59), Anna develops a death wish which manifests itself as an invalidism which returns Francine to her bedside as nurse to change the bandages on her head and fan her "with a palm-leaf fan" (27).[16] Anna plays out the lack of robustness attributed to the white creole during the late nineteenth and early twentieth centuries, acquiring it by deliberately standing too long in the tropical sun. "The creole whites, owing to the enervating influence of the climate, are not a robust race" ("Creole"). There are, too, in *Voyage in the Dark* several sickbed scenes in England, linked with an oppressive sense of enclosure and airlessness related in large part to Anna's nega-tivity of response to English constructions of foreign women. The airlessness recalls the punishment—burial alive—which was meted out to vestal virgins who transgressed their office by losing their virginity.[17] In Hester's memory of Anna's father, the sign of his "failing" is his criticism of English hypocrisy and repudiation of England. The "failing" is elaborated as "such a brilliant man poor man buried alive you might say [in Dominica] yes it was a tragedy a tragedy" (53).

In the first version of Part IV, Anna's sickbed, presided over by Francine in an early memory, is now (in a conflation of her illness and her mother's) tended by Meta. What is repressed in Anna's desire to sustain an oceanic identification with Francine—the fraught legacy of race- and class-inflected history—returns in the menacing and violent figure of Meta. As if to resist this return Anna remem-bers lines of a patois song Francine must have taught her: "Ma belle ka di maman li/Petit ke vini gros." As the words make no sense to Hester, Anna has to give their meaning: "My beautiful girl is singing to her mother The little ones grow old The little ones [grow] old."[18] Anna's memory then shifts to Hester's reception of her enjoyment of black music: "she picks out all the nigger tunes by herself [. . .] I dislike that song."

Anna's defiance of Hester in Dominica (entailing her attachment to Francine and black oral culture) is compressed in the memory of "hiding behind the oleander bushes the oleander trees" singing "Ma belle ka di maman" and "all the songs I knew twenty songs one after the other all the songs I knew and my voice went thin thin but I went on singing."[19] Her next memory is of leaving Dominica, and singing Francine's only English song: "Now all good times I leave behind Adieu sweetheart adieu" (382). It is as if the intense investments of libidinal energy in the relationship with Francine and defiance of Hester have been a defense against the fear of Meta and the negativity she represents. But the memories of Meta are insistent, and they lead to terrified conflations of Anna's sexual experiences with a sickening fear of a zombie ("his hands had such a lot of hair on them," 387) and of a duppy or shadow (the black woman with yaws she sees on her ride to Constance Estate—relived in memory—is a duppy).[20] Interpreting Anna waiting for blackness to come as her imminent death, Michael Sadlier, Rhys's editor at Constable, asked her to revise Part IV to "give the girl a chance" (qtd. in Morris 2); among other changes, Rhys cut the references to Meta, the physical and verbal violence of their relationship, and the zombie.

That the foreboding figure of the duppy has yaws is significant. Sander Gilman argues that Nana's smallpox (a pun on pox) unmasks "the disease buried within, the corruption of sexuality," providing "a visual icon of decay" (*Difference* 105). Like Nana's disease the disease of the duppy is connected with venereal disease. As a monitory figure for Anna, the woman is connected with the syphilophobia that marked 1910s discourses about the amateur. Yaws was a major and ineradicable public health problem in Dominica and other tropical regions during the nineteenth and early twentieth centuries.[21] During Rhys's childhood the facial disfigurement of the woman Anna meets—"her nose and mouth were eaten away" (*Voyage* 130), making her speech unintelligible to Anna—would have been diagnosed as syphilis by H. A. Alford Nicholls, for many years the medical superintendent of the Yaws Hospital and author of an 1894 *Report on Yaws*. In his report he specifically contests the diagnosis of such symptoms as yaws by J. Numa Rat, who also practiced in Dominica and had published on yaws. Rhys's father, William Rees Williams, a doctor, who had been district medical officer for the Yaws Encampment at the Soufrière at least from 1882 to 1884 and regularly treated patients with yaws, is less certain than Nicholls of the distinction between yaws and syphilis (Nicholls, *Report on Yaws*). There was a medical debate during the 1890s and 1900s over whether yaws was "syphilis modified by race and climate" (Rat 210). In 1950 medical opinion was still divided:

Yaws is caused by a spirochaete, a minute organism indistinguishable on microscopical examination from the organism responsible for syphilis, and related, in some degree, to the spirochaete of relapsing fever. The relationship of the spirochaetes of

yaws and syphilis is very close indeed, so much so that some medical authorities regard them as identical, and the two diseases as different manifestations of one process. This is not, however, the view generally accepted. (Wilcocks 82)

Nicholls attests to the social disgrace of white people contracting yaws, a disease
from which their generally better living conditions normally protected them.   In
Disease and Representation, Sander Gilman argues that:

It is the fear of collapse, the sense of dissolution, which contaminates the Western
image of all diseases[.] . . . But the fear we have of our own collapse does not remain
internalized. Rather, we project this fear onto the world in order to localize it and,
indeed, to domesticate it. For once we locate it, the fear of our own dissolution is removed. Then it is not we who totter on the brink of collapse, but rather the Other.
And it is an-Other who has already shown his or her vulnerability by having col-
lapsed. (1)

The duppy's symptoms and Anna's witnessing of them alone give visual and
aural form to Hester's figuring of the contamination of the white lady through
unintelligible speech and loss of English control over the social boundaries between races. Detail of Anna's ride supports a reading of it as obliquely sexual in
import: Anna's "habit-skirt" has a tear; her destination—Constance Estate—
suggests firmness and regularity. The menace of the duppy is of a sexualized
dissolution and loss of control:

*I thought I'm going to fall nothing can save me now but still I clung desperately with
my knees feeling very sick*

"I fell," I said. "I fell for a hell of a long time then." (158)

The feverish Carnival-fall sequence of corporeal memory that accompanies
Anna's experience of a botched abortion resonates with a highly conflicted and
ambiguous metaphoricity of blackness. Anna's sexual performances and "fall" in
London—metaphorized in terms of dance and horse riding—are replayed nightma-
rishly to the music-rhythm-song of 1902 Carnival, to the tune of "There's a
Brown Girl in a Ring" (and also "Charlie Lulu" in the first version).[22] She is
represented as "whirling round and round" (157, *Voyage* IV 387), protesting fee-
bly, crossing giddily, not rationally or volitionally,[23] beyond the bounds of a
white middle-class propriety of the body, to the voice of Uncle Bo saying "you
can't expect niggers to behave like white people all the time," and catching up
the idea, identified as Hester's in the first version, that "it ought to be stopped."[24]
"Well it's only nigger music but it does make you want to dance," her voice
says in the first version; Anna's dancing is "rhythm of seeds of seed," a compressed reference to the chak-chak, vitality and possibly conception of her baby
(387). Anna's joining in the dance may allude to (and twist) Marlow's refusal in
Heart of Darkness to give in to the temptation to "go ashore for a howl and a

dance." He claims he "had no time"; work "was surface-truth enough . . . to save a wiser man" (Conrad, *Heart* 69–70). The allusion may imply that Anna lacks the "deliberate belief" Marlow says is needed to sustain the veneer of evolutionary racial "progress" "out there"; more importantly, however, it points to the material circumstances and prospects that push her into becoming a kept woman and an amateur.

In the first version the novel closes with Anna waiting for "blackness" to come, blotting out consciousness; in the original published version an infernal repetitive cycle of promiscuity is implied. "Blackness" has acquired metaphorical and primitivist resonances in the text. As Toni Morrison argues of Marie Cardinal's *The Words to Say It*, "black or colored people and symbolic figurations of blackness are markers for the benevolent and the wicked; the spiritual . . . and the voluptuous; of 'sinful' but delicious sensuality coupled with demands for purity and restraint" (ix). Anna's wait catches up the "blackening" of Anna's creoleness in English racial typologies; her fear of and desire for blackness—and the manichean possibilities it represents for her; the pressure of the body in pain on her consciousness; and the depressive negativity that has begun to overwhelm her with the return of the memory of Meta. Imminent death is also a possible reading.

In complying with Sadlier's request to exclude Anna's death, Rhys had to cut some of the potential topicality of the original ending. During the 1930s the Ministry of Health conducted a long-ranging enquiry into maternal mortality. Abortion was acknowledged as one of the causes of maternal mortality, and there was much public debate over abortion law reform. In "Triple Sec," Suzy's abortion is performed by doctors and under chloroform; in *Voyage in the Dark*, Anna's abortion is performed by a Mrs. Robinson with an instrument that Anna intimates in a draft held in the British Library "felt its way up to where my life was & opened out tearing me in two so slowly so slowly" (Add. Ms. 57856). In 1931 doctors expressed particular concern about deaths from puerperal sepsis contracted through instrumental abortion.[25] In the second version of the ending Rhys gives the doctor more prominence; his medical intervention ("like a machine that was working smoothly") promises to bring her back inside the "machine" of oppressively and mean-heartedly discriminatory socioeconomic relations and discursive regimes. Anna's consciousness picks up his voice saying "'She'll be all right[. . . .] Ready to start all over again in no time, I've no doubt.'"[26] She thinks "about starting all over again. And about being new and fresh. And about mornings, and misty days, when anything might happen. And about starting all over again, all over again . . ." (159). The repetition of "all over again" in the final sentence and the closing ellipsis are ambiguous: they may imply a feeble warming to the idea of a new start (ironized by the prospect of the machine) or a loss of energy (and breakdown of the machine) as Anna loses consciousness. Either way her chances are slim.

NOTES

1. See, for example, Staley 5; Davidson 4–5; Tiffin, "Rites" 33; O'Connor, *Jean Rhys* 30–37; and Frickey 9. Gregg offers fine, detailed readings of Rhys's representations of black people, but does not examine the dynamics of modernist primitivism in her writing.

2. JanMohamed identifies four subgenres based on the manichean allegory; they include "the story utilizing Africa as an alluring, destructive woman—from Haggard's *She* and *Nanda the Lily* to Marguerite Steen's *Sun Is My Undoing*—that recalls Kurtz's fixation on the dark, satanic woman; and the story presenting Africa as a dark labyrinth—which Conrad seems to have inaugurated and which finds its more recent manifestations in such novels as Graham Greene's *Heart of the Matter*—wherein a European journeys into Africa in order to discover his own identity as well as the meaning of life and death" (71). These subgenres are ubiquitous in colonial and postcolonial fiction. They inform texts as diverse as Patrick White's *A Fringe of Leaves*, Margaret Atwood's *Surfacing*, Bessie Head's *A Question of Power*, and Katharine Susannah Prichard's *Coonardoo*. The subgenre may be ambivalently used explicitly or implicitly to question racial stereotypes.

3. I articulate this point as a deliberate allusion to an argument of Irigaray in "Women on the Market," an essay that addresses women's status as commodities and objects in the exchange-relations of Western patriarchal discursive and libidinal economies: "*So commodities speak. To be sure, mostly dialects and patois, languages hard for 'subjects' to understand.* The important thing is that they be preoccupied with their respective values, that their remarks confirm the exchangers' plan for them" (*This Sex* 179).

4. My articulation of this point is based on a reading of Iris Marion Young's critique of political theories of community based on an ideal of small-group, face-to-face relations in "The Ideal of Community and the Politics of Difference" 312–17.

5. Rhys seems occasionally to fix the Dominican landscape in formulated phrases. For example, in response to the playing of Martinique music, "Maladie d'amour, maladie de la jeunesse," Sasha Jansen remembers lying in a hammock: "The hills look like clouds and the clouds like fantastic hills" (*GM,M* 77). The indifference of the stars is experienced by Phoebe in "Good-bye Marcus, Good-bye Rose" (29) and of the landscape by Antoinette in *Wide Sargasso Sea* (107).

6. The protagonist of Rhys's "Temps Perdi" says she is "almost as wary of books" as she is of people. "They also are capable of hurting you, pushing you into the limbo of the forgotten. They can tell lies—and vulgar, trivial lies" (*TWC* 145). The motif is discussed by Helen Tiffin in "Rite of Reply."

7. As a child, Cixous, too, sought to transcend colonial realities by losing herself in a world of books. I discuss the implications of this flight into textuality in "Difference, Intersubjectivity and Agency in the Colonial and Decolonizing Spaces of Hélène Cixous's 'Sorties.'"

8. In "'Women Must Have Spunks': Jean Rhys's West Indian Outcasts," singled out for critical canonization by Pierrette Frickey in *Critical Perspectives on Jean Rhys*, Lucy Wilson notes in passing many of these features of Rhys's representations of African Caribbeanness, but does not identify them as primitivist or consider their historical provenance.

9. Letter to Francis Wyndham, 14 Sept. 1959, *Letters* 171.

10. She is discussing a similar problem in feminist discourse.

11. Julian Pefanis discusses the way Georges Bataille and other French intellectuals took up Mauss's work on the gift-economy in *Heterology and the Postmodern: Bataille, Baudrillard, and Lyotard.*

12. The address suggests Leslie Tilden Smith was trying to market the piece in 1930–1931. The typed title, crossed out in favor of the one I have given, is "Down Along: A Fragment of Autobiography." It is held among the Jean Rhys Papers. The "crowds of masks" would defy white people "because they had their feet well on your necks; and they paid you barely enough to live on and then called you 'lazy devil of a nigger' for not doing more work; and imagined that you envied them, their pale faces and their pursed-up mouths, half-cruel, half-sanctimonious, and the stiffly-wooden gestures of their bodies" (12). In criticizing white people Rhys's autobiographical voice here identifies herself with the masks through the second-person plural pronoun "you"; white people are "they" and "them." Rhys reworks many of the memories in this autobiographical piece as Anna Morgan's in *Voyage in the Dark.* Meta's poking out of her tongue through the mask when Rhys was "seven or eight" brought on "a fit of hysterics," and she "had to be put to bed and pacified by a handkerchief saturated with eau-de-cologne tied round" her "head" (10).

13. A Dominican historical allusion dates these memories as being of the 1902 Carnival. See my article "William Rees Williams in Dominica" 14, n. 64.

14. White slavery was a topical issue in pre–First World War London and still in 1934. Suffragettes, particularly Emmeline and Christabel Pankhurst, made the issue central to their 1913 Moral Crusade. League of Nations efforts to address the problem are summarized in Vern and Bonnie Bullough 287.

15. This passage is also quoted by Emery as an example of "Hester's attempts to maintain the prevailing order" against a Carnivalesque "play of many voices, languages from all strata of society" (74).

16. In *Jean Rhys,* O'Connor notes the death wish (95) but does not connect it with primitivist racialized conceptions of the body or racial ideas about the white Creole. O'Connor offers a detailed and subtly nuanced examination of Rhys's representations of her mother in *Smile Please* and the Black Exercise Book (23–40). O'Connor argues that "there is a connection between her [Rhys's] relationship to her mother and to her feeling about the blacks of Dominica and, of course, to all women. . . . It is a queerly turned relationship, mixed with love, hate, envy, fear and guilt" (31). The twists she follows differ from mine, even though we cite some of the same passages. She does not identify the primitivisms of Rhys's personal myth of her mother or examine the ways Rhys's representations of maternal figures and African Dominican people are constructed by and operate within particular historical discursive regimes.

17. I want to thank my student Robert Cullen for drawing this to my attention and so wittily. He also elaborated the links between Hester and Vesta, or Hestia.

18. This song is also featured in "Temps Perdi."

19. When Antoinette Cosway Mason wants to force a confrontation with "Rochester" over the truth about her mother, she imitates "a Negro's voice, singing and insolent" (*WSS* 106). In "Let Them Call It Jazz," Rhys adopts the first-person narrative voice of Selina Davis. It is her only piece of fiction told from the point of view of a black Caribbean character and in patois. Interestingly, it is a story in which she contests first-wave British feminist narratives. See my essay "Modernity, Voice and Window-Breaking."

20. In the folklore imparted by Meta, zombies are "black shapeless things" with hairy hands (*SP* 30). In West Indian folklore duppies may take the shape of strangers on the road; having passed them one should be wary, for one may meet them again further along the way. On the ride to Constance Estate, Anna meets the woman with yaws: "I was frightened; I kept on looking backwards to see if she was following me, but when the horse came to the next ford and I saw clear water I thought I had forgotten about her. And now—there she is" (*Voyage* 130).

21. In "Lost Island," Rhys says that yaws is a "form of leprosy" (2). Gilman notes that in the late nineteenth century syphilis was thought to be a "a form of leprosy that had long been present in Africa and spread into Europe in the middle Ages. The association of the black and syphilophobia is thus manifest" (*Difference* 101).

22. Morris notes that "There's a Brown Girl in a Ring" "connects in irony with Anna's insistence that her mother was white, not coloured" (5), but does not place Anna's taking of the part of the "brown girl" in the context of racial constructions of the white creole or her desire to be black.

23. Compare Emery 66. Giddiness is reported by Perry in 1932 as an effect of use of quinine as an abortifacient. Laurie's lie about quinine covers up the involvement of Mrs. Robinson, who could have been charged with using an instrument with intent to procure the miscarriage of Anna Morgan—and with manslaughter if Anna were to die.

24. Under the 1895 Peace Preservation Act permission to masquerade was given by the governor in council. Masqueraders were ordered to be "decently clothed" and to conduct "themselves in an orderly manner." (See, for example, the published Order in the *Dominican* 21 Feb. 1895: [3], and in the *Dominica Guardian* 16 Feb. 1906: [3].) As Joseph Hilton Steber reminded 1905 masqueraders, "lighted torches are not to be used; and . . . the blowing of shells and the carrying of dangerous weapons are prohibited by law." In 1904 the Catholic clergy tried "to have the carnival suppressed" ("The Approaching Carnival," *Dominica Guardian* 25 Feb. 1905: [2]).

25. The Ministry's *Report on an Investigation into Maternal Mortality* was finally presented to Parliament in April 1937. An Interim Report of the Departmental Committee on Maternal Mortality and Morbidity was published in 1930. A representative advocate of legalized abortion was F. W. Stella Browne. A shortened version of her contribution to *Abortion* (1935), "The Right to Abortion," is reprinted in Rowbotham. In the *Times* on 26 July 1932, a Dr Pollock of the Wandsworth Branch of the British Medical Association is reported to have said: "It would never do for the British Medical Association to seem to be adopting an attitude of laxity towards moral problems, and he did not think it would ever be the policy of the association to advocate the termination of pregnancy as a cure for moral laxity" ("Treatment in Hospitals"). Concern about instrumental abortion was commented on by the Right Hon. Lord Riddell, president of the Medico-Legal Society, in the *Journal of Obstretrics and Gynæcology of the British Empire*. He specifically cites T. W. Eden's "The Prevention of Puerperal Sepsis: Mother and Child" (March 1931). The Ministry of Health's *Report of the Inter-Departmental Committee on Abortion* was published in 1939.

26. In early fragments of the ending held in the British Library (Add. Mss. 57856), the abortionist makes a variant of this comment. A woman is taking down Anna's feverish words. British doctors were advised during the 1930s to have a dying statement of women who had had criminal abortions taken down. The statement was regarded legally as having "a solemnity equal to that of a deposition made on oath" (Perry 124). A statement identifying the abortionist could be admitted as evidence in her or his trial.

Chapter 6 ──────────────────────────────

"Just a Cérébrale or You Can't Stop Me From Dreaming"

Sasha Jansen's perception of the complexities of her world in *Good Morning, Midnight* (1939) is indicative of the self-absorption and self-pity that characterize her depression: "My life, which seems so simple and monotonous, is really a complicated affair of cafés where they like me and cafés where they don't, streets that are friendly, streets that aren't, rooms where I might be happy, rooms where I never shall be, looking-glasses I look nice in, looking-glasses I don't, dresses that will be lucky, dresses that won't, and so on" (*GM,M* 40). For her a "room is a place where you hide from the wolves outside" (33), a place in which she can "pull the past" over herself "like a blanket" (49), "shut the damned world out" ([68]). Her memory peoples her loneliness with ghosts from her past: her dead baby, a husband, the midwife who attended her, acquaintances, friends, former employers.

Rachel Bowlby has elegantly elaborated the "impasse"—a "narrow, cobble-stoned" street "going sharply uphill and ending in a flight of steps" (9)—as the novel's leitmotif. "But," Bowlby writes, the novel "is structured like a rhetorical impasse too, since all its positive terms are already excluded with the force of impossibility (once there might have been hope for change, for a long time there has been none). As an impasse, and as the story of an impasse, the novel does not pretend to go very far. But as a woman's story written by a woman, it claims with ironic precision to be unconvincing" (Bowlby 57). In finally sentencing Rhys to inauthenticity, Bowlby alludes to a thought of Sasha's during a conversation with René, a gigolo, who has seemingly fetishized her as a "luck-bringer" (*GM,M* 127). Sasha describes herself to René as "no use to anybody . . . I'm a cérébrale, can't you see that" (135). This self-representation then figures for Sasha a relation of women to writing: "Thinking how funny a book would be, called 'Just a Cérébrale or You Can't Stop Me From Dreaming.'

Only, of course, to be accepted as authentic, to carry any conviction, it would
have to be written by a man. What a pity, what a pity!" (135)

The cérébrale is a monstrosity for both Sasha and René and is likened in Sasha's mind to the spectacle of a self-satisfied "little black boy in a top-hat"
(136). The monstrous identity of the cérébrale haunts Sasha in the closing pages
of the novel, as she turns René's contemptuous definition of the cérébrale into a
self-accusation: "'You don't like men, and you don't like women either. You
like nothing, nobody. Sauf ton sale cerveau. Alors, je te laisse avec ton sale
cerveau. . . . '" ['. . . Except your dirty brain. Then I leave you with your dirty
brain. . . .'] (157). Her words also echo the harassing commis voyageur's abuse
of her after René visits her hotel, leaving a note for her. The commis voyageur,
whose sexual advances she has rejected, shouts at her from his doorway, "'Vache!
Sale vache'" ['Cow. Dirty cow'] (125). After pushing René away as lover, she
reassures herself and the René she wills in fantasy to return to her bed:

. . . I am very tired.
    Not me, no. Don't worry, it's my sale cerveau that's so tired. Don't worry about
that—no more sale cerveau. (158)

Transcendence of the monstrousness of the identification, a will to purge the
"sale cerveau," motivates Sasha as she waits for the door of her room to open
and even as she accepts, shockingly for most readers,[1] the substitution of the
commis voyageur for René, saying in echo of James Joyce's Molly Bloom:
"'Yes—yes—yes. . . .'" ([159]).

The sexological, evolutionary, and literary discourses that circulated in the
early twentieth century around the cérébrale and the dreaming woman, types of
the "sexless" intellectual woman, are, to date, unrecognized intertexts of the
novel. In these discourses the "sexless" woman is often figured as sleeping and
the man's kiss is a threshold to the possibility of wakening to (hetero)sexuality
and an idealized or, less frequently, abjured femininity. Bowlby is disturbed that
Rhys's characters do not "have backgrounds and histories known to themselves
and to others who know them, including the narrator," that are "connected to
cultural as well as private events" (54).[2] I argue that Sasha's background and
history are broadly implied by Rhys through discourses and a poetics of sexual,
racial, and class hygiene, which do connect Rhys's protagonists with contemporary culture. I link Rhys's negotiation of these discourses to her representation of
Serge, the Russian Jewish artist, and his painting of the banjo player, which
Sasha purchases.

"SHE REPRESENTS INDIFFERENCE OR RESISTANCE TO THIS ACTIVE TEMPO"[3]

For Sasha the most habitable life is one of a depressive indifference ordered
by ritual. Indeed she seems to become dependent on the stupefaction it promises.

Indifference is one of Weith Knudsen's categories of "deficient sexual sensibility" in *Feminism* (1928). He claimed that twenty-five percent of women are indifferent in terms of their "sexual responsiveness" (Jeffreys 170). "I have no pride—no pride, no name, no face, no country. I don't belong anywhere. Too sad, too sad. . . . It doesn't matter, there I am, like one of those straws which floats around the edge of a whirlpool and is gradually sucked into the centre, the dead centre, where everything is stagnant, everything is calm. Two-pound-ten a week and a room just off the Gray's Inn Road," Sasha thinks (*GM,M* 38). Temporarily "excited" at the prospect of having an apéritif with René, Sasha defensively reasserts self-control: "And, after all, the agitation is only on the surface. Underneath I'm indifferent. Underneath there is always stagnant water, calm, indifferent—the bitter peace that is very near to death, to hate. . . ." (128). Indifference amputates feeling and pain, as in Julia Martin in *After Leaving Mr Mackenzie*. Sasha's language of surface and depth implies that indifference is now her true self.[4] She certainly believes that indifference offers a prospect of transcendence of the materiality of her circumstances and her anxieties about aging:

People talk about the happy life, but that's the happy life when you don't care any longer if you live or die. You only get there after a long time and many misfortunes. And do you think you are left there? Never.

As soon as you have reached this heaven of indifference, you are pulled out of it. From your heaven you have to go back to hell. When you are dead to the world, the world often rescues you, if only to make a figure of fun out of you. (75–76)

"[D]ead to the world," asleep, she is comforted and composed by a fantasy of being outside the historical time represented by the "whirlpool" and the Paris Exhibition of 1937.[5] The Exhibition, formally the Exposition Internationale des Arts et Techniques Dans La vie Moderne (International Exposition of Arts and Technics in Modern Life), had as its "twin gods peace and progress," and as its theme the "division that had grown up between the arts and technology" (Chandler [283]–84). In *Good Morning, Midnight* it is a metonym of French and, by extension, European internationalism in the late 1930s. Sasha desires peace and stagnation, inertness. "I'm a bit of an automaton," she thinks (10), using an image that suggests she has internalized the order of a society "grown mechanical in head and in heart, as well as in hand" (Carlyle 37). Later in the novel she will explictly imagine the world as "an enormous machine made of white steel" against a grey sky (*GM,M* 156). Sasha's turn inwards entails, in London, withdrawal to a "little life," deciding to drink herself to death, getting old, looking "at this . . . at that . . . at the people passing in the street and at a shop-window full of artificial limbs" (11); and, in Paris, a room in a cheap hotel located on an impasse, "a place to eat in at midday, a place to eat in at night, a place to have my drink in after dinner" (9). "Saved, rescued" by the inheritance, relieved of the necessity to earn a living, she feels "[t]he lid of the coffin shut down with a bang. . . . No more pawings, no more pryings—*leave me alone*. . . ." (37). The "coffin" is the place to which the Englishness of her "extremely respectable" middle-class family—"inward-looking . . . nice, decent, essentially private . . . about self-effacement and retreat" (Light 11)—relegates the "wild" Sophia, renamed Sasha.[6] The "bit of the public scene where transformations are played out" (Cixous 67), which Sasha desires to enter actively, is the realm of the feminine consumer. The "transformation act" (*GM,M* 53) she promises herself involves a new hair color, a new hat, and new clothes—a fresh surface, but, as Sasha observes, she is judged and classified on her surface appearance.

The fantasy of indifference usually integrates Sasha's identity sufficiently to stop her from bursting into tears. She fears making a spectacle of herself by crying in public. Mary Russo writes generally about women's fear of becoming a spectacle: "Making a spectacle out of oneself seemed a specifically feminine danger. The danger was of an exposure. Men, I learned somewhat later in life, 'exposed themselves,' but that operation was quite deliberate and circumscribed. For a woman, making a spectacle out of herself had more to do with a kind of inadvertancy and loss of boundaries . . . anyone, any *woman*, could make a spectacle out of herself if she was not careful" (213). Sasha's response to her fear is retreat—a desire for "radical negation, silence, withdrawal, and invisibility"— rather than bold affirmation of the spectacle through parodic "performance, imposture, and masquerade" (Russo 212).

Between October 1938 and January 1939 the English public could have visited an exhibition featuring many studies of weeping women, the Guernica Exhibition. Pablo Picasso's *Guernica*, the artistic centerpiece of the Spanish pavilion at the Paris Exhibition, and over sixty preliminary studies for the composition, many of them portraits of weeping women, had been shown to aid the National Joint Committee for Spanish Relief. The summer 1937 issue of *Cahiers d'Art* featured essays on the painting and reproductions of preparatory studies and photographs of the painting-in-progress. The grieving woman in wartime is a stock figure. "The regularity" with which the tears of the woman weeping because of "infringement of her physical integrity . . . or else bereavement are mentioned in every variety of war narrative is both impressive and frightening," writes Nancy Huston (275). Picasso's weeping women have been described as "among the most wrenching [portraits] in the history of art" (Freeman 14). In *Guernica* itself the grief is represented as tear-shaped eyes and droplet-shaped nostrils on a woman cradling a dead baby and on a woman who has apparently jumped from a burning house. Reviewing the Guernica Exhibition in the *London Bulletin*, Herbert Read describes *Guernica* as "the modern Calvary, the agony in the bomb-shattered ruins of human tenderness and faith" (218). Sasha's tears are a comment on the psychological and epistemic violence of civic and civil relations based on predation, cruelty, "market value" (*GM,M* 25), and obsessive placing of people on planes and within hierarchies of value. Those relations are imaged as a "fray" (25) and are part of a world beyond redemption in which "Venus is dead; Apollo is dead; even Jesus is dead" (156). A woman showing publicly the traces of the violence in tears in depression will make a spectacle of herself.

René finds the Star of Peace at the Paris Exhibition "vulgar" and "mesquin" [shabby] (137), and his comment resonates in the novel as a reflection on the temporality of European internationalism. The Exhibition was the first to be termed "international" rather than the standard "universal." The fountained area in which Sasha and René speak at the Exhibition was flanked by the imposing Soviet and German pavilions, the positions and styles of which suggested ideological confrontation and militaristic tension. They faced each other. The roof line of the Soviet pavilion was stepped up in planes, culminating on its highest level with a dynamic sculpture of a young worker and a collective-farm woman holding a hammer and sickle, icons of the worker's revolution. It implies the revolutionary spirit that enables an evolutionary progress. The German pavilion was a low, rectangular building with a towering front section of tall pilasters capped by a roof surmounted by a statue of "the German eagle, its talons clutching a wreath encircling a huge swastika" (Chandler 288). The roof line seems to be designed to suggest the soaring evolutionary spirit of Nazism. The architecture of the Exhibition itself produces a "narrative of imperial Progress" as *consumer spectacle*" (McClintock 33), nationalistic, propagandistic, and intensely competitive. "Cold, empty, beautiful," the Exhibition at night is, Sasha thinks, what she "wanted" after talking ribaldly with René about the English and love (*GM,M* 137).

Internationalism is a facade, a glossily packaged ideological commodity in a pervasive commodity culture. Travel is controlled by passport regulations. Before the First World War only Russia and the Ottoman Empire had passport regulations; Fussell notes that after 1915 they became "a fixture of the European scene" (25). Both Sasha and René have difficulties with passports, Sasha because of nationality by a failed marriage that belies her English appearance, René says because he is a French-Canadian deserter from the Foreign Legion who has arrived in France through Franco Spain with no papers or passport. Bowlby observes: "[n]ational identities and names . . . become part of a set of signs to be interpreted, personal coordinates available for deciphering, without there being any reason to suppose that they correspond to a truth, of origin or legal fact" (42). National "styles" and popular cultures are commodified to keep money and luck circulating. Sasha's husband, Enno, for instance, has a French friend who "sings at the Scala," calling himself "Dickson because English singers are popular at the moment" (*GM,M* 97). Sophia renames herself more exotically Sasha when Enno buys her "a Cossack cap and the imitation astrakhan coat" (11), thinking it might change her luck. Sexuality, too, is commodified, a spectacle of parading and exhibiting, of seduction technique. Even poverty is exhibitable. Sasha remembers an English medical student in Paris presenting to her gaze "as if he were exhibiting a lot of monkeys" people so poor that they pay to sleep "close-pressed against each other" at tables and on the floor in a café (35).

The colonial, too, is commodified as spectacle, stereotype, style, fashion, sexual object. The French colonial exhibit at the Exposition was located "in isolated splendor on the ile des Cygnes in the Seine. This was the familiar

French 1001 Nights dreamland, the exotic Orient and darkest Africa made real by theme pavilions and dusky natives hawking wares in the *quartier d'outre mer*" (Chandler 287). The exhibit of masks from Gabon and the Ivory Coast was said by Marc Chadourne, "the official chronicler of the colonial exhibit," to cry out the message: "'I am black, but I am beautiful'" (Chandler 287). Serge makes imitation West African masks, "straight from the Congo," he remarks to Sasha, confusing both his geography and their origin (*GM,M* 76). They adorn the walls of his studio. Despite his interest in "primitive" style and familiarity with fashionable beguine and "negro" music, what he says about Montparnasse and his story about meeting a "mulatto" woman from Martinique in London are permeated by racial stereotypes. Both Sasha and René have sexual pasts they recall in the routines of the "seduction" scene after their kiss. Sasha remembers the "practice" of delay and betrayals; René, the techniques of the gigolo and, faced with a recalcitrant Sasha, of the gang rapes in which he participated in Morocco, a French "protectorate" where he claims to have served as a Foreign Legionnaire: "'in Morocco it's much easier. You get four companions to help you, and then it's very easy. They each take their turn. It's nice like that.' He laughs loudly." (152) His "tourism" in the colonial military includes sexually commodifying local youngsters to sample through homosexual acts. "'I don't like boys; I tried in Morocco, but it was no use'" (134), he had earlier confessed to Sasha.

Stories of anticolonial nationalist resistance and efforts to contain it are unvoiced. René does not want to talk or think about Morocco, where he was stationed from 1934 until his desertion in 1937. He would have had to sign a contract "to serve with honour and fidelity" unconditionally for five years (Laffin 14). In 1937 the Legion was involved in the violent suppression of the Comité d'Action Marocaine, a Moroccan nationalist party that was campaigning for a return to indirect rule (Turnbull 55–56). These aspects of René are not accounted for in 1939 reviewer John Mair's characterization of him as a "deplorably familiar" figure "facsimilied" from the "second-rate international novel" in his "naive greed, lovable viciousness, childish amorality, etc." (614). Through René, Rhys hints at the violence, commodification, and exploitation that sustain the French colonial presence in Morocco.

The sense of deracination that permeates Sasha's indifference—"no pride, no name, no face, no country"—may be compared with the "splitting off of consciousness" Virginia Woolf writes of in *A Room of One's Own*. Judith Kegan Gardiner and Bowlby have drawn attention to Rhys's apparent allusion to Virginia Woolf's argument that a woman who wants to write needs £500 a year and a room of her own in Sasha's description of herself as having "[t]wo-pound-ten a week and a room just off the Gray's Inn Road" (Gardiner 245–46, Bowlby 52–53). Helen Carr comments: "For Woolf a room of one's own is privacy within the bourgeois home: for Rhys a room is never a home, only the latest bleak retreat from a hostile world" (51). Woolf says that "if one is a woman one is often surprised by a sudden splitting off of consciousness, say in walking down Whitehall, when from being the natural inheritor of that civilisation, she becomes, on the contrary, outside of it, alien and critical" (Woolf, *Room* 146). The splitting off is produced by exclusion from and circumscription of movement in public spaces, sexist denigration, and restrictive middle-class feminine propriety.

For Sasha, Paris and especially her room is "saturated with the past" (*GM,M* 91); it is "all the rooms" she has "ever slept in," "all the streets" she has "ever walked in." Her "undulating procession of memories," however, begins with "escape from London" through marriage to Enno after the First World War (109). Sasha remembers coming to Paris, a place on which their hopes of "the good life" are focused (96), and the fresh starts (fresh self-inventions) as wife, mother, mannequin, dress-house guide, teacher of English to foreigners, and ghost writer, indeed as Sasha. London, to which she returned in 1932, is synonymous with the imprisoning force of English hypocrisy, love as a "matter of hygiene" (132), the monotony of "jam, ham . . . lamb, and . . . roly-poly" (38), and the temporality of its "extremely respectable"—the "cliché," "a sentimental ballad" (36).

Sasha's early life there, apart from an allusion to a convent schooling, having no money of her own, a memory of her drawers falling down, and a sentence and a half of a letter denouncing her marriage as imprudently "mad" (*GM,M* 96), is compressed in the image of "a little room, smelling stuffy, with my stockings hanging to dry in front of a gas-fire. Nothing in that room was ever clean; nothing was ever dirty, either. Things were always half-and-half. They changed one sheet at a time, so that the bed was never quite clean and never quite dirty" (95). The sources of pollution are identified as her own physicality, and the standard of the accommodation and female servants, the visibility of whose labor, McClintock would suggest, improperly exposes "within the middle-class formation the economic value of women's work" (164). The dirty sheet, turned to a joke, bears the memory trace of physicality, of sex, of the fundamentalness of working-class female labor to the production of middle-class domestic purity, propriety and stuffiness and conspicuous middle-class feminine leisure: it marks for Sasha "a crisis in value" (McClintock 154).

Elucidating the work of Mary Douglas, Frazer Ward comments on the hybrid, the half-and-half: "hybrids disturb structures of ideas, schemes of things based on systematic inclusion and exclusion: fitting neither one definition nor another, the hybrid exposes the permeability of those bounded systems modeled on the body" (30). McClintock would suggest that in the Victorian "iconography of dirt" the permeable boundaries are those "between 'normal' sexuality and 'dirty' sexuality, 'normal' work and 'dirty' work and 'normal' money and 'dirty' money" (154). Sasha thinks that love in England is usually a question of "racial" hygiene: it is "a stern virtue," an "indecent necessity—and who would spend money or thought or time on the indecent necessity? . . . We have our ration of rose-leaves, but only because rose-leaves are a gentle laxative" (*GM,M* 132). In this scheme voluntary desire (want rather than need) is racialized as not-white, not-English, made "dirty" and "sinful." The repudiation of the room is foundational of Sophie/Sasha's adult identity. Her family, childhood, the "crisis in value" form its "constitutive outside," that "site of dreaded identification against which—and by virtue of which—the domain of the subject will circumscribe its own claim to autonomy and life" (Butler, *Bodies* 3). The expectations that Sasha focuses on marriage to and the "good life" with Enno (suggestive of her family's disapproval) promise to clarify the crisis in value. The refrain that runs through the memory of the room at the Steens' in the Netherlands, the first room of her life with Enno, is "not to go back" to London (*GM,M 95*).

Sasha's past in England returns to terrify her as the grey sky which is the neutral ground of her vision of the world reduced to the indifference of a machine. Woolf's Mary Beton's aunt's legacy "unveiled the sky" to her, "and substituted for the large and imposing figure of a gentleman, which Milton recommended" for her "perpetual adoration, a view of the open sky" (Woolf, *Room* 59). In *A Room of One's Own* the open sky is a figure of "release from sex-conscious Gothic psychological and economic captivity" (Thomas, "Battlefield" 165), of the purging of the "poison of fear and bitterness bred" in Mary Beton by the rigors of earning a living, of "effort and labour" and "hatred and bitterness" ceasing, because no man can hurt her or has anything to give her (Woolf, *Room* 57). It transfigures her relation to patriarchal authority. Sasha's aunt's legacy of £130 a year is, by comparison, figured as a path to the coffin. The legacy may have released Sasha from the need to earn a living, but she is still "very much afraid of men," "even more afraid of women," "very much afraid of the whole bloody human race" (*GM,M* 144). Her view of the grey sky is partially blocked by her vision of the machine. For Sasha a "grey day" is a reminder of "walking in London"; its greyness is a pathetic fallacy for a bleak mood, occasioned by thinking there is "not a hope" of her "good life" being realized (102). The novel's title is an allusion to an Emily Dickinson poem, which serves as epigraph:

Good morning, Midnight!
I'm coming home,
Day got tired of me—
How could I of him?

Sunshine was a sweet place,
I liked to stay—
But morn didn't want me—now—
So good night, Day! [5]

In Sasha's memories of travel to the "good life" of Paris happiness, Enno, eating exotic food, and escape from London are compressed in an image: "A door has opened and let me out into the sun" (104). The grey sky figures return, genteel poverty, the cliché, the English (Sasha relishes "English" jokes), the excoriated room. In Helen Corke's alternative version of a man's novel about a dreaming woman, *Neutral Ground*, her title is her figure for sexual indeterminacy.

"BRIDEBED, CHILDBED"

"'Bridebed, childbed, bed of death': thus woman's trajectory is traced as she inscribes herself from bed to bed in Joyce's *Ulysses*. . . . Molly, wife and adulteress, voyages in her memories. She wanders, but lying down. In dream. Ruminates. Talks to herself. Woman's voyage: as a *body*," writes Cixous, of the sleeping woman in patriarchy, for her an Everywoman, aroused from her dream by the man's kiss which initiates the story of her woman's body (66). Sasha charts her voyage as a woman's body "from bed to bed, until the age at which the thing isn't 'woman' for him anymore" (Cixous 66), but rather a sexual bore (to Enno), socially "dead" (to a male family member, identified only as an "old devil" [*GM,M* 36]), a dirty cow (for the commis), or, as Sasha realizes, a "rich bitch" (to gigolo René) (*GM,M* 64). "The night is coming," thinks Sasha (120).

Sophia/Sasha stakes a lot on her bridebed, and the crisis in value epitomized by the prearmistice room is not resolved by marriage, escape from London, or motherhood. Marriage promises "normal" sex; her most extended memory of an incident in London involves sex outside marriage and humiliation. She had evidently not been sexually awakened by an unidentified man who says to her, "'Can you resist it?'" She resists what she seems to read as an assumption of racialized sexual availability by adopting a "Nordic" coldness (*GM,M* 113). "'Stupid, stupid girl,' he says, doing up buttons" (114). (Her drawers fall down at the bus stop afterwards.) After "about a month" in Paris, Enno announces to wife, Sasha, that their sexual relationship is unsatisfactory: "You don't know how to make love[. . . .] You're too passive, you're lazy, you bore me" (107). Only at one point, secure in the knowledge of her love for him, does she accept the "musty smell, the bugs, the loneliness, this room which is part of the street outside." "[T]his," she declares, "is all I want from life" (109). The dominant, indeed overwhelming, theme of Sasha's coming-to-Paris and returning-to-London narratives is money. "Money circulates; it circulates—and how!" (108), but Sasha and Enno do not have a steady supply or constant luck. "I haven't any money. He hasn't any either. We both thought the other had money," remembers Sasha (96). They "[s]wing high, swing low, swing to and fro" (across many planes) to the rhythm of money circulating through their hands. Money means the difference among "A room? A nice room? A beautiful room? A beautiful room with bath?" (118) Sasha's fake astrakhan coat is a sentimental reminder of swinging high. For Sasha swinging low means "shabby clothes, worn-out shoes, circles under your eyes, your hair getting straight and lanky, the way people look at you" (102).

Sasha's anxiety about money is most intense after the birth of her "beautiful" but "unfortunate" son (*GM,M* 50–51). Destitute, with Enno away to seal a job, she worries "about money, money, money for my son; money, money. . . ." The midwife is a crone figure, who speaks an "old, old language of words that are not words" during births and "doesn't approve of chloroform."[7] Rhys suggests that, because Sasha has to give birth in a "place for poor people," she experiences a natural, primitive childbirth, in which her body becomes "an instru-

ment" (50) of ancient female wisdom. In May 1934 an appeal had been launched
in England to raise funds to provide anesthetics for poor mothers ("Safer Motherhood")—Rhys suggests such women have more pressing concerns. Sasha experiences initial doubts about her maternal love, and only gradually begins to "like
taking" the baby in her arms and "looking at him" (*GM,M* 51). Her sense of
herself as a bad mother because she does not have the money to nourish and support him, maternal love expressed as "torture" (50), is exacerbated when insomnia and anxiety dry up her milk. The midwife's "solution" is to bandage Sasha's
body so that there will be "no trace, no mark, nothing" of her childbirth (51).
When the baby dies at five weeks, Sasha's body may have "not one line, not one
wrinkle, not one crease" (52), but her heart and memory are "heavy as lead,
heavy as a stone" (116). "Everything" is "all spoiled" (contaminated by the corruption of the corpse). Sasha thinks God "very cruel," and when Enno goes out,
she tries to cope with her grief by not thinking, fixing her gaze blankly (116).

Sasha is pressured by the uncertainty of money, the smell of sulphur from
the fumigation of a rented room in the Rue Lamartine, and a sense that she is
"dragging" Enno "down" (*GM,M* 109) to seek work, "normal" money, rather
than the "dirty" money (101) she acquires in Brussels from a Mr. Lawson by
trading on her sexual attractiveness to him, a show of helplessness, and his
pleasure in the "unlimited right to scorn" her (101). Ironically her first marketable skill is her native-speaking fluency in English—she gives English lessons
to foreigners. Her subsequent working life in France in "dreary" or "boring" jobs
(16, 19) turns her dream of Paris to nightmare, and, tormented by the flies in her
room near the Place de la Madeleine, she writes a begging letter to "England," to
her family (119). Her earning money seems to give her employers the "unlimited
right to scorn" her, a right played out most fully in her memory of a labyrinth of
passages in a dress shop and the "Persian garden" setting of a story she is paid to
ghost write. Mr. Blank, the English manager of the shop, mispronounces a
French word in an instruction, and Sasha panics at the thought of seeming "a
fool" (23) by not knowing where to go. The labyrinth of passages becomes emblematic of her working life and her poor "market value" (25): "they will always
see through me. The passages will never lead anywhere, the doors will always be
shut" (28). She clings to the idea of having a particular black dress; it is an idea
of transformation, of confidence, of rising a social plane, a shred of the good life.
Retrospectively Sasha understands that by marking her "an inefficient member of
Society" (he has spoken of her "complete imbecility"), Mr. Blank can pay her
miserably, "lodge" her "in a small, dark room," "clothe" her "shabbily,"
"harrass" her "with worry and monotony and unsatisfied longings" till he gets
her "to the point when" she will "blush at a look, cry at a word" (24–26).

Like Mr. Blank, the rich woman in Antibes who employs Sasha to write up
her fairy stories says one thing and means another, making it difficult for Sasha
to understand instructions. René has also been "employed" by this woman, as a
gigolo it is implied. The woman's stories feature plants, and she anxiously insists that her stories are allegories. "'You understand that, don't you?'" Sasha

remembers her asking. "'Yes, I understand,'" responds Sasha, recalling that the woman "was never very explicit about the allegory" (139). If the stories are allegories, they will speak doubly through a sentimental language of flowers. As Christopher Looby points out, "while the language of flowers was expressly designed for the purposes of heterosexual courtship, it seems to have accreted other, unstable meanings and associations that opened onto less normative realms of desire, including forms of racialized eroticism, sexual deviance, and gender heterodoxy" (121). Sasha does not understand the allegorical language, and so cannot play the sexual game in the way that she writes up the woman's scenarios. The woman comes into Sasha's room "very early in the morning in her dressing-gown, her hair hanging down in two plaits." Her stories are about a cactus, a white rose, a yellow rose or a red rose (remembered in this order), which signify, respectively, warmth of feeling, "I am worthy of you," "Decrease of love. Jealousy," and "Bashful shame" (*Language of Flowers*). Sasha does not even recognize what is required of her when the woman asks her to set the allegory in a Persian garden, an orientalist signifier of decadence and exotic sensuousness. The woman's husband, Samuel, does not like Sasha's stories, but still the woman cannot say directly what Samuel means. They are not getting (sexual) value for money. His reported complaint that Sasha writes "in words of one syllable" and desire for long words may function as a reminder that the stories are for an adult audience. Sasha remembers the woman's mind as "washing about, like the bilge in the hold of a ship, all washing around in the same hold—no water-tight compartments," her snobbery, her sense of property, her shrewdness and her hardness (*GM,M* 140).

"BED OF DEATH"

Sasha identifies herself with a diseased kitten owned by upstairs neighbors in London, and the identification suggests the ways that she thinks about her middle-aged sexuality. The cat is a readily available and recognized euphemism for the female genitals (pussy). Torgovnick has examined the changing functions of the cat in Manet's *Olympia* and parodies of it. When Olympia's genitals are covered, a cat is used to figure them (Torgovnick 102). Sasha's response to René's technique implies that she is practiced in picking up men, but her memories are not explicit about this aspect of her life. Sasha becomes obsessed by the comment a young Englishwoman makes about her in a rather expensive restaurant, recalling it as "What the devil (translating it politely) is she doing here, that old woman? What is she doing here, the stranger, the alien, the old one?" This memory and the spectacle of a man shouting after a little girl (probably his daughter), "'You have a drop on your nose'" (*GM,M* 46), makes Sasha start to think about "that kitten," a creature she gives human psychological traits: "an inferiority complex and persecution mania and nostalgie de la boue [longing for the lower depths]." The traiting of the cat links it with the hunted "madwomen" on upper floors so common in Rhys's fiction. Mrs. Greiner, the kitten's English

owner married to a German man, thinks the cat "'ought to be put away.'" The
kitten was "thin, scraggy and hunted" and "snarled at caresses." The "sore on the
neck," which is getting "worse," seems to be linked to the attentions of "all the
male cats in the neighbourhood." After Sasha shooes her from her room, she
runs "right out into the street" and is run over by a taxi. Sasha thinks the taxi
"merciful" (47). Shortly after remembering the kitten, Sasha, haunted by her
"terrible" eyes, thinks her eyes were "like that kitten's eyes" when she looks in
the mirror (49). (Rhys may be making a mordant private joke here. Kitten was
Lancelot Hugh Smith's pet name for her, and Tony's pet name for Suzy Gray in
"Triple Sec.")

In the restaurant, Sasha recalls an old French gentleman having described the
English as a sore and decides that if she cries she "shall really have to walk under
a bus" when she goes outside. Nostalgie de la boue is Sasha's psychoanalytic
descriptor of the kitten's sexual desire. Wilhelm Stekel describes nostalgie de la
boue as a "downward urge" apparent in women in attachment to "'rounders,' inferior men and even criminals" (1: 39). He interprets this urge as revenge on parents "for their rigid negations and arbitrary delimitations" of "freedom" in the
interests of "culture" (1: 39–40). The Frenchman, he writes, calls the "attitude of
mind" entailed in "choice of love objectives from among the lower ranks . . .
Épater le bourgeois! Shocking the philistine!" (1: 39). He ties this downward
urge to dreams of falling, of abysses opening up (1: 40, 43). Sasha's concern
about the planes on which she is put is one expression of anxiety about falling.
When René persists in questioning Sasha about her fear of him, she thinks:
"You are walking along a road peacefully. You trip. You fall into blackness.
That's the past—or perhaps the future. And you know that there is no past, no
future, there is only this blackness, changing faintly, slowly, but always the
same" (GM,M 144). The blackness is glossed in her spoken response to René as
"the whole bloody human race [. . .] a pack of damned hyenas" (144). Blackness is also the color of what night implies in the novel: growing old alone
(118), surviving the failure of dreams of the "good life," becoming the stranger
(etranger), going "to pieces" (119), and in relation to Dickinson's poem,
"coming home" [5].

Serge chooses to tell Sasha a story of having been sexually importuned by a
crying, drunken unnamed "mulatto" woman in London, another hunted female on
upstairs floors, and Sasha wonders initially whether he is trying to get at her by
identifying her with the woman, but he says not, by implicitly identifying Sasha
as a "white woman" (79); this identification helps bring about a positive transformation in Sasha's mood. He may, however, be reading Sasha as sexually importuning him through watching him dance wearing the mask, and talking with
him about "negro music," or constructing her consumption of alcohol, in popularized eugenic thought a "racial poison" (Saleeby 205–45), as a point of similarity between the women. For Serge the mulatto woman is no longer sexual
woman (in Cixous' sense), having cried "so much that it was impossible to tell
whether she was pretty or ugly or young or old" (79), and he feels he was

"talking to something that was no longer human, no longer quite alive" (80). The child of a neighbor had told her that "she was a dirty woman, that she smelt bad, that she hadn't any right in the house" (81).

Serge reads the mulatto woman through stereotypes. He claims that the woman wanted him to "make love to her and that it was the only thing that would do her any good" (81). That he may have read her blackness stereotypically as a sign of promiscuity is suggested by his image of suffocation, which compresses his disgusted hatred of the house after this incident: he felt "as if a large derrière was sitting" on him, a feeling analogous to entering a space of immurement ("one of those walls where people are built in, still alive"), a punishment for Roman vestal virgins and Roman Catholic nuns who broke vows of chastity. A large derrière, originally an ethnographic marker of the Khoikhoi (colloquially Hottentot) woman, became during the nineteenth century a sign of the promiscuity of the black woman and the prostitute (Gilman, *Difference* 90, 99). Serge's disgust seems to be focused on his own unkindness (sending her away with the dregs of his whisky); what he reads as her transgressive sexual forwardness, which reduces him to a threatening passivity (she is on top sexually in his image); the contamination of himself by her desire; and the cruel racism of the child, which reduces him to speechlessness ("'Well, what can you say to a story like that?'") after having offered, he thinks, the "reasonable" advice: "'Don't let yourself get hysterical, because if you do that it's the end'" (*GM,M* 80). There may also be a play on kind in his sense that his recoil entailed his being not kind (of the same race). Gilman charts the emergence of a stereotypical myth of the Jewish person as a "white Negro" (*Difference* 31): "the black and the Jew were associated not merely because they were both 'outsiders' but because qualities ascribed to one became the means of identifying the difference of the other" (35). Gilman notes that Eastern European Jewish people were thought by some to have "mulatto" features and that Jewish people "responded" to the "white negro" model of race "as if confronted with the reflection of their own reality" (*Difference* 31). Sasha is relieved when Serge identifies her as white, rather than as a racialized hybrid.

Serge's disidentification from the mulatto woman marks a disidentification from a "white negro" model of Jewishness, which his donning of the mask and dancing to beguine music for Sasha might have made literal, especially as Serge thinks his own head Jewish. Remembering being costumed in a fine suit in London, he says he had "looked quite an Englishman from the neck down. I was very proud" (*GM,M* 79). Arguably, too, Serge's body is effeminized by its nervousness, given that neurasthenia was so often represented as a modern affliction of women brought on especially by their "increased mental activity" (Showalter 135).[8] Torgovnick observes that "Dadaist and Surrealist works almost obsessively superimpose or juxtapose the white female with primitive masks, often creating a collage of white female body against African head, or white head against black; the absence or substitution of heads seems of special interest (see, for examples, Man Ray's *Kiki*, also called *Noire et blanche* . . . ; Hannah

Hoch's *Monument to Vanity II*; Max Ernst's *Elephant of the Celebes*)" (102). In racist and primitivist frames of perception dancing to beguine music was associated with "African" sexuality.[9] Serge's dancing recalls to Sasha's mind the words of a man from Lille trying to make sense of her drunkenness as they left the Café Buffalo: "*Have you been dancing too much?* [. . .] *Mad for pleasure, all the young people*" (*GM,M* 77). Sasha urges Serge not to stop dancing. This may be an intertextual reference to the carnival-fall sequence in *Voyage in the Dark*, implying that Sasha is not the kind of prude who would insist, as an unidentified voice does there, that Masquerade "ought to be stopped" because "it's not a decent and respectable way to go on" (*Voyage* 156). Sasha, however, does not join in the dance, as Anna Morgan does in imagination, moving, as I argued in chapter 5, beyond the bounds of a white middle-class propriety of the body.

In Paris, Sasha becomes the object of the sexual attentions of the man in the room next door, dubbed the "ghost of the landing" and a commercial traveler (commis voyageur) by Sasha, and of René, men who are doubled in various ways. The commis voyageur loiters and parades sexually before Sasha among the signs of female domestic labor, a clutter of "brooms, pails, piles of dirty sheets and so forth—the wreckage of the spectacular floors below," dressed in a flannel nightshirt "yelling" for the maid Marthe (a play on martyr), or in dressing gowns, a "beautiful dressing-gown, immaculately white, with long, wide, hanging sleeves," which makes him look like "the priest of some obscene, half-understood religion" (*GM,M* 30), or "a blue one with black spots" (13). Sasha resists as a misrecognition the sexual availability his "cringing, ingratiating, knowing" gaze (13) sees in her, the "plane" of the relationship he desires, snubbing him, pushing him away from her room when he stands "in the doorway, smiling. (Now then, you and I understand each other, don't we? Let's stop pretending)": "It's like pushing a paper man, a ghost, a something that doesn't exist" (31). Sasha's class differentiation of herself from him produces him as a disembodied figure of nightmare; René, by contrast, is effeminized and bodied by his exhibition of himself before her physically as Sasha has exhibited herself before men whom she wanted to pick up (61). Rhys pointedly uses the word "exhibiting"—"exhibiting himself, his own person" (61)—and Sasha sharply observes and recognizes the cross-gendered technique that renders him "calm, indifferent, without a glint in his eye" (132–33). Her observation of the technique critically distances her from René's performance. Sasha's fright at the commis voyageur, her subjective sense that the hall "smells like a very cheap Turkish bath in London," a descent "into a fog of stale sweat—ten, twenty years old" (31), pushes her one day to seek "most respectable" accommodation (31) in order to exist "on a different plane at once . . . if only for a couple of nights" (32). Stallybrass and White note that "[a]t one level smell was re-formed as an agent of class differentiation" during the nineteenth century. "Disgust was inseparable from refinement: whilst it designated the 'depraved' domain of the poor, it simultaneously established the purified domain of the bourgeoisie" (140).

The commis voyageur is doubled in nightmare with a wounded father figure and in his sexual importuning of Sasha with René. In her nightmare a man dressed rather like the commis voyageur in "a long white night-shirt" urges her to remember that he is her father and begins shouting "murder" (*GM,M* 12). The blood streaming from a wound in his forehead marks him as a Goliath figure, a champion of the Philistines, despite his small stature. In stock breeding blood signifies "recorded and respected ancestry; pure-bred breeding" (*Macquarie Dictionary*). Sasha's failure to acknowledge her parentage and loss of respect for the father's authority and the family's sense of a loss of pure breeding in the "wild" Sophia are represented in the wound. If the snubbed Sasha is "dead" in the eyes of her family, then who has "killed" whom? Sasha may be announcing their "murder" of her when she begins to shout, "'Murder, murder, help, help'" (13). The doubling of the father figure and the ghost of the landing (the "family" resemblance does not extend to their noses) works to suggest that Sasha's failure to respect the commis voyageur's genealogy (he is anonymous to her) and patriarchal authority has caused his deadness for her. His "bird-like face" with its "sunken, dark eyes" (13) feasts sexually at the end of the novel on what the "pack of damned hyenas" (144) have left of Sasha.

Sasha, insisting, as a means of resisting a sexual advance, that she is different from other women, urges René to recognize her as a cérébrale, "'I'm no use to anybody . . . I'm a cérébrale, can't you see that.'" He demurs, commenting, "'I should have thought you were rather stupid. [. . .] I don't mean stupid. I mean that you feel better than you think'" (*GM,M* 135). Sasha's "no use" echoes René's admission of sexual failure with "boys in Morocco" (134). Perhaps playing along with René's sense of her stupidity, Sasha questions his understanding of the term cérébrale by acting dumb. He informs her, "'A cérébrale [. . .] is a woman who doesn't like men or need them,'" but is not, as Sasha infers from this, lesbian: "Ah, but a cérébrale doesn't like women either. Oh no. The true cérébrale is a woman who likes nothing and nobody except herself and her own damned brain or what she thinks is her brain'" (136). (Sasha had conceded to René that she had on one occasion felt an unrealized lesbian desire for a particular woman.) René implies a perverse narcissistic sexuality, in which not the flesh but the conceited idea of the brain becomes the autoerotic object of desire. Sasha thinks:

So pleased with herself, like a little black boy in a top-hat. . . .
"In fact, a monster."
"Yes, a monster."
"Well, after all that it's very comforting to know that you think I'm stupid. . . ."
(136)

Sasha has been called stupid or imbecilic by other men too, and Rhys has undermined their judgment by showing, for instance, that Sasha is afraid to blame Mr. Blank publicly for the error caused by his mispronunciation and that the man who witnesses her drawers fall down was motivated by his own conceit

and sexual disappointment. Sasha mordantly mocks the triviality, empty polite-
ness, and compliance of her "usual conversation"—"'I believe it's going to be
fine today—yes, I hope it is—yes—yes—yes—'" (135)—but in her inner dialogue, as Gregg notes, "Sasha interprets her 'life' through language, books, music, painting, writing, and memory" (154). Sander Gilman observes that by the
eighteenth century the black person had become an "icon for deviant sexuality in
general, almost always, however, paired with a white figure of the opposite sex"
(*Difference* 81). That the "little black boy in a top-hat" is for Sasha an icon of
autoerotic sexuality might suggest that the top hat is a euphemism or sexual
symbol. He reappears later in her imagination wearing a top hat and a G-string.
The top hat may make explicit what the G-string conceals yet draws attention to;
the scaling of the boy's littleness against the tall hat and of his chronological
immaturity against the sexual knowingness of striptease performance invokes
racial stereotypes of phallic size and sexual precociousness respectively. The
cross-racial pairing figures the brain of the cérébrale as oversized unheterosexing
phallus.

The cérébrale and the dreaming woman were late nineteenth- and early twentieth-century types of the "sexless" woman, of the modern woman disordered by
her intelligence and education. Sheila Jeffreys has charted the emergence of the
"frigid woman" as a sexological category during the late 1920s (165–85), and
appropriately points out that frigidity is evaluated in relation to heterosexuality.
In D. H. Lawrence's elaboration of the dreaming woman in 1912, he implies her
fundamental sexual frigidity. Laura Marholm's account of the cérébrale in *Studies in the Psychology of Woman* (translated into English in 1899) is not as
sexually explicit. Her cérébrale anticipates "surging waves of life" she has read
about, but until she reorders her brain properly her "glance" becomes "dull," her
"breath weaker, and the just-awakened woman falls asleep again" (71). The signs
of disorder are drawn from a late nineteenth-century symptomatology of the
"chronic female masturbator" (Dijkstra 74).

Marholm's book is permeated by her commitment to "a temporality of evolution, as an an organic process of development or growth" (Felski 148) and ve-
hement repudiation of the revolutionary emancipation of women proceeding
around her. Emancipation, termed "war against men" (Marholm 41), has produced, she suggests, "half-woman . . . this most absurd of all intermediate
stages" (Marholm 40), a devolution of proper femininity. She analyses three
main types ("differentiation[s]") of the modern lady—the cérébrale, the détraquée,
and the grande amoureuse[10]—explicitly eschewing consideration of "those
women who have fallen from the fortifications of society's great citadel and live
upon a lower plane,—the fallen, the erring, the led astray, or whatever one may
term them; that mass of wantonness and duped simplicity " (50). (Sasha places
herself on the plane of the born lady in identifying herself as a cérébrale.) For
Marholm the spinal cord is the normal site of feminine morality and intelligence. Wilhelm Stekel discusses the model of

the double-chamber arrangement of our nervous system. The lower a person stands upon the cultural level the more strongly developed is his love life. But that love is purely animal-like, perhaps we should say vegetative,—a function of the spinal cord. The spinal cord, the lower center, contains the centers controlling the sexual organs. The lower the animal stands upon the biologic scale, the simpler is the arrangement of his sexual organs; the special senses stand at the service of the spinal cord. The man of culture possesses also an upper center,—the brain. The brain is the seat of all inhibitions and of all the artificially induced and acquired stimuli; it is the organ of judgment and deliberation; it governs sexual inhibitions. The specific character of every love is determined by the struggle between brain and spinal cord. (1: 4–5)

The class relations he describes between higher and lower, brain and spinal cord, could be mapped across various kinds of scaled difference: sexual difference, racial difference, differences in social class, for instance.

Marholm defines the cérébrale, "a very frequent type among 'intellectual' women" (65) who have "enjoyed a thorough and well-assimilated education" (67),[11] as "on the one hand verging towards masculinity, and on the other towards the unripeness of a clever, precocious child" (63). "They all write,—these intelligent young women—either openly or in secret. They write in order to feign to themselves a contentment" (73). In women of the cérébrale type, according to Marholm, "constant, regular, mental activity" develops into "sexlessness" under the "pressure of their surroundings and by the restraint of their natural impulses. . . . The grounds in their own natures for this change were, firstly, a very feminine characteristic,—sharp observation; secondly, a very common feminine defect,—lack of poetical feeling" (63–64). The quality of their writing relegates them to the ranks of the "scribbling woman" (73). "La cérébrale" is for the French, the Parisian in particular, Marholm writes, "the woman who loves with her head and not with her heart, the woman whose sexual sensibility needs mental consent, who must have reasons for loving" (64). (Sasha's marriage to Enno is twisted up with her expectations of the "good life" and the resolution of her "crisis in value.")

Marholm's characterization implies a privileging of reason over the passionate spontaneity of the spinal cord, a privileging false to a feminine "nature" and precocious. Marholm's citation of the "clever, precocious child" is a reference to evolutionary theory. Early precociousness and permanent arresting of "intellectual faculties" at puberty were held to mark the intellectual development of women and nonwhite men and justified an "equation of the intellectual capacities of women and children" (Dijkstra 167). Carl Vogt in his *Lectures on Man* equated the intellectual capacities of the "grown-up Negro," "the child, the female and the senile white" (qtd. in Dijkstra 167). Marholm states that the "woman who loves thinks with the brain of the man she loves." While the cérébrale has "intact her instincts and sexual nature, she still tries to think with her own brain" because "she has no man with whose brain she can think" or "because she deems herself above the man whom she has" (67–68). Because her "instincts and sexual nature" are still "intact," however, she is capable of evolving into the highest type, the grande amoureuse, if she raises her heterosexual love object "above herself" and "set[s] herself under him" (79).

Sasha's posing of "Just a Cérébrale" and "You Can't Stop Me from Dreaming" as alternative titles for a book about a particular female type suggests she is referring to the "dreaming woman."[12] D. H. Lawrence refers explicitly to the type in *The Trespasser* (1912) in the character of Helena, modeled on Helen Corke, who had had an intimate relationship with Herbert Baldwin Macartney, her married music master, with whom she spent a brief holiday, after which he committed suicide. She and Lawrence had been "colleagues and friends as elementary school teachers in Croydon" (Corke, *Lawrence* [iii]). Lawrence based *The Trespasser* on her retrospective writings on the relationship and conversations with her. She later published a novel based on her relationships with Macartney and Lawrence and focused around questions of the protagonist's sexual indeterminacy, *Neutral Ground* (1933), largely written in 1918. The reviewer of the novel in the *Times Literary Supplement* complained that Corke's treatment of the holiday in a "somewhat cursory" manner diminished the "balance" of the narrative (538). Lawrence's examination of psychology in *The Trespasser* had been commended: "the psychology is penetrating and convincing," wrote B. S. (Basil de Selincourt) in the *Manchester Guardian* (Draper 47); the novel "leads the mind to a deeper understanding of the inexorable physical and moral laws which, holding humanity in bondage, work out for every trespasser a certain doom," opined the reviewer for the *Westminster Review* (Mansfield 27).

Jane Heath has argued that the protagonist Ellis Brooke's "unfocused, unplaced, and unnamed" sexuality would today be classified as lesbian, but Ellis "lacks the identity which the term lesbian now confers" (51). Ellis thinks of herself as between "Man" and "Woman" (Corke, *Neutral Ground* 312). Corke represents Ellis's aversive response to heterosexual touch as a matrophobic disgust at women's reproductive potential—she thinks that reproduction is a "senseless and mechanical fury" (164) and an inhibition of women's freedom. The response is also a product of her socialization into a belief that "while the body, with its passions, was in necessary subjection to moral law, the mind moved above it in a state of exalted and unchallenged freedom" (123). Ellis rejects what other women represent to her as woman's duty, desire and prudence: the rooting of self in a marriage partner, "his money and his plans" (96). Angus Rane, modeled on Macartney, eroticizes Ellis's spirituality and self-containment (so different from his wife, Cora's, slatternliness and reproductive excess), comparing people like Ellis with the double stock: "They fulfil themselves in their own lives. Their energy doesn't go to seed. It isn't diverted for reproduction. They are free to express in their own persons the fullness of the life charge they hold" (157). He allegorizes himself and family-oriented people as pansies, the petals of which develop, "but not to the full measure of one's vitality. More than half one's life power is drawn to the production of seed and pollen" (156).

Lawrence's narrative voice says of Helena in *The Trespasser*:

She belonged to that class of "Dreaming Women," with whom passion exhausts itself at the mouth. Her desire was accomplished in a real kiss. The fire, in heavy flames, had poured through her to Siegmund, from Siegmund to her. It sank, and she felt herself flagging. She had not the man's brightness and vividness of blood. She lay upon his breast dreaming how beautiful it would be to go to sleep, to swoon unconscious there, on that rare bed. She lay still on Siegmund's breast, listening to his heavily-beating heart.

With her, the dream was always more than the actuality. Her dream of Siegmund was more to her than Siegmund himself. He might be less than her dream—which is as it may be. However, to the real man she was very cruel.

He held her close. His dream was melted in his blood, and his blood ran bright for her. His dreams were the flowers of his blood. Hers were more detached and inhuman. For centuries, a certain type of woman has been rejecting the "animal" in humanity, till now her dreams are abstract, and full of fantasy, and her blood runs in bondage, and her kindness is full of cruelty. (64)

(After feeling "love, youth, spring, happiness, everything" she thought she had lost, return in her embrace of René, Sasha's desire is initially satisfied by a kiss: "We kiss each other fervently, but already something has gone wrong" [Rhys, *GM,M* 148].) Ellis Brooke, "[i]n resisting demands that became more and more urgent"—Angus's kisses and embraces—"felt that she was measuring her strength, not against Domine [her nickname for Angus] but against an impersonal force that used him pitilessly as its instrument. She believed that Domine's higher nature fought with her against its subordination to this force" (Corke, *Neutral Ground* 190). Ellis glosses this "impersonal force" elsewhere as "animalism" and "sheer sensuality" (153), but one might also read it today as compulsory heterosexuality.[13] The reviewer of *The Trespasser* in the *Nottingham Guardian Literary Supplement* had roundly deplored Lawrence's philosophy of "animalism" (Mansfield 27).

Lawrence's term "Dreaming Women" is an allusion to Rachel Annand Taylor's *The Hours of Fiammetta* (1910).[14] Hilary Simpson suggests that Taylor, on whose poetry Lawrence lectured in 1910, "reinforced, from the woman's point of view, conclusions about 'spiritual women' which he was already formulating" (49). Taylor distinguishes between "two great traditions of womanhood": the Madonna "brooding over the mystery of motherhood"; and the "dreaming woman," celebrated as existing "complete in herself," "the acolyte, the priestess, the clairvoyante of the unknown gods": "Strange, wistful, bitter, and sweet, she troubles and quickens the soul of man, as earthly or heavenly lover redeeming him from the spiritual sloth which is more to be dreaded than any kind of pain" (Taylor [5]). Sloth, one of the seven deadly sins, had become racialized as an attribute of a decadent aristocracy, the working class, and nonwhite people. Modern dreaming women, Taylor insists, find that "[t]heir intellectual forces, liberated and intensified, prey upon the more instinctive parts of their natures, vexing them with unanswerable questions. So Fiammetta mistakes herself to some degree, loses her keynote, becomes embittered and perplexed. The equilibrium of soul and body is disturbed; and she fortifies herself in an obstinate idealism that cannot come to terms with the assaults of life" (6). In "The Epilogue of the Dreaming Women" (first published in the *English Review*) Taylor offers a "new vision" (6) of dreaming women reintegrated as muses of Love:

Give mercies, cruelties, and exultations,
    Give the long trances of the breaking heart;
And we shall bring you great imaginations
    To urge you through the agonies of Art. (75)

This promise is predicated on the women having had men give up to them "souls" to be wakened. Armour, justice, orb, and scepter for women are abjured in favor of "veils mysterious and delicate," and "thuribles" (75). In *Neutral Ground*, Ellis draws a parallel between Angus Rane's allegory of the double stock and Taylor's idea of the dreaming woman, dismissing Taylor's idea as "picturesque" and "poetic," overly literary in relation to her own experience of need (157).

Lawrence's elaboration of the dreaming woman, insisting on her destructive rather than redemptive spiritual aspect, is so central to *The Trespasser* that he proposed to Edward Garnett as one of three alternative titles "The Man and the Dreaming Woman" (*Letters* I, 1 April 1912, 378). Lawrence reports to Edward Garnett that Ford Madox Hueffer (later Ford), the first reader of the manuscript of his young protégé, said that it "is a rotten work of genius. It has no construction or form—it is execrably bad art, being all variations on a theme" (*Letters* I, 18 Dec. 1911, 339). Ford's comment reminds me of his praise for Rhys's "singular instinct for form" in his preface to *The Left Bank and Other Stories* (25).

Lawrence's dreaming woman is an untainted Sleeping Beauty figure, who fails to awaken to her sensuous physicality at the man's kiss. Instead, she dreams of sleep or a faint into insensibility in an aestheticization of passivity, which implies a disengagement from her body to become a detached observer of an artifice. Hampson, usually read as an authorial mouthpiece, comments to Siegmund that "deep, interesting women" find "natural" men a source of personal and romantic degradation and argues that this leads this type of woman to harbor destructive desires towards such men (112). Hampson's "supersensitive" woman "refined a bit beyond humanity" (112) is similar to Marholm's ladies prone to "super-sensitiveness," who carry in their "blood an over-sensitive chastity-barometer": "nothing to them is so distressing, so debasing, as to feel a stain upon themselves" (53).

Lawrence sets up a dichotomy between the man whose sexual desire melts a mind/body split and the highbrow woman who rejects the incarnation of her dreams, repudiating the healing of the split.[15] The domesticity of Siegmund's marriage to Beatrice is represented as "years of soilure," "dirt of misery" (89), slovenliness (171); their children are for him "great brown stains" on a "dirty" tablecloth and a litter of boots, shoes, and clothes (50). He seeks "purification"

of soul and body, the feeling of being "perfectly clean and free, fresh" in his relationship with Helena (89) and fetishizes Helena's whiteness, fixing his gaze on
her characteristic "white dress," "full white arms" (66), "white, sloping shoulders" (67), "moonlit ivory of her face" (71), her breast "as the breast of a white
bird" (87). If her whiteness seems to promise a cleansing, it finally reveals itself
as a fundamental iciness[16] and inviolability (72). Lawrence racializes Siegmund's
disgust at Beatrice by associating her with foreignness. In Siegmund's memories
of the origins of his relationship with Beatrice he recalls her French convent
schooling and her having been "brought . . . out" by knocking about with the
army in Egypt (her father was an improvident army officer). The youthful Beatrice is remembered ironically in the romantic setting of a conservatory with
white star-like narcissus and hyacinths among the green, "a keen, fresh scent on
the warm air" (123). Cora's mother's family in *Neutral Ground* is Spanish. Angus speaks of Ellis's purity without fetishizing her white skin. The huge ice-
crystals he dreams about while on holiday with Ellis suggest both Ellis's sexual
inaccessibility and his own withdrawal into himself preparatory to committing
suicide.

The conversation about the cérébrale haunts Sasha in her subsequent dealings
with and desire for René, which are punctuated by three graphic erotic scenarios
in her imagination that emblematize her unspoken sexual fears. The first scenario occurs during a conversation with René in which he tries to dissuade Sasha
from her insistence that sexual intercourse between them is unimportant and will
not happen. After he gestures the sexual touch that will transform her (she likens
it to the technique of a baker kneading dough), she watches "the little grimacing
devil" in her head: "He wears a top-hat and a cache-sexe and he sings a sentimental song—'The roses all are faded and the lilies in the dust'" (*GM,M* 146).
Sander Gilman observes that during the "rise of modernism" in Europe the act of
"seeing the black" is associated with "the fantasy of the genitalia" (*Difference*
109), the "sign of decay and destruction, a marker against which the Western
world can judge its own degeneracy and decline" (125). The song Sasha's "devil"
sings links the striptease and genitalia with decay and death; roses are conventional symbols of love, lilies of purity. His grimace suggests his own disgust.
He may be fused in her imagination with the boys René has "tried in Morocco"
(*GM,M* 134). While the monitory image confirms her desire to be left alone and
she articulates the desire to René, she allows him to accompany her on her taxi
ride home.

The setting of the second scenario, a product of Sasha's "film-mind," is "a
little whitewashed room" in a hot climate. The relationship between the foregrounded male and female figures is constructed on a master/servant model (rather
like the relationship between Mr. Howard and Rhys in his serial story). Sasha
identifies with the woman-maid, whose costume (black dress, felt slippers, bare
legs) resembles that of a dishwasher in a tabac Sasha had observed earlier, salut-
ing her as "the girl who does all the dirty work and gets paid very little for it."
The similarity suggests that the whitewash, the semblance of respectability,

covers over what is hidden by the woman's sexual abasement and dependence: the space of labor, represented earlier as an "unbelievable smell" that "comes from the sink" (87), a metaphorical "coffin" that would seemingly make Sasha faint (87), and of exploitation. It is the abasing labor that the man, who is whistling the march of the Foreign Legion while cleaning his shoes, seems to eroticize: "He often brings home other women and I have to wait on them, and I don't like that" (147). At many points in Sasha's narrative a highbrow, ironical, respectable, often humorous,[17] inner voice engages with her desiring self. The split becomes apparent in her response to the abasement narrative. Sasha's highbrow recognition that the narrative is shaped by melodramatic conventions of popular cinema— "My film-mind. . . . ('For God's sake watch out for your film-mind. . . .')" (147)—makes her laugh.[18]

The "voluptuous simplicity of the preliminaries" (Cixous 66) to Sasha and René's fervent kissing is short-lived, and she has to contend with an exacerbated split between her two voices (here constructed as body and mind). She feels "uneasy," half of herself "somewhere else": "Did anybody hear me, was anybody listening just now?" (*GM,M* 148). Her fear of intimacy is twofold: on the one hand she is afraid to lose respectability, to make "a scene in this hotel" (151); on the other she desires a kindness she does not see in René's "ironical" eyes (149). She resists being thought "Easy, easy, free and easy. Easy to fool, easy to torture, easy to laugh at" (150). As he attempts to force her she hears her "high, clear, cold" respectable voice rise to take command of the situation, to insult and mock René so that he will leave. After he departs, she senses that "Madame Vénus is angry" and Phoebus Apollo, symbol of shining light, "is walking away [. . .] down the boulevard to hide himself in la crasse." The reference to Phoebus Apollo's action recalls Dickinson's poem: "Day got tired of me—" Sasha compresses her mood in an image of an irredeemable world. What is left

is an enormous machine, made of white steel. It has innumerable flexible arms, made of steel. Long, thin arms. At the end of each arm is an eye, the eyelashes stiff with mascara. When I look more closely I see that only some of the arms have these eyes—others have lights. The arms that carry the eyes and the arms that carry the lights are all extraordinarily flexible and very beautiful. But the grey sky, which is the background, terrifies me. . . . And the arms wave to an accompaniment of music and of song. Like this: "Hotcha—hotcha—hotcha. . . ." And I know the music; I can sing the song. . . . (156–57)

Visually the image alludes to European futurist art; its temporality is a musical idiom thought of in the day as earthy and "American Negro"—the image synchronizes the stereotypically highbrow and lowbrow. The foreground emphasizes human artifice—machine, makeup, lights—and, as Emery notes, is created "through a movement of condensation and unification," picking up "its meaning from associations with artificial limbs she has glimpsed in a shop window, the makeup she wears, the steel hand in her dream that points the way to the exhibition, and the stage lights that expose the crudity of a song that she knows well"

(167). I would add, too, the four arms of the banjo player in Serge's painting. William Leiss argues persuasively that in representations of the machine as a sign of the degeneration of human society and social relations the root metaphor is master and servant, developed as domination and servitude (149), with mechanization marking an internalization of an inversion of the (proper) hierarchy human/machine. If the neutral ground, the grey sky, terrifies Sasha, the music is reassuringly familiar. Hotcha, hot jazz, is a 1920s and 1930s musical style, the solos characterized by a "frenetic quality, an urgent sense of rhythm, agitated syncopation, eager anticipations of the beat, and an earthy or 'dirty' tone" (Kernfeld 540). "Hot expression" was thought to be "purely Negroid in its peculiar aesthetic, in much of its melody and in virtually all of its rhythm" (Sargeant 212).

Sasha's vision of the machine against the grey sky contrasts with her vision as the beguine music from Martinique prompts her to imagine or remember herself "lying in a hammock looking up into the branches of a tree. The sound of the sea advances and retreats as if a door were being opened and shut. All day there has been a fierce wind blowing, but at sunset it drops. The hills look like clouds and the clouds like fantastic hills" (*GM,M* 77).[19] Sasha's meeting with Serge and consumerist appreciation of his paintings does bring about a transformation in her mood: the studio "expands," "the iron band" around her "heart loosens," and she is miraculously "happy" (83). She chooses to purchase from the impromptu exhibition a painting of "an old Jew with a red nose, playing the banjo" in a gutter (83). Contemplation of the figure first catalyses the return of her memories of her marriage and later Sasha identifies herself with the man.

The image of the machine against the grey sky pushes Sasha to "stop" her mocking, highbrow, snobbish, respectable voice "talking." Serge "speechifies" about the creative genius of Van Gogh: "'the terrible effort, the sustained effort—something beyond the human brain, what he did'" (79). In sexually willing René back to her room ("the effort, the enormous effort, under which the human brain cracks"), Sasha promises a reinvention of herself in which her dirty brain is "no more," and she has exchanged love objects, and will be "simple" (158).

The commis voyageur enters Sasha's room rather than René. He has certainly heard René mockingly shout for help in a "high falsetto voice" (151) and loudly describe the methods of gang rape that he learned in Morocco, possibly muffled voices and sounds of a sexual struggle, the door shut as René leaves, Sasha crying, a key dropping, and Sasha's door being left "a little open" as Sasha anticipates René's return (158). "[L]ooking down" at her, the commis voyageur's eyes are not kind, but "mean" and "flickering" (159). Sasha writes:

I look straight into his eyes and despise another poor devil of a human being for the last time. For the last time. . . .
    Then I put my arms round him and pull him down on to the bed, saying: "Yes— yes—yes. . . ." [159]

"For the last time" echoes her thought when René, "his hard knee" between her resisting knees, asks her whether she understands that "'everything's going to be all right.'" She thinks the "ritual answer" to his "'T'as compris?'": "'Yes, I understand.' Thinking 'For the last time.' Thinking nothing." (153) The scene is interrupted by her ironical voice. The echo of this at the novel's end emphasizes that the other voice now speaks and that it offers a ritual answer to the man's sexually objectifying gaze.

What does Sasha affirm with her yeses? Molly Bloom's yeses, which close *Ulysses*, affirm her acceptance of Leopold Bloom's proposal of marriage. She encourages his proposal: "he said I was a flower of the mountain yes so we are flowers all a womans body yes that was one true thing he said in his life and the sun shines for you today yes that was why I liked him because I saw he understood or felt what a woman is and I knew I could always get round him and I gave him all the pleasure I could leading him on till he asked me to say yes" (Joyce 703). Her yeses are an embrace of the "love, youth, spring, happiness" (*GM,M* 148) twisted up in the memory. The moment had brought Molly Bloom to think "as well him as another" (Joyce [704]). With different intonations, Sasha has said three yeses before, once in fearful agreement with Mr. Blank, when he asks her to affirm that she is "[j]ust a hopeless, helpless little fool" (*GM,M* 24), and once to herself in self-mocking agreement with René's sense of her stupidity (135). They are the self-censored yeses of the complying, self-abasing woman which her interlocutors want to hear. The commis voyageur, "another poor devil of a human being" ([159]), is represented visually as a vampire figure, with his emaciated body "thin as a skeleton," "bird-like face and sunken, dark eyes" (13), and his liminal living/dead, human/animal form for Sasha. The "long, wide, hanging sleeves" of his white dressing gown (30) give an impression of bat's wings, and, as is usual in Rhys's fiction, the whiteness is associated with coldness and death. He will taste Sasha's bloody lip, which René has tasted in the bite that caused it. The shared taste seals a homosocial exchange.

Sasha's yeses may be read in this undeveloped thematic as the necessary enervated, indifferent compliance of the vampire's prey. Here Rhys, as in "Triple Sec," turns back on the male party to casual sex the disease metaphor used of "amateurs" during the moral panic around venereal disease in the 1910s: "vampires upon the nation's health" (M.D.). As in "Triple Sec," *Quartet*, and *After Leaving Mr Mackenzie*, the disease of the amateur is depression (see chapter 4). If the cérébrale needs reasons for loving, having rejected the cérébrale identity to conform with René's desire, Sasha needs no reason for loving. In the commis voyageur's gaze and Sasha's yeses the psychological and epistemic violence of a European culture structured by relations of predation, cruelty, market value, and hierarchizations of people are mirrored as monstrosity. So, too, is the monstrosity of the psychological coercion of women into consenting to sexual intercourse through their fear of the implications of the labels cérébrale or dreaming woman and the racial consciousness that structures that fear.

"AUS MEINEN GROSSEN SCHMERZEN"

Serge's friend Delmar tells Sasha that two years before Serge had been living in the gutter ("'La crasse'") rather than the "beautiful, respectable room" in which she saw him (*GM,M* 85–86), information that links Serge and the Jewish man in his painting, "double-headed, double-faced," four-armed, "standing in the gutter, playing his banjo" (91). The painting suggests that highbrow modernist art may be created from an artist's experience and observation of the socially "low." The Jewish man may be read as a portrait of the artist, literally or metaphorically down-and-out, fragmented by his economic and racial subordination, or exhibiting a modernist disintegration of realistic unity of character. The doubling might also be read as a sign of Serge's identification with the artist-figure in his painting. As a banjo-playing musician and social outsider on the basis of race, the man recalls Banjo in Claude McKay's bestselling novel *Banjo*. African-American Banjo's creativity is drawn from his vagabond life in "The Ditch," a Marseilles ghetto. The banjo is an instrument of African origin, introduced to the Americas by slaves.

For Sasha the man in the painting is "gentle, humble, resigned, mocking, a little mad. He stares at me" (91). Under the pressure of his gaze Sasha relives her past (given the immediacy of present-tense narration) and imagines a future in which she *remembers* "about being young, and about being made love to and making love, about pain and dancing and not being afraid of death, about all the music" she has "ever loved, and every time" she has "been happy" (155). She identifies so closely with the man that she imagines herself saying "'I know the words to the tune you're playing. I know the words to every tune you've ever played on your bloody banjo'" (155). To cope with Mr. Blank, Sasha recites a line from Jewish Heinrich Heine's "Lyrical Intermezzo," "aus meinen grossen Schmerzen mach ich die kleinen Lieder" ["out of my great pains I make the little songs"] (21). While at the end of the novel Sasha insists in response to her ironical voice that she "mustn't sing any more" (155) and links her tears over this with "the light" in her "sale cerveau" going out (158), as first-person narrator of her story she becomes "her own maker of fiction," with the "power to build texts and to articulate her own narratives" (Le Gallez 176).

NOTES

1. Gregg reads Sasha's acceptance of the commis voyageur as a "morality tale about the responsibility of the artist" not "[t]o turn away from that which appears horrible or repugnant" and about the "moral responsibility of the Other to forge a practice of the self that is inclusive rather than exclusionary" (160–61).

2. Bowlby constructs Rhys as lacking in technique by comparison with Virginia Woolf in *Mrs. Dalloway*.

3. Cixous 67.

4. I am aware that Kristeva cites indifference as the "foreigner's shield" in *Strangers to Ourselves* (269). That citation is part of her essentialization of the foreigner in

a single set of psychological traits, which are not historicized.

5. By contrast, Ezra Pound, in his vorticist manifesto in the first number of *Blast* (1914), states that hedonism "is the vacant place of a vortex, without force, deprived of past and of future" (153).

6. This kind of Englishness can be heard in Frank Swinnerton's review in the *Observer*. Swinnerton describes *Good Morning, Midnight* as "not at all 'nice.' Miss Rhys has written several ruthlessly disagreeable studies of women whose lives, casual, improvident, and inescapably draggled, have fallen into misery."

7. The stereotype of the crone in scenes of childbirth is discussed by Cosslett 31–35.

8. The body Sasha watches dancing in the mask is "thin, nervous" (*GM,M* 77), and when Serge offers her a cigarette after speaking of Van Gogh's genius, "his hand is shaking" (79). Rhys is drawing on a stereotype of the Jewish person as neurasthenic, a stereotype elaborated by Sander Gilman, who observes that the "interchangeability of the image of the neurasthenic and the Jew" ambiguously integrates the "Jews into the negative image of modern civilization" (*Difference* 156).

9. The primitivist black Jamaican writer Claude McKay writes in *Banjo: A Story without a Plot* (1929) of "Negroes" dancing to Martinican beguine, American jelly-roll, Jamaican burru or Senegalese bombé (variants of each other)—that they "are never so beautiful and magical as when they do that gorgeous sublimation of the primitive African sex feeling. In its thousand varied patterns, depending so much on individual rhythm, so little on formal movement, this dance is the key to the African rhythm of life" (105). In a letter to Oliver Stoner dated 7 August 1970, Rhys says that she knows McKay's work. The letter is held among the Jean Rhys Papers. *Banjo* had a strong influence on the development of négritude.

10. Marholm distinguishes the cérébrale from a higher and a lower type of born lady. She uses "French expressions" for her types because "our beloved German is quite too plain for such subtleties" (60–61). The grande amoureuse, enthuses Marholm, "not only embodies the growing ardor of womanly devotion, but represents in the highest degree refined nature, culture which has become nature . . . She is the flower of feminine intelligence and the moral refinement of her time; she appears as the embodiment of the highest feminine intellect. A third characteristic is the warm, full, nourishing passion that she wraps about man, fostering but not scorching, like the warmth in which the mother carries the child in the womb" (62). Her love is "without repletion, a love of unlimited surrender, of intellectual devotion, and of psychic enthusiasm, fully as much as of physical enjoyment; a love in which the physical is transformed without loss into vibrations of the soul; finally, a love of long duration, of joyful self-surrender to one man, without intervals of emptiness and lassitude" (62). She is "perhaps the only woman-genius there is," all her "passive womanly qualities" having "stepped from their home in the spinal cord and formed a closer communion with the brain" (61). By contrast with the other types the détraquée, translated as "Disordered, unbalanced" (53), is a creature of "inflamed desire," fluttering "covetously from man to man, unable to settle to rest beside any one of them; finds nothing but disappointment in the final satisfaction of her wants; undervalues her husband; converts marriage into a torture; and—strange as it may seem—in spite of her eternal circling about it, rarely comprehends the physical basis of the relationship between man and woman or enjoys spontaneously the relation itself" (52). Her love is marked by disease—inflammation (which it carries to her partners) and hys-

teria (62)—and is animalized: she has "outstretched devil-fish arms"; "stretches forth her antennae and gropes for him [the decadent man] again" (54). She has a "sharp glance" (linked with "cunning") and "quick judgment for trivialities only" (58).

11. In summarizing and criticizing Marholm's classifications in *The Feminine Note in Fiction* (1904), W. L. Courtney says that he may "for the sake of terseness . . . be pardoned for calling the cérébrale 'the brainy type'" (xxiv).

12. There are other points of comparison between *Good Morning, Midnight* and *The Trespasser*. Like Beatrice in *The Trespasser*, Sasha is "in disgrace" with her family because of her marriage. Both Lawrence and Rhys use a protagonist's identification with a kitten to articulate reflections on sexuality and include a scenario in which a person works up the courage to ask after the health of a married loved one at their marital home only to find that their loved one died during their procrastination. Siegmund and Helena watch a female kitten owned by a little girl having a "'run on the sand.'" It scampers after a more adventurous dog. At the prospect of entering the water it walks "a few steps," turns "its small face this way and that," and mews "piteously." Helena pities it; Siegmund smiles, saying, "Crying because things are too big, and it can't take them in." Helena understands its fright. Siegmund laughingly acknowledges his own fright, commenting that the gods "won't be kind enough to put me in their pinafores." Siegmund articulates his awareness of Helena's diffidence. The kitten's name (Tissie) may be a cross-lingual pun ('tis Sie, German for you). Sensing something is amiss when she doesn't hear from Siegmund after his return to Wimbledon, Helena procrastinates, but eventually she decides to buy a local paper in his neighborhood for news of him or, as a last resort, to visit his home to inquire after his health. She reads of his funeral in the paper. In *Good Morning, Midnight* a fat man tells Sasha a story about a man trying to pluck up the courage to inquire after the health of the married woman he loves. By the time he asks the woman is dead (117).

13. Compulsory heterosexuality has been influentially theorized by Adrienne Rich.

14. Reviewers of *The Trespasser* did not pick up and give wider currency to the term "Dreaming Women," although some depicted Helena as a dreamer. In the *Manchester Guardian*, Basil de Selincourt described Helena as an "absorbent, dreamy creature" (Draper 46), and in the *New York Times Book Review*, she was characterized as "the woman of dreams, the seeker after extreme sensations, not physical, but psychic . . . Helena searches for psychic sensation in physical experience" (Draper 50). The *Athenaeum* opined that Helena is "more egoistic [than Siegmund] . . . a woman who cannot lose sense of her own identity even in the supreme intimacy of love" (Draper 45). Rebecca West in the *Freewoman* says of Helena: "She used to withdraw to the sentimentalist's voluptuous chamber of self-torture to become a self-scourging moralist, and would distress his [Siegmund's] simplicity with her sobs. Continually she receded from him into the nook of some obscene fastidiousness, some icy distaste for life" (46). For her *The Trespasser* is "magic," on a "different plane" (44) than the other books she was reviewing. She closes with a call for "novels written by women about men. Very few men have ever succeeded in creating men as they have succeeded in creating women" (47).

15. Lawrence returns to the figure of the woman satisfied by a kiss in "The Witch *a la Mode*." The sexual tension between Bernard Coutts and Winifred Varley culminates in "the first kiss she had genuinely given." While he reels "conscious of the throb of

one great pulse, as if his whole body were a heart that contracted in throbs," "[a]lready she had had enough." "[C]lose below his eyes, were the half-sunk lashes of the woman, swooning on her unnatural ebb of passion," and "his heart grew dead with misery and despair. This woman gave him anguish and a cutting-short like death" (69). In a rage he accidentally knocks over a lamp stand. He rescues Winifred from the fire. The story closes with Bernard Coutts "running with burning-red hands held out blindly, down the street" (70). The term dreaming woman is not used in the story.

16. At one point Siegmund dreams of "huge ice-crystals" (119).

17. Streip offers a shrewd and illuminating discussion of Rhys's humor.

18. Bernstein points out: "The distinction between 'lowbrow' and 'highbrow' culture invokes primitivist discourse since the higher position of the brow indicated for Victorian anthropologists a later evolution of primates with superior intelligence" (235).

19. Emery argues that Sasha "experiences a moment of carnivalesque community that truly, though temporarily, transforms her. The catalysts of her metamorphosis are the West African masks that line the painter's studio" (157). She interprets the moment of community as a reconnection with the Caribbean. Rhys does reuse the image of hills and clouds in *Smile Please* to describe the Dominican landscape with which she wanted to identify herself as a child (81), but she does not mark Sasha's vision as a memory of a Caribbean childhood. Interpreted as a Caribbean scene it recalls tourist advertizing and consumption of leisure.

Chapter 7

The Labyrinths of "a Savage Person—a Real Carib"

Dominica has one of the two significant Carib Indian communities of island Caribbean countries, the other being on St. Vincent. Recently, Dominica's historian Lennox Honychurch has begun using the people's name for themselves in the men's language, Kalinago (21), but Carib is still the general term used in Dominica (*Destination Dominica* 5). In 1891, the year after Rhys's birth, Dominica's population comprised approximately 300 Caribs, 26,841 African Dominicans, and 335 white people (Cracknell 85, 57). The meanings given the differences between white colonists and Carib Indians historically form part of Rhys's Dominican racial consciousness. Those meanings are played out in her representations of Carib Indians in *Voyage in the Dark* (1934) and "Temps Perdi" (1967), a story Howells argues is "Rhys's most complex questioning of her Caribbean inheritance" (141).[1] In a letter to Francis Wyndham in 1962, Rhys mentions an unfinished novel, "Wedding in the Carib Quarter," the manuscript of which "disappeared completely."[2] Rhys's representations of Carib Indians and figurations of the Carib are integral to the racially inflected formation of her modernism.

The unnamed narrator of "Temps Perdi," an immigrant in England, remembers her gendered Dominican difference within the hypocritical indifference of the English state. Imagining herself emerging from the experience of being lost in the labyrinth of involuntary memory—a labyrinth figured as "the Inner Circle," metaphorically both the heart of the London underground and a "limbo of the forgotten"—she knows she shall have gone native, that she "shall be a savage person—a real Carib." In *Gone Primitive: Savage Intellects, Modern Lives* Marianna Torgovnick uses the terms "primitive" and "savage" interchangeably; in Rhys's fiction the "savage" and the "primitive" are not so casually elided, probably because there is a sedimented stereotype of Carib "savagery" integral to her Dominican colonial heritage. Her discrimination between the "savage" and the "primitive" distinguishes Carib and African Caribbean peoples. Torgovnick argues that "gender issues always inhabit Western versions of the primitive ... the connections between Western conceptions of the primitive and issues of gender and sexuality are utterly crucial. . . . Views of the primitive become implicated in forms of Western self-loathing" (17–18). Rhys's representations of the Carib—her discourse and her tropes of "savagery" in *Voyage in the Dark* and "Temps Perdi"—are used to figure issues associated with transcendence of womanly embodiment and feminine colonial mobility. Issues of gender and sexuality "inhabit" Rhys's representations of the "savage," producing implicit and explicit links or analogies between the positionalities of alienated white Dominican women and Carib Indians. These links or analogies are marked by anxiety effects and an extravagance that is, to adapt Nancy K. Miller, "a form of insistence about the relation of [Dominican] women to writing: a comment on the stakes of difference within the theoretical indifference of [colonial English] literature itself" (39). Rhys's theme of the relation of Dominican women to writing is also developed in "Temps Perdi" through a juxtaposition of oral and chirographic economies of cultural production and the temporalities they enjoin.

Like Nancy K. Miller, I use and extend Luce Irigaray's concept of indifference:

a) Within the masculine order, the woman is indifferent in the sense of non-different or undifferentiated because she has no right to her own sexual difference but must accept masculine definitions and appropriations of it.
b) As a consequence, she is indifferent in the sense of detached or remote because of the imposture of her position. (*This Sex* 220)

Racial and ethnic others within specific cultures or systems of domination are pressured to accept indifferent definitions and appropriations of their racial and ethnic differences and may sense their impostures within those definitions, stereotypes, and appropriations.

In early twentieth-century colonial discourse about Caribs discrimination is made between a then and a now, a past and a present condition, with the nineteenth century as the turning point. Peter Hulme, in a discussion of the linguistic construction of the Carib/Arawak distinction, argues that an ethnic stereotype of the Carib is embedded in apparently neutral Western historical and ethnographic information about them. "[T]he stereotype," he states, "operates principally through a judicious combination of adjectives which establish characteristics as eternal verities immune from the irrelevancies of historical moment: 'ferocious,' 'warlike,' 'hostile,' 'truculent and vindictive'" (*Colonial Encounters* 49). Hesketh Bell, the Mr. Hesketh of Rhys's *Smile Please: An Unfinished Autobiography*, produces a plethora of such attributes for the Carib in his 1902 report to the House of Commons on Dominican Caribs: "savages" is qualified, at various points in his brief history of the race and its resistance to colonization, with "warlike," "indomitable," "dauntless," "man-eating," "formidable," "redoubtable," and "bloodthirsty" (*Administrator Bell to Mr Chamberlain* 3–11). But, he avers, and his comment is an excellent example of the paternalism the "now" aspect of the stereotype justifies, the Carib "is now as law-abiding and mild a subject as any the King has. . . . The hundred years of peace and protection have arrested, almost at the last gasp, the extinction of this interesting remnant of one of the world's races" (10–11). Virtual extermination, extinction, and, in the words of the commissioners appointed to inquire into the "Carib War" of September 1930, "loss of the qualities and characteristics which distinguished their ancestors" are the marks of the Carib now. At times the commissioners, J. Stanley Rae and Sydney A. Armitage-Smith, imply a racial degeneration (24). The stereotype of the Carib then is strategically used to inauthenticate the Carib now. Resistance to colonization now does not confer distinction: it is, as Rae and Armitage-Smith represent it, "felonious"; the tribe becomes "a mob"; the "War" Chief is "unfitted" for leadership.

The first-person white Dominican narrators of *Voyage in the Dark* and "Temps Perdi" give potted histories of Carib Indians drawn from childhood reading. In *Voyage in the Dark*, set before the First World War, Anna Morgan's knowledge of Caribs is all second hand; in "Temps Perdi" the narrator recalls in detail a visit to the Carib Quarter (the Carib Reserve) in about 1936, a visit prompted by her fascination with an array of images of Carib Indian people drawn from a colonial archive. The visit is precisely dated for the reader by a reference to a recent special issue of *L'Illustration* for the Tricentenaire des Antilles Françaises dated 23 November 1935. Peter Hulme and Neil L. Whitehead reproduce the image to which she alludes in *Wild Majesty: Encounters with Caribs from Columbus to the Present Day* (1992). Rhys herself had revisited Dominica in early 1936, staying at Hampstead on the north side of the island, mixing socially with people from Melville Hall, less than three miles from the Carib Reserve, and touring the Reserve.

Anna Morgan reproduces, in a quotation from a Dominican book or lesson, part of a convent schooling, "then" and "now" attributes of Carib "savagery" embedded in seemingly bland factual information: the Caribs "were . . . warlike . . . fierce"; they are "now practically exterminated" (*Voyage* 91). Her thoughts of the Caribs are produced by an associative drift away from the words of a music hall song she tries to recall. She remembers:

"The Caribs indigenous to this island were a warlike tribe and their resistance to white domination, though spasmodic, was fierce. As lately as the beginning of the nineteenth century they raided one of the neighbouring islands, under British rule, overpowered the garrison and kidnapped the governor, his wife and three children. They are now practically exterminated. The few hundreds that are left do not intermarry with the Negroes. Their reservation, at the northern end of the island, is known as the Carib Quarter." (90–91)

Mary Lou Emery argues that the transition from the song to the memory of the text about the Caribs "inscribe[s] the dynamics of sexual and colonial relations in a search for community that is also an experiment in fiction" (29). Emery's interpretation of the dynamics of Rhys's politics and modernist aesthetic is structured by dualisms integral to an idealized model of feminist community: "separated self/shared self . . . individualism/community . . . masculine/feminine, public/private, calculative/affective," inauthentic/authentic (Iris Young 306). In fitting Paul Ricouer's hermeneutics of sedimented and prospective symbolism to this dualistic model to interpret the representation of the Caribs, Emery has to read Anna's recitation as a transformative subversion of what she reads as the sedimented—stereotypical—feminine symbolism of the song performance. Anna's uncritical recirculation of the indifferent sign of Caribness sedimented in the colonial Dominican racial unconscious, however, reproduces an epistemic violence, rather than creates, as Emery proposes, the possibility of a "recognition" of difference. The immediate effect of Anna's recitation is, in fact, to make palatable some of the stock boarding house food that has come to epitomize for Anna the sameness of Englishness.

The passage occurs shortly after Anna, abandoned by her lover and protector Walter Jeffries, has tried to compose a letter to him in which she talks about her feelings (90–91). Its stylistic mimicry of Molly Bloom's inner monologue in its paucity of punctuation only serves to highlight for the reader Anna's relative sexual naivety and her largely bookish knowledge of that feminine best-seller, romance. She writes: "I've read books about this and I know quite well what you're thinking . . ." Her letter, "sheets of paper all over the bed," is interrupted mid-sentence by her hearing the words of her desire as chatter: "And *going on like that*" [italics added]. Having internalized masculine scorn of women's chatter, she ceases writing, and later burns the sheets.

The recitation about the Caribs is part of a strategy of dealing with the despair over the excess femininity of her own writing by seeking distractions—in noises, objects, memory. It is a strategy similar to her recitation of the multiplication table to ward off tears during a confrontation with her stepmother (61). Rhys alludes obliquely to a common motif in women's writing, the look from the window as a figuring of women's desire for transcendence of the materiality of their gendered circumstances in the house; this prospect is denied Anna by the cumbersomeness of the window—and so she keeps the "curtains drawn all the time." The recitation from memory marks a return to the unquestioned colonial verities of Anna's origins—it is a writing (and an interpellation of her own ethnic identity) that consoles. The differences of racially "other" women in the English boarding house are objectified and exoticized as mantel ornament: among dogs, a pig, and a swan are "a geisha with a kimino and sash in colours and a little naked woman lying on her stomach with a feather in her hair" (90).

For Peter Wolfe, "Temps Perdi" lacks narrative focus: "wayward plotting and dim character portraits keep us outside the narrator's psychological cage" (58). In what for Wolfe seem to be "signs apparently without meaning and value—empty and excentric" one may decipher "*supplementary framings*" (Bhabha, "'Race'" 201)[3] of European literature and Dominican modernity that elaborate the decay of colonial literary and political authority.

The narrator of "Temps Perdi" exhibits the sense of transcendental homelessness that Georg Lukacs and Ricardo J. Quinones argue is central to the "negative typology" of modernity. For Lukacs transcendental homelessness is "a form of absolute (though reversible) alienation from the self, from society, and (source of all other alienations) from 'immanent totality'—a phrase that denotes the effortless awareness of meaning and purpose, the complete correspondence of personal desire and cosmos, the presence of secular grace" (summarized in Torgovnick 227). Quinones locates the "Modernist point of departure" in the disintegration of the sense of the family "as a source of continuity and value." During the nineteenth century, he argues, "the problems of time and history . . . were brought home into the family—it having become the great shelter for the burdens of continuity and remembrance." Early modernist texts, though, represent not a comfortable sense of homeliness—a secure sense of "linearity and lineality"—but an "unresponsiveness of alien surroundings that seriously questions humanistic ideals or simple endeavor, and even . . . the dissolution of the known, ordinary, solid world" (40, 45). The transcendental homelessness of Rhys and her white Caribbean female protagonists is crucially linked to interrogations of the homeliness of the family. An "effortless awareness of meaning and purpose" achieved through a secure sense of linearity and lineality is absent. The domestic polities of houses and family relations in Rhys's fiction allegorize in complex ways troubled colonial and gender relations in, as critics are becoming increasingly aware, precisely detailed historical times. Such allegorization is familiar: colonial pieties, for instance, are often figured through family romance (parent culture, mother country, colonies and the colonized as children); and in psychoanalysis psychosexual development is allegorized through family romances.

Transcendental homelessness in Rhys's fiction is also crucially linked to what Homi Bhabha in another context terms "an estrangement of the English Book." In colonial discourse, he argues, there are signs of an "'imperial delirium' . . . signs of a discontinuous history, an estrangement of the English Book. They mark the disturbance of its authoritative representations by the uncanny forces of race, sexuality, violence, cultural and, even, climatic differences which emerge in the colonial discourse as the mixed and split texts of hybridity" (Bhabha, *Location* 113).[4] The estrangement of the English Book is produced by the burden of representation of colonial difference in a cultural tradition of the selfsame, in which, to extend Irigaray, the universal is "the equivalent of a[n English] male ideolect, a [colonial] masculine Imaginary, a sexed world— without neutrality" ("Is the Subject" 61). The narrator of "Temps Perdi" reads the neutrality of the English sitting room as a "hypocrite's mask"; its library of books gives the "lie"—and "vulgar, trivial" lie—to her gendered colonial memory and senses (*TWC* 145). The "unresponsiveness" of the middle-class English masculine values of the English Book to her existential reality fragments a unified subjectivity; she is alienated from the Book's linearity and lineality. The books of the English domestic library, she thinks, are "capable of hurting you, pushing you into the limbo of the forgotten" (145). They are linked with the hypocritical civility of the metaphorically beige-masked locals, who engage in "smothered . . . silent, sly, shy laughter" behind her back (147).

To supplement a remark by Elizabeth Grosz about the way feminists need to uncover the "unspoken yet privileging assumptions about masculinity" in phallocentric models of universality, in re-membering her story the narrator has "to clear a space within the 'universal' and to reclaim [colonial] women's places in it" (97). That space is structured by a female modernist gothic aesthetic that functions in a dialogic relation to the universal English book and a Proustian aesthetic of memory. Like other gothic fiction, it also "conducts a dialogue *within itself*, as it acts out and defeats subversive desires" (Jackson 96).[5] In "Temps Perdi" those desires are focused on "going savage," and the internal dialogue is conducted through an extravagant tropological subtext. Rhys gives modernist inflection to two of the stock generic layers of colonial fiction based on the manichean allegory of racial stereotype outlined by Abdul R. JanMohamed (71): a white Dominican woman, now resident in England, journeys into the maze of her colonial memories to discover her own identity and come to an appreciation of the decay of colonial authority; at the core of the labyrinth is a beautiful, "destructive" Carib woman. Rhys reinscribes these generic layers, and motifs drawn from Joseph Conrad's *Heart of Darkness*, including the lie and London as a place of darkness. She also reinscribes the then Carib chief's evidence to a Royal Commission in 1893 and available representations of the Carib War.

"Temps Perdi" has three geographical and temporal settings, each a site of international, racial, ethnic, and misogynistic tensions. In the present of the story the narrator is living in "Rolvenden," a house on the outskirts of an English village under threat of enemy fire during the Second World War; she recalls her times in two other houses—a flat she had in post–First World War Vienna when she worked as a secretary for the Japanese Commission, and "Temps Perdi," the plantation house in Dominica from which she journeyed to the Carib Quarter and photographed a beautiful Carib girl with a physical disability. Her experiences of each of these houses are marked by hostility fragilely and slyly masked as civility. A representative range of that hostility includes feeling herself the enemy within as foreigner and woman in wartime Britain; knowing of the disgust at interracial contact beneath the diplomatic manners of Colonel Hato; witnessing what she assumes is a "love dance" in which Yoshi looks "at the women of the party very slanting-eyed and mocking" (150); and visiting the Carib Quarter in the aftermath of the Carib War, dreading "hostile criticism" (158). The Creole patois phrase "Temps Perdi" comes to encapsulate the tenor of her mobile colonial expatriate experience and its seeming termination in Rolvenden with her an aged, "helpless" woman on her own (145) menaced by the locals, who steal her coal or direct misogynist abuse at her. "Temps perdi," the narrator explains, alluding to Proust's *Á la recherche du temps perdu,* does not mean, poetically, lost or forgotten time, but matter-of-factly wasted time, lost labour. There are places which are supposed to be hostile to human beings and to know how to defend themselves. When I was a child it used to be said that this island was one of them. You are getting along fine and then a hurricane comes, or a disease of the crops that nobody can cure, and there you are—more West Indian ruins and labour lost. (155)

The words "Temps Perdi" had been carved on a tree trunk by an early would-be colonizer defeated by the capricious spirit of place (and what is not literally spoken: Carib hostility).[6] The narrator's appropriation of the words and her determination to write them in Rolvenden heal the rift produced by a failure of colonial meaning-production marked by banal symptoms of hysteria: a physical passivity that mimics the constrained mobility of the Carib women she meets, and a move to a second-person address. "The hysteric," Irigaray argues in *Parler n'est jamais neutre*, based on empirical research, "cannot assume his/her own discourse; everything is referred for validation to the 'you'" (summarized by Whitford 35).

The failure of meaning-production needs to be placed in the context of the Carib War. The history of the Carib War contains an incident that is a "ghostly repetition"[7] of an uncanny scene from the fictional *Heart of Darkness*. In September 1930 the H.M.S. *Delhi* fired star shells and trained searchlights into the Carib Reserve, a mountainous and fairly inaccessible 3,700 acres. The visit of the ship to Dominican waters was authorized by the island's colonial administrator, Edward Carlyon Eliot, to put down what became known locally as the "Carib War." On 19 September a riot among Caribs had followed a raid by six policemen searching for smuggled rum and tobacco, and the police were, in the words of the subsequent Report to the House of Commons, "compelled (a) to release their prisoners; (b) to abandon their seizures; (c) to retreat. They had been disarmed completely, beaten and injured" (Rae and Armitage-Smith 20). In the report it is stated that two Caribs were killed and two injured by police shooting; in his autobiography Eliot says "three young Carib lads were killed" (227). Conrad's Marlow found the sight of a gunboat firing into a colonial landscape "incomprehensible[.] . . . There was a touch of insanity in the proceeding" (41); the commissioners appointed to inquire into the Dominican "Incident" declared: "We have no hesitation in expressing our conviction that the *display* of overwhelming force by H.M.S. *Delhi*, which obviated the actual *use* of military force altogether, was the only wise course to pursue, and that the demonstration by H.M.S. *Delhi* and the landing of Marines restored the sense of respect for lawful authority which had been shaken by the incident of the 19th."

Dismissing the distress the measures caused the Caribs, the Commissioners, J. Stanley Rae and Sydney A. Armitage-Smith, pronounced them "anodyne" and "salutory" (21)—they certainly calmed the commissioners. Anxieties haunt the text of the report: anxiety produced by what they describe as felonious resistance to "lawful" police action (including the behavior of the Carib chief "who made no attempt to control the mob," 17); and anxiety produced by Carib claims to distinction in British law. These claims to distinction—that Dominican Caribs "occupied a position analogous to that of a small Indian Native State, subject only to the suzerainty of the Crown and not amenable to the ordinary jurisdiction of any local court"—were dismissed for lack of chirographic evidence (4). Claims of cultural distinction, too, were dismissed for lack of proffered evidence of "any trace of primitive customs or traditions" (24)—the Caribs could not be placed in the "primitive" cultural time of the ethnographic other. The one Carib claim to distinction eagerly acknowledged as legitimate is the claim of "pure" Carib women to physical distinction: "long tresses of bluish-black hair" rendered to the photographic gaze of the commissioners with "obvious pleasure" (23). (Carib participation in the tourist economy of looking has been integral to demonstration of continuing Caribness and title to the Reserve.)[8] The commissioners were impressed by the apparent tractability of the Carib women and schoolgirls, even recommending that a Carib girl (rather than a boy) should be trained as an agricultural missionary. Thomas Jolly John, the Carib chief, was dismissed from office. The commissioners found him "either unable or unwilling to collaborate with the Government in the preservation of peace and order" (27) and reported the absence "of anyone possessed of the character and intelligence required to occupy a position of primacy over his fellows" (26). The office of chief, an important element of Carib ethnic self-definition, was abolished and the royal mace removed to Roseau, the colony's capital. The chieftaincy was officially reestablished in 1953 "at the request of the Carib people" (Owen 389, 391).

In "Temps Perdi" colonial decay in Dominica, accompanied by male African Dominicans becoming agents of absentee colonial landowners or authority, is troped as the empty plantation house being engulfed by everything running "wild"—a centipede even falls out of a book in the library as the narrator opens it. The decay of colonial authority—including the authority of the English Book—displaces the narrator from the colonial "family" and its pieties. The gaudily illustrated Englishman's book of the 1880s about the Caribs that fascinated her is also "capable of hurting you, pushing you into the limbo of the forgotten" and hysteria. The narrator's desire to visit the Carib Quarter is prompted by curiosity—"because," she says, "of a book I once read, pictures I once saw" (156). In the pictures of Carib people she recalls—stock variants of European representations of the primal encounter between Caribbean and European people, "idealized tribute" and "fierce hostility" on the part of native Caribbean people (Hulme, *Colonial Encounters* 14)—she has read a subtext of fear and sadness.

In the retrospective narration of the visit to the Carib Quarter the narrator's anxiety, like the anxiety of John Smith in telling the story of Pocahontas, is "coped with through the deployment of a variety of tropes" (Hulme, "Polytropic Man" 25); the subtext of her own impressions of the Carib Quarter may be read in tropes and displaced metaphors: for instance, extreme weather (hurricanes, wind, and sun), wind-tormented as opposed to the "tame" trees around the plantation house, and the "morose, obstinate" appearance of horses, "the price of survival in hostile [African Dominican] surroundings" (155–58). The exercise of a "bloody" imagination—in broaching more openly the menace of potential Carib or African Dominican hostility or English misogyny expressed in unrepeatable words (left "blank, blank" and "blank, blank, blank," 146)—may open "a traumatic breach [in the narrative] no trope could close" (Hulme, "Polytropic Man" 25). Hulme uses trope "to imply . . . a crux at which the discourse is most visibly dealing with difficulties of various kinds or, in a word, exercising power" ("Polytropic Man" 28, n. 14). The narrator was fascinated by accounts of a secret language among Carib women; the cryptic tropological subtext of "Temps Perdi" registers anxieties associated with white Dominican female embodiment in hostile surroundings.

To the narrator the Dominican earth is "sometimes red and sometimes black. Round about here it is ochre—a Carib skin. In some lights like blood, in others just pretty, like a picture postcard coloured by somebody with a child's paintbox and no imagination" (160–61). The description is consistent with an essentialist metonymy, or, to use Morrison's term, "metaphysical condensation" (68) in the text that figures Carib people through nature. Lack of imagination, it is implied, conceals the hostile Carib recalcitrance that bloodies the earth. Only a veiled awareness of "hostile" recalcitrance is apparent. Most of the Carib people hide in the bush "riddled with narrow paths" when visitors come (159). When the policeman points out the king's house the narrator thinks, "So, there's still a king, is there" (159). The rebuilt police station and its row of rifles with bayonets are "new and clean." The African Dominican policeman tells the story of Carib hostility to the colonial authority the presence of the police station represents: "They burnt the first one down, and they burnt twenty feet off this one" (159). He states casually, in a voice that "might have been an Englishman talking," that the second incident in which "only two or three Caribs" were killed was retaliation for the failure of a petition to the government for a hospital.

The presence of the police station prior to the Carib War is Rhys's invention, and she translates the actual resistance to police authority during the Carib War into one modeled on her usual symbol of defiance of colonial authority: the firing of the police station by Carib people is modeled on the firing of the white plantation house by African Caribbean people. The plausible and sympathetic pretext for the fictional rebellion is drawn from the time of Rhys's Dominican childhood. On 7 December 1893 the Carib chief, Auguste François, had petitioned a British royal commission inquiring "into the condition and affairs of the island of Dominica" for a school and a hospital;[9] the school was provided in 1894, a resident health nurse during the 1960s. The hospital pretext effectively links what Rhys represents as Carib "degeneration" and disease with colonial government neglect. What becomes literally unspeakable in the narrator's hysteria is the complicity of a European Dominican woman in this neglect.

The hysteria is brought about by an initial inability to assimilate the meaning of "the sun, the flamboyance, the girl crawling (because she could not walk) across the floor to be photographed. And the song about the white cedar-trees" (161). The ambiguity of "the sun, the flamboyance"—the words may refer to either the climate and vegetation, or the Carib girl who "appeared in the doorway of the dark little bedroom [of the Carib hut], posed for a moment dramatically, then dragged herself across the floor to the sun outside to be photographed, managing her useless legs with a desperate, courageous grace"—effectively reinforces the essentialist metonymy that figures the racial other through nature. The visit to the Carib Quarter has culminated in the narrator and a probably Carib guide, Charlie, photographing a picturesque "Carib" girl with long hair against a background of her and her mother's Roman Catholic icons.[10] The icons—virgins and saints—function as metonyms of fetishistic colonial civility and a desire for transcendence of the materiality of their embodiment in the mercy (the quarter) of religious faith. Her mother is standing by, gesticulating, exclaiming, "Hélas! . . . Hélas, hélas!" at her daughter's diseased physical condition and her own constrained mobility. No longer part of a mobile colonial expatriate economy (as servant), the Carib mother moans: "Now I must stay because I am old, I am old and who will take me away?" (160) The "limbo of the forgotten" refers also both to the Caribs generally ("Whenever the Caribs are talked about, which is not often, the adjective is 'decadent,'" 156) and through a play on limbo (limb-0) to the constrained mobility of the women.

The taking of a photograph is, Christian Metz argues, an "act of cutting off a piece of space and time, of keeping it unchanged while the world around continues to change, of making a compromise between conservation and death" (85). It preserves and represents implicitly the "immobility and silence" of the object photographed that are central to "photographic *authority*." In the narrator's remembered account of the visit the off-frame of the "picture postcard coloured by somebody with a child's paintbox and no imagination" (161) preserves the condescension of that authority—displaced on to the male guide—and the "obvious pleasure" of compliance with it. The narrator also brings in her colonial cultural baggage a preconception about a pure Carib physical essence ("the Carib type"), which allows her to split the mother/daughter pair of the visible Carib polity into pure and creole, just as Rae and Armitage-Smith labeled the photographs of adult Caribs they appended to their report (not reproduced in the printed copy) "pure" and "mixed" blood. The ethnographic and picturesque economy of looking of the narrator and Rae and Armitage-Smith is inextricably linked with ideas of racial purity and degeneration. The disease of the Carib girl and the "strange, small, womanish face" of a "fierce" warrior in a probably early eighteenth-century visual representation seem to be constructed as aspects of the decadence of the Caribs. Fixed in a Western economy of representation, the warrior carries weapons "useless" against laughter (157). Colonial ethnographic aestheticization distances and disarms opposition. The pure/impure taxonomy of blood the narrator invokes is challenged by the implied spiritual grace of the Carib girl.[11]

In a state of hysteria—given the immediacy of present-tense narration—the narrator imagines herself "caged under a mosquito-net . . . a prisoner in a cell full of small peepholes" (160–61). Using a racialized language of "they" and "we" she tries to come to terms with her relation to "up-to-the-minute" African Dominican male graffiti, part of a misogyny that crosses racial and cultural boundaries and is expressed in different forms, and her failure to remember the words of an "old" African Dominican women's song about the "light and fragile" flowers of the white cedar trees. The graffiti on "thick, fleshy leaves edged with thorns" reads "over and over again 'Girls muck, girls muck,' and other monosyllabic and elementary truths" in place of the "hearts pierced with arrows . . . and 'Z loves A'" (161) the narrator and her childhood friends would write. In the "natural" cycle of seasonal regeneration the old-fashioned romantic innocence of the white children is succeeded by an aggressively abject representation of female sexuality. The particular women's song is no longer sung and is now recoverable only as a small fragment in the narrator's memory; in the oral economy of the song's cultural production it is now "part of the past with no immediately discernible relevance to the present" that has "simply fallen away" (Ong 48). As African Caribbean and African American peoples often used to sing obliquely about their masters and mistresses, this falling away could imply that the white cedar flowers of the song are a metaphor for white European colonists who "fell with the first high wind and were blown away as soon as they fell" (155). As I noted in chapter 1, William Davies uses a horticultural trope, the exotic species, to figure white settlers, and Rhys figures the violence of Mr. Howard's second touch through this familiar tropology. In the narrator's modernist remembering and inscription of "home," the orality of the African Dominican women's song means it can only be preserved as fragment, another symptom of colonial decay ("West Indian ruins") and linguistic degeneration, a different kind of limbo of the forgotten.

Proust urges that the recovery through involuntary memory of Time Lost "in the face of which all the efforts of . . . memory and of . . . intelligence came to nought" entails an "extra-temporal being" that appeases "apprehensions" of mortality (216). For the narrator of "Temps Perdi" the merging of past and present in involuntary memories of Dominica offers no intimations of immortality or personal grace, but a bleak affirmation of decay and exile from both the "truths" of the English and a canonical modernist book and the distinctive economies of linguistic and cultural production of Carib and African Dominican women.

NOTES

1. "Temps Perdi" was first published in *Art and Literature* 12 (Spring 1967): 121–38 and later collected in *Penguin Modern Stories 1*, ed. Judith Burnley (1969). A version of the story was part of the collection "The Sound of the River," which was turned down by Constable in 1946. In the published version Rhys recycles and reinflects parts of the "War Material" section of the version of "Vienne" that appeared in *The Left Bank and Other Stories*. An earlier version of "Vienne" had appeared in *transatlantic review* (1924)—it is reprinted in *The Gender of Modernism*. Howells does not read "Temps Perdi" historically.

2. Letter to Francis Wyndham, 22 July [1962], *Letters* 213. She says: "I found some notes on it the other day, and they made no sense at all any more."

3. Bhabha is summarizing Michel Foucault, "The Art of Telling the Truth" 91.

4. Tiffin has discussed Rhys's relation to the English book in other texts in her current work on canonical counter-discourse. See her "Rites of Resistance" and "Rite of Reply."

5. Jackson is summarizing an argument of David Punter's in *The Literature of Terror*.

6. Rhys's account is general, but she may also be making a private allusion to a specific piece of Lockhart family history. In 1879 a case brought by Mrs E. Lockhart, Rhys's maternal grandmother, against her neighbor Mrs. Shillingford, owner of Perdu Temps estate, was heard in the Circuit Court of Dominica. Lockhart, as attorney for the children of her husband by the terms of his will, was trying to recover some five acres of land that she claimed her brother had leased to Mrs. Shillingford. The jury found in Mrs. Shillingford's favor. Much of the testimony concerned the conflicting chirographic evidence of several surveys of the land. Mrs. Shillingford stated that Messrs. Finlay and Letang, who surveyed the estate when she "took possession" of it twenty-five years before, "showed her a piece of land in the middle of the river, on which stood a tree; that was, they said, her boundary line" ("Lockhart *v.* Shillingford" [2]). The new surveys by Mr. G. B. Blanc, the surveyor general, questioned her memory of which of two islands was the boundary and confirmed that the land in dispute belonged to Geneva Estate. In his evidence he suggested that "[i]slands sometimes form in rivers and sometimes disappear," making them unreliable as "marks to survey by." Rhys uses "blank, blank" and "blank, blank, blank" to signify expletives in the story.

7. I borrow a term of Homi Bhabha's. In "DissemiNation" he discusses the "ghostly repetition" of the "time and space" of black British peoples in the film *Handsworth Songs* (307).

8. The Carib Reserve was gazetted in 1903, but the "Caribs' right to occupy the land was never actually guaranteed by formal ordinance." Caribs therefore, writes Owen in 1975, "make a point of displaying their most Indian-looking members to visitors to the reserve. Also, mixed Caribs underplayed their dark features either by emphasizing their close relationship to persons of purer Carib ancestry or by attributing these features to cause other than ancestry" (389).

9. Hamilton, Appendix C, No. 25. The letter bore an Anglicized version of his name, August Francis. The second fact given "as a cause of discontent" in the letter is that a "hospital is also needed, and our own sick are taken to town with great difficulty. The distance to town is considerable, and the roads are in very poor condition."

10. Hulme and Whitehead observe that "[i]t is not uncommon for visitors [to the Carib Territory] to focus on an adolescent girl" (273).

11. Gregg suggests that as "[i]n much of Rhys's writing, the Creole's ability to feel empathy with the female West Indian Other depends on a sufficient admixture of white 'blood'" (191).

Chapter 8 _____

A Place-to-Be-From

"I have seen it before somewhere, this cardboard world where everything is coloured brown or dark red or yellow that has no light in it. As I walk along the passages I wish I could see what is behind the cardboard," thinks Antoinette as she remembers her escapes from Grace Poole's custodial care (*WSS* 148). Her sense of déjà vu attests to the pre-scriptive power of print, the books that codify an imperial English planetary consciousness, and interpellate colonial subjects. The English and "their world," England, are at once both familiar and strange (*WSS* 148). As Antoinette voices her experience of the "cardboard world" readers, too, may experience a strong sense of déjà vu. Rhys defamiliarizes the colonial assumptions in Rochester's and Jane Eyre's accounts of Bertha Mason in *Jane Eyre*. The very familiarity with Bertha's end, however, has tended to foreclose readings of the predetermination of Rhys's narrative and its intertextual scope. In this chapter I read *Wide Sargasso Sea* in relation to *Jane Eyre* and *Othello* and to several of Rhys's historical intertexts in order to elucidate Rhys's representations of self/Other relationships and to critique some of the slippages, worldings and blind spots that inform and subtend Gayatri Chakravorty Spivak's influential reading of them in "Three Women's Texts and a Critique of Imperialism."

Historical allusions in *Jane Eyre* to Jamaican slave rebellions and to the abolition of slavery precisely date the action of the novel; Rhys transposes her fictional "life" of Brontë's "'paper tiger' lunatic" Bertha Mason (*Letters* 262) to a later period. I appreciate that the established critical opinion is that "*Jane Eyre* is unspecific about its dates" (Hulme, "Locked Heart" 25). That view, however, overlooks the allusions to Caribbean history in the novel. In banter positioning herself as missionary to the sexually despotic Rochester's harem (Brontë 297–98), Jane Eyre alludes to the part Sam Sharpe's rebellion, also known as the Baptist War, an 1831 uprising of Jamaican slaves, played in bringing about the abolition of slavery, the role missionaries were supposed to have played in inciting the rebellion, and the abolition of slavery, resolutions in support of which were passed in the House of Commons in June 1833. In the "fiery West Indian night" and "wind fresh from Europe" scene (Brontë 335–36), Rochester alludes obliquely to an 1823 slave rebellion in Jamaica. The references date the marriage of Rochester and Bertha as having taken place in 1819, with Bertha's incarceration in England commencing in 1823–1824.[1] The discourse of white creole moral degeneracy offered Brontë a type, which might be construed as perverse, in accord with James Cowles Prichard's theory of moral madness (Grudin 147). "There is a phase of insanity," Brontë explains to W. S. Williams on 4 January 1848, "which may be called moral madness, in which all that is good or even human seems to disappear from the mind, and a fiend-nature replaces it. The sole aim and desire of the being thus possessed is to exasperate, to molest, to destroy, and preternatural ingenuity and energy are often exercised to that dreadful end. . . . Mrs Rochester, indeed, lived a sinful life before she was insane, but sin itself is a species of insanity" (Shorter 383–84).

The persistent anxiety for Rhys in imagining a life of Bertha Mason was plausibility. "She must be at least plausible with a past, the *reason* why Rochester treats her so abominably and feels justified, the *reason* why he thinks she is mad and why of course she goes mad, even the *reason* why she tries to set everything on fire, and eventually succeeds," wrote Rhys in 1958 (*Letters* 156). She says that she fabricated the Caribbean experiences of her characters by working through material she called "Creole": "getting down all I remembered about the West Indies as the West Indies used to be. (Also all I was told, which is more important). . . . [I]t had no shape or plan" (*Letters* 153). In *Wide Sargasso Sea* the marriage of Antoinette and Rochester takes place circa 1840. I address some of the implications of Rhys setting her novel "between 1834 and 1845 say" (*Letters* 297). Rhys's temporal shift places "Bertha" Mason's life in a starkly transitional phase of Jamaican and Dominican history.

That phase is an interregnum in which "[t]he old is dying, and the new cannot be born" and "there arises a great diversity of morbid symptoms" (Antonio Gramsci, qtd. in Gordimer 263). The slave labor system, which sustained a plantation economy and a ruling elite (white and colored, European settlers and Creoles), was replaced in 1834 by an apprenticeship system as an interim measure towards emancipation. Emancipation of apprenticed labor occurred in Jamaica and Dominica in 1838. Local political and economic power was concentrated in the hands of elites. Political independence from Britain was attained in 1962 in Jamaica and 1978 in Dominica.[2] In the 1830s and 1840s ruinate lands were those areas of decaying plantations that had reverted to tropical vegetation and on which maroons (runaway slaves) and former slaves often squatted, developing a market economy. The ruinate lands are an important setting in *Wide Sargasso Sea*.[3] In this setting Tia and Antoinette's relationship develops; Antoinette acquires an ability to transcend the materiality of place and her isolation by "[w]atching the red and yellow flowers in the sun thinking of nothing" (24);[4] and

Rochester's fear of a "green menace" (123) is sharply exacerbated. If one reads the motif of flight in the third installment of Antoinette's dream as "fulfilling the traditional slave wish for wings with which to fly 'home,'" as Emery does (57), then "home" for Antoinette is the ruinate land of the Coulibri of her early adolescence. Michelle Cliff writes:

The civilizer works against the constant danger of the forest, of a landscape ruinate, gone to ruination.

Ruinate, the adjective, and *ruination*, the noun, are Jamaican inventions. Each word signifies the reclamation of land, the disruption of cultivation, civilization, by the uncontrolled, uncontrollable forest. When a landscape becomes ruinate, carefully designated aisles of cane are envined, strangled, the order of empire is replaced by the chaotic forest. The word *ruination* (especially) signifies this immediately; it contains both the word *ruin*, and *nation*. A landscape in ruination means one in which the imposed nation is overcome by the naturalness of ruin.

As individuals in the landscape, we, the colonized, are also subject to ruination, to the self reverting to the wildness of the forest. (40)

Rhys's consciousness of the Caribbean shares many of the modernist primitivist metonymies of Cliff's mythologization of black nationalism in maroon history and the "natural" justice of an indigenization of African Caribbean people, but with a differently complex articulation. Cliff's reclamation of "wildness" entails an embrace of "the aboriginal mother . . . imagination, emotion, spontaneity, history, memory, revolution, flights of fancy . . . [f]lesh . . . Caliban" (38–39). In *Wide Sargasso Sea*, Rochester racializes the ruinate land around Granbois and constructs it as a site of spiritual conflict. That process is integral to "a triple conflation of 'White,' 'Europe' and 'Christian,'" which "imparted moral, cultural and territorial content to Whiteness" from the late seventeenth century (Bonnett 175).

RHYS'S CHRISTOPHINE

Rhys's inscription of Christophine—reputed Obeah woman, in Antoinette's mind a surrogate mother figure, and critic of Rochester and colonial authority— has become, since Spivak's brilliant and provocative essay "Three Women's Texts and a Critique of Imperialism," a contentious site in postcolonial feminist debate bearing on the theorization of Other and self and whether a subaltern can speak. Spivak's reading of Christophine, Benita Parry's critique of it, and comments on their dispute by Anne Maxwell are relatively indifferent to the historical specificities of Christophine's and Rhys's sites of enunciation. Indeed, in "Theory in the Margin," in which Spivak addresses Parry's criticisms, she describes Rhys as Jamaican (161). Spivak reads Rhys's representation of Christophine as an allegory of a deconstructive maxim. Her object of study mirrors a "truth" she has assimilated from theoretical sources. Christophine is, she writes, an aporia of différance, an "Other" who cannot be selved, an excess that "cannot be contained by a novel which rewrites a canonical English text within the European novelistic tradition in the interest of the white Creole rather than the native. No perspective *critical* of imperialism can turn the Other into a self, because the project of imperialism has always already historically refracted what might have been the absolutely Other into a domesticated Other that consolidates the imperialist self" ("Three Women's Texts" 253).

A footnote directs her readers to her essay "Can the Subaltern Speak?" There her theorization of self and Other is grounded in Jacques Derrida's "critique of European ethnocentrism in the constitution of the Other" in "Of Grammatology as a Positive Science." In her account the "project of imperialism" produces the "domesticated Other" through processes of consolidation of an inside for "some domestic benefit," recognition by assimilation, and containment (292). Referring Christophine's leavetaking of Rochester in Dominica back to her maxim, Spivak questions its motivation, its plausibility. Christophine is, she writes, forced out of the novel "with neither narrative nor characterological explanation or justice," and this immediately after she has highlighted the different positions she and Rochester occupy in legal terms ("Three Women's Texts" 252–53). In Spivak's model of self/Other relations, Otherness is, as Asha Varadharajan observes, "privileged as the anti-West or the West's limit-text, as the vanishing point of the intelligibility of the discourse of imperialism. . . . Spivak keeps theory chained to the allure of an elusive subaltern being that is to be found neither in the text of imperialism nor in that of insurgency—indeed, not even between the two" (96).[5]

I reread some of the important functions Christophine has in *Wide Sargasso Sea* in relation to materials that formed part of Rhys's worlding as a Dominican: a turn-of-the-century Obeah case, and the "Letter of the Law" in the British Caribbean of the 1830s. In addressing the meanings of the "Letter of the Law," I will be engaging with a defining moment in the emergence of the Mulatto Ascendancy and Rhys's compensatory inscription of Lockhart family history, complementing Peter Hulme's work in "The Locked Heart: The Creole Family Romance of *Wide Sargasso Sea*," and endorsing his "insistence that the local and the particular," "even the familial . . . do matter" "if one of the strategies of colonial discourse is the homogenisation of cultural differences" (30).

The promulgation of "The Obeah Act 1904" in the Leeward Islands Federation (to which Dominica then belonged), Roman Catholic Father Meister's comment in a letter to the *Dominican* that "After all, there is something in 'obeah!'", the grisly murder of ten- to twelve-year-old Rupert Mapp in St. Lucia (in which severed hands and extracted chest bone, heart, and left lung were cited as conclusive proof of Obeah practice),[6] and a libel suit brought by William Wallace Wyllis against Joseph Hilton Steber, the editor of the *Dominica Guardian*, generated a public discussion in Dominica about what was in Obeah. The material on Obeah that was published in Dominican newspapers around 1904 circulated as part of a moral panic. Sermons against Obeah were preached and the terms of the Act were widely publicized. (Rhys turned fourteen in this year.)

Steber explained Obeah to his readers: "Obeah . . . for the most part is based upon the use of spell or charm, and some psychical processes mostly in connection therewith: and includes communication with 'departed spirits [sic] (Duppies) in a species of mantic phrenzy; the protection of fields and crops by means of glamour and 'nature spirits', some Ceremonial Magic, the cure and infliction of disease, causing death, and the whole supplemented by a wide knowledge of poisons and other vegetable drugs, &c., &c." ("What Is Obeah?" [3]).[7]

The Obeah Act 1904, which legislated "stringent" measures[8] against "Supernatural practice" and Obeah practice, against consultation with practitioners, and against "Publication of matter promoting Obeah,"[9] was, Steber suggested, "rendered necessary partly on account of the extent to which obeah is believed in and practiced both in Dominica and Montserrat, above all the other Presidencies" ("Obeah Legislation"). The Act, passed by the General Legislative Council on 8 February, set in train a rash of prosecutions.[10] The villages of Coulibristie (Meister [3]), and Canefield, Massacre, Fromagé, and Mahaut were singled out as areas of intense activity ("Dominica" [2]). (In *Wide Sargasso Sea*, Rhys situates the Dominican honeymoon estate Granbois in this locality; the village of Massacre is named.) Penalties under the Act were severe: for Obeah practice, for example, imprisonment for up to twelve months and possibly police supervision for up to two years after release, and "if a male, in addition" to imprisonment "or in lieu thereof," a whipping of up to twenty-four lashes; for consultation, a fine of up to £50 or imprisonment for up to twelve months; and for "Publication of matter promoting Obeah" a fine of up to £50 or "in default" up to six months imprisonment. The Act reintroduced whipping as a punishment and penalties for consultation. By August 1907, Steber, who had issued a call to "arms" against Obeah belief and practice in November 1904 ("What Is Obeah?"), was questioning the evidence on which convictions were being secured ("The Obeah Question"). On 15 January 1905 Ann Tuitt from Montserrat, who had at one time worked as a cook for the Rees Williams family at Bona Vista, was convicted of Obeah practice on the strength of possession of objects used in Obeah practice, and having been seen dressed in white at midnight in the Anglican burial ground in Roseau. She was sentenced to six months hard labor, the judge, the Honourable William Coull, having taken into account, he said, her age (about sixty-five years) and "apparently broken state of health" ([Righton], "Another Obeah Case").[11]

Simon Watney has observed that "moral panics do not speak to a 'silent majority' which is simply 'out there' waiting to listen. Rather they provide the raw materials, in the form of words and images, of those moral constituencies with which individual subjects are encouraged to identify their deepest interest and their very core of being" (qtd. in Walkowitz 121). In the Obeah Act itself "obeah and other pretended supernatural or occult practices" are stigmatized as "certain vulgar frauds," and belief in their efficacy is termed "superstition."[12] (During the 1830s Dominica law spoke of the "pretended art of witchcraft or obeah.")[13] Steber constructed measures against Obeah as a stage in the emancipation of black people, a removal of the "shackles of ignorance" ("What Is Obeah?"); in an editorial, Righton described them as "elevation" of the Dominican masses from "perpetual mental servitude under the demoralising mastery of the doctors of the Black Art" (12 November 1903 [2]). Both Steber and Righton were educated and Christian.

Patrick L. Baker argues that people from the Ascendancy "eschewed recognition of their slave ancestry and imitated, where possible, their white ancestry, which often enabled them to obtain a better education, an inheritance of some capital, and a different life style." As a "centring strategy of competition for control" at the local Dominican level, it contrasted sharply with the cultural affiliation of the nonwhite majority, which tried to remove itself "from metropolitan control" as far as possible (125). The measures against Obeah are represented in the press as part of a contest between two "moral constituencies": the forces of civilization, humanity, real (as opposed to nominal) Christianity, education, and "right thinking" on the one hand and Obeah and humbug, "part of the creed of most Dominicans," on the other.[14] Believers and practitioners are excoriated by Steber, believers as ignorant, credulous, prone to base superstition and appeals to their lower instincts ("What Is Obeah?"), and "simple-minded" ("Murder and Superstition"); those engaged in "supernatural practice" (telling fortunes, cure of injuries or disease, use of charms) as humbugs ("Obeah Legislation"); and Obeah practitioners as dark, evil, and barbarous, at their worst, propitiaters of "the evil spirit by human sacrifice" ("What Is Obeah?"). In the polarizing moral scheme of Steber and Righton the syncretic religious faith of the "masses" (drawn from African, indigenous, and Christian sources), implicitly referred to as a nominal, rather than "real" Christianity,[15] is framed in terms of the black racial stereotype of manichean allegory. Steber called to "arms" all "good-minded and noble-hearted citizen—strangers and natives, white and coloured; the press; legislators, clergymen, schoolmasters; men in authority; judges, magistrates, employers of labour, &c., &c., against any further incentives to ignorance, superstition and crime": "We want Church and State to unite in the education of the masses" ("What Is Obeah?").[16] Both Steber and Righton saw education as a key to improvement of the socioeconomic level and "civilization" of nonwhite people and used the occasion of the moral panic to press this claim.

The "personal" and gendered stakes in bringing charges of Obeah practice against another were highlighted in the evidence given in the libel suit that William Wallace Wyllis, a shopkeeper in Roseau, brought against Steber. Two years earlier Wyllis had lost a court case he had brought against Miss Appoline Emanuel for Obeah practice. I cite this case in some detail, because Rhys seems to have drawn on elements of it in her representation of the triangulated relationship among Christophine, Antoinette, and Rochester. My account of both cases is based on reports of the libel trial in "Wyllis v. Steber." While a written judgment was given in the Obeah case, no transcript of the trial seems to have been made. Wyllis's wife and Emanuel had lived in the same house before Wyllis and his wife married, and Emanuel lived with the Wyllises after the marriage. In evidence at the libel trial Wyllis stated that "Appoline Emanuel used to make threats at him saying she is going to make his wife leave him and cling to her for they (Appoline and Mrs Wyllis) were living together quite good before and he came and disturbed them. Sometimes he would be speaking to his wife and this woman would call her and she would leave him and go to her."

Wyllis was upset that he and his wife "could not agree" and also by Emanuel's influence over his wife. He seems to have found Emanuel a threat to his sense of his proper masculine authority over his wife and to have been troubled by the intimacy of the female friendship. Within six months of marriage he brought the charge of Obeah practice against Emanuel, convinced by rumor and the finding of an assumed "obeah bundle"—"pins, threads of different colours, bones, an egg, bits of the woman's dress, etc."—in the pocket of Emanuel's red dress by a Mrs. Spooner, a washerwoman. Encouraged by Mrs. Eugene Duverney, his wife's aunt, Wyllis had visited an unnamed "hypnotiser," who "hypnotised herself and told him that the woman [Emanuel] was trying to drive him away from his wife, etc." He wrote down recipes the hypnotizer gave him in a notebook, which his wife then produced as evidence of his own Obeah practice. Called as a witness in the libel suit, the clerk at the Roseau Magistrate's Court at the time, Albert Charles Shillingford, remembered the names of two of the recipes, "A powder to let us live lovingly" and "A powder to drive away the woman." The magistrate who heard Wyllis's case against Emanuel dismissed the charge and commented, how seriously is unclear, that "it was Wyllis himself who was practising obeah." (Wyllis was not formally charged with Obeah practice.) The case brought about a separation between Wyllis and his wife, who moved to Trinidad. What became of Emanuel is not mentioned. At the original trial she was examined by the defense, two prosecutors, and the magistrate. Men's voices retell the women's stories in the libel trial.

Father Meister, who had been transferred from his Coulibristie parish because, he claimed, of a campaign orchestrated against him by the unnamed "leading obeahman of Coulibristie," wrote on 9 March 1904 to the *Dominican* that "After all, there is something in 'obeah!'" Wyllis concurred in a letter to the *Dominican*, recirculating publicly his charge against Emanuel and stating that "Mr. Steber *knows* very well I am sure, *that 'There is something in Obeah.'*"[17] Feeling that he had been accused of hypocrisy (and, subtextually, tainted by the stereotype he had been wielding against Obeah), Steber railed against Wyllis in a piece titled "Victim or Impostor?," referring to the earlier court case, and shortly afterwards reprinted in the *Guardian* a paragraph from the Montserrat *Herald* in which Wyllis's letter was described as "despicable" and "calculated to work untold mischief in the minds of the ignorant and superstitious" and Wyllis as "undoubtedly, a most degraded specimen of humanity." Wyllis brought a libel suit against Steber over "Victim or Impostor?" and the reprinted paragraph. Steber had advocated the prosecution of Wyllis for promotion of Obeah ("Obeah Legislation"). Steber was found guilty of libel over the reprinted material, damages of £2 were awarded to Wyllis, and Steber had to pay costs ("Wyllis v. Steber [Concluded]"). The *Guardian*, by recording laughter in court in its reporting of the libel case, tried to make a fool of Wyllis. In his editorial of 2 June 1904 on Steber's reportage of the case, Righton defended Wyllis as "a well behaved and respectable citizen" ([2]).

The cases highlight investments of various kinds that complicate the demarcation of and potential identification with abstract moral constituencies, which might subtend construction of a normative white Creole self in relation to the racially and culturally other. At stake are questions of gendered authority and loyalty, romantic disappointment, and class and cultural affiliation. In *Wide Sargasso Sea*, Rhys's Rochester, the European book (*The Glittering Coronet of Isles*), and the colonial laws of Jamaica and Dominica invoke a Christianity versus Obeah opposition. Rhys's Rochester is disconcerted by Christophine's influence over Antoinette and Antoinette's intimacy with Christophine: their talk in a Dominican patois he cannot understand;[18] Antoinette's clinging to Christophine; and Antoinette's ability to explain signs of cultural difference, which exacerbates his growing xenophobic sense that she is not "English or European either," even if she is a "Creole of pure English descent" (*WSS* 56). Rhys demonstrates the interestedness of Rochester's resort to citing the power of colonial law against Obeah to Christophine, after Christophine articulates a direct threat to his marriage and his greed, a proposal that she and Antoinette go away together with half of Antoinette's dowry. In effect, Christophine proposes a cross-racial counter-family. Like Wyllis with Emanuel, Rochester blames Christophine (and her assumed Obeah) for "all that has happened here" (*WSS* 131). Christophine herself says to Antoinette when she first leaves Granbois for her own house: "Too besides the young master don't like me so much. If I stay here I bring trouble and bone of contention in your house" (*WSS* 84).

Rhys rescripts the intimacy between Emanuel and Mrs. Wyllis in Christophine and Antoinette's relationship as a nurse/charge, servant/mistress relationship, in which Antoinette's hugging and kissing of Christophine is a mark of open affection on Antoinette's part for her former nurse and of a need for comforting in times of emotional distress. Christophine and her voice are for Antoinette a nurturant corporeal presence and memory, a construction with modernist primitivist resonances. Christophine signifies for Antoinette the female body as pleasurable and desirous, rather than (as with her mother, Annette) as withdrawal, listlessness, and trauma. In Rhys's cross-racial reworking of the Wyllis-Emanuel conflict, Rochester's response to the intimacy of his wife and another woman in the house is xenophobic—"'I wouldn't hug and kiss them,'" Rochester says, "'I couldn't'" (*WSS* 76)—and characterized by jealousy of Antoinette's access to the physical comfort and ease of the familiar. While Rochester is, Antoinette says, "'always calling on God'" (*WSS* 105), Antoinette calls on Christophine or Pheena. Christophine is, for him, a rival for Antoinette's affection and loyalty. He associates Christophine with the seeming caprice of a strange domestic order (*WSS* 75), complains to himself about Antoinette citing what "'Christophine wants'" at him (*WSS* 75), and is taken aback by her forthrightness as a servant and black woman in using "horrible" language in his presence (*WSS* 71), questioning his masculinity through comparison, he thinks, with the "magnificent body" of Young Bull (*WSS* 72), which he makes an issue of blood, and judging him. Like Mrs. Wyllis, but not publicly, Antoinette accuses her husband of Obeah practice: "'Bertha is not my name. You are trying to make me into someone else, calling me by another name. I know, that's obeah too'" (*WSS* 121). Where necessary in Part II of *Wide Sargasso Sea*, Rhys has Antoinette's voice interrupt Rochester's narrative to provide readers with details of her visits to Christophine's home. Christophine is called to account by Rochester to describe her "influence" over Antoinette.

In *Wide Sargasso Sea*, Christophine's speech is reported in the narratives of Antoinette and Rochester, most extendedly in Rochester's account of the scenes in which Antoinette returns to Granbois, having turned to Christophine for solace after overhearing Rochester and Amelie's sexual encounter, and in which Rhys lets Christophine confront Rochester with sharp criticism of his conduct. Christophine, Spivak suggests, engages in unromanticized "individual heroics on the part of the oppressed" ("Three Women's Texts" 251). The letter from retired magistrate Mr. Fraser concerning Christophine has provided Rochester with a "recipe" to "drive away the woman." Rhys often juxtaposes scenes with cognate motifs. Antoinette's overhearing of Rochester and Amelie together is juxtaposed here with Rochester's overhearing of Christophine's comforting of Antoinette. Rochester's steeling of himself here to "what would happen" and what he "must do" (*WSS* 119) through waking from the hypnotic influence of Christophine's "judge's voice" (*WSS* 126) is comparable to Antoinette's remembering of "something" she "must do" on waking from the dream she dreams for the third time (*WSS* 153): in Spivak's formulation, to "act out the transformation of her 'self' into that fictive Other, set fire to the house and kill herself," thereby securing *Jane Eyre* a place in the British feminist canon ("Three Women's Texts" 251).

What allows Christophine's voice to be heard in Rochester's narrative of her return and confrontation and what Rochester hears at particular points are twisted up with Rochester's upper-class English masculinity and his struggle to maintain what he sees as a rational Christian self-command in unfamiliar social and topographical settings that he totalizes as hostile, founded on secret economies, and Obeah. Spurned by Antoinette, rebuked by Christophine, imagining that even the telescope "drew away and said don't touch me," Rochester experiences a return of the terror of being lost in the forest as the "green menace"—"the shadows of the trees moving slowly over the floor." "There was nothing I knew, nothing to comfort me," he narrates (*WSS* 123). Registered through a Dominican distinction between exotic (European) and local vegetation, as discussed in chapter 1, and an early twentieth-century tropology of colonial paternalism current in Dominica, the terror is of a palimpsestic erasure of imperial Christian enterprise by Obeah and of the entanglement of his lower body in plant emblems of the "native" that threaten to bring him to the ground. In the vicar-general's address to the new Catholic bishop of Roseau, Dr. Phillipe Schelfhaut, on 5 June 1902, the paternalism of colonial rule is represented as a "civilizing administration, which understands the good, and desires to do it, as fitly as possible by God and His Church," offering its "shade and protection." The diocese is figured as a "garden" ("Arrival" [3]).[19] Rochester's anxieties about the "green menace" of what for him are foreign trees reinflects this discourse. Rochester overhears Christophine soothe Antoinette with patois songs and endearments. The nurse/child talk is threatening, "dangerous. I must protect myself," he thinks. Yet at the same time it is vicariously soothing enough to this tired warrior to make him "feel sleepy" (*WSS* 123).

Rochester's sexual arousal by and "encounter" with the servant Amélie had been initiated when she took on the role of nurse. She brings him food after the illness he blames on Christophine's poison, cuts some of it up, and feeds him with one arm while supporting his head with the other as she would a child (115). The night scent of the river flowers habitually giddies Rochester. Christopher Looby has analyzed the ways in which Thomas Wentworth Higginson's descriptions of the color and odor of flowers in his *Army Life in a Black Regiment* (1869) encode "powerful intimations of guilty eros. In the normative masculine olfactory *imaginaire* of the time, odor sensations . . . were invested with a host of threatening and disorienting associations" (133). In Rochester's narrative the scent of tropical flowers is also invested with "threatening and disorienting associations." On an earlier occasion the scent of the river flowers returned him to a site of childhood, of corporeal intimacy and pleasure with the nurse, the situation, Antoinette's melancholy, scripting for him playing the part of the nurse for Antoinette, rocking her "like a child" and singing to her "an old song" he "thought" he "had forgotten" (*WSS* 70).

In the confrontation scene Rochester opens the window, letting the perfume in while Antoinette is berating him. Rochester's "dazed, tired, half hypnotized" state (*WSS* 130), which permits what he thinks a "useless conversation" with Christophine to continue (*WSS* 129), bears the memory traces of a space before the Oedipal prohibition, a prohibition inscribed in Rochester's narrative as learning "to hide" his feelings (*WSS* 85), the articulable motor of time of upper-class English phallic speaking subjectivity and reality. These memory traces of an unspeakable, unrealizable desire make possible the breach "in the social cell" (Cixous and Clément 150) that permits readers to hear Christophine's critique within Rochester's narrative. Our hearing Christophine's voice and Rochester's temporary loss of self-command are founded on the bodies of other "women," principally the anonymous nurse's but also Antoinette's and Amélie's, and Rochester's in a woman's part as nurse, "bodies despised, rejected, bodies that are humiliating" to him "once they have been used" (Cixous and Clément 154). The memory traces and the "forbidden" desires they produce form a "constitutive outside" of Rochester's identity, a "site of dreaded identification against which—and by virtue of which—the domain of the subject will circumscribe its own claim to autonomy and life" (Butler, *Bodies* 3).

Because of Rochester's sleepy, dazed state, Rochester and readers hear parts of Christophine's speech differently. Rochester hears Christophine's version of the story of Antoinette's romantic disappointment in him as a loud echo in his head. He hears reverberated: "(*Leave her alone*) [. . .] (*Why?*) [. . .] (*No more love*)," and his own cold voice saying "'And that [. . .] is where you took charge, isn't it? You tried to poison me.'" The echo tells a summary narrative: "(*Foolishness foolishness*) [. . .] (*Too strong for* béké. *Too strong*) [. . .] (*She cry and she beg me*) [. . .] (*For love*) [. . .] (*Break her up*) [. . .] (*Marionette, Antoinette, Marionetta, Antoinetta*) [. . .] (*Force her to cry and to speak*)" (*WSS* 126–27). The narrative catalyzes Rochester's remembering of Daniel's words "'Give my love to your wife—my sister [. . .] You are not the first to kiss her pretty face'" (*WSS* 104) as "'*Give my sister your wife a kiss from me. Love her as I did—oh yes I did*'" (*WSS* 130). This suggests that the narrative exacerbates Rochester's sense of the perversity and indiscriminate profligacy of the colonial white woman's desire and that he might even have heard a lesbian subtext ("*She cry and she beg me* [. . .] *For love*") in the reverberated story. Rochester hears Christophine as a threatening subject of desire when she utters the word "money" (*WSS* 130)—he quickly and defensively resumes his "ingrained Protestant rationality and fear of heretical ecstasy" (Harris 146) and invokes the law against Christophine.

In his subsequent dream-image of an English future for his marriage—a drawing of an English house, a "child's scribble" of a woman contained on the third floor, English trees (*WSS* 134)—his desire and body are inscribed by Rhys as infantile representation of the woman who embodies for him colonial difference, as material property, and as English landscape. The landscape is emptied on its two-dimensional surface of its mythologized and mythologizing relation to colonial history and a history of the production of sexual and capitalizing desire that resolutely includes colonial lands and peoples and a xenophobia encompassing racial, cultural, class, and gender difference. Rochester "domesticates" Christophine through surface repudiation and erasure; his fantasy erases Antoinette's connections with women to produce her as an isolated individual. His libidinal investment in the English landscape, with its comforting English trees, is grounded in relation to what Anne McClintock describes as an imperial "pornotropics for the European imagination—a fantastic magic lantern of the mind onto which Europe projected its forbidden sexual desires and fears" (22). That investment is an instance of what Jacqueline Rose, drawing on Roland Barthes's *Mythologies*, describes as "the way belief-systems write themselves as nature, dissolve into the landscape[.] . . . Emptied of its history, the land is packed with appropriating, mythological, intent" (25).

Antoinette's difference and, for Rochester, her intemperance are condensed in her red dress; it releases into Antoinette's subjective space and time at Thornfield Hall the benign spirit of the Caribbean registered in horticultural tropes: "[t]he colour of flamboyant flowers," "the smell of vetivert and frangipanni, of cinnamon and dust and lime trees when they are flowering" (*WSS* 151). The Dominican landscape has been pre-scripted by Rochester as Obeah, "green menace," perverse desire, and excess—for which Christophine becomes a metonym in his narrative—and by Antoinette as "indifferent" (*WSS* 107) to the projections of human desire and conceptualization in terms of a "versus complex." The term is Kamau Brathwaite's. He explains it as a "missilic tendency to see issue/discussions as aspect of whose VICTORY a given (fought-over) i-tem is" ("Post-cautionary Tale" 77). In representing Dominica as a woman scorned by England, returning the scorn as indifference to English authority, Froude makes such projections and such a conceptualization. "'It is not *for* you and not *for* me,'" Antoinette says of the landscape.

Readings of Christophine's physical disappearance tend to foreclose some of the ambiguities in Christophine's speech and to validate unquestioningly a sense of reality based on sight and tangible presence. Lee Erwin observes that "Christophine's obeah . . . guides the outcome" of Antoinette's fire and death:

Before "Rochester" leaves the West Indies, he is driven by his long last talk with Christophine to cry, "I would give my eyes never to have seen this abominable place." Christophine replies, "You choose what you give, eh? Then you choose. You meddle in something and perhaps you don't know what it is" . . . Thus, when Antoinette dreams her dream for the third and last time, in Thornfield Hall, she cries out to Christophine for help and sees that she has been helped by a wall of fire—and we know from *Jane Eyre* that Rochester loses exactly what he "chose" to lose. (143)[20]

Judie Newman argues of the blinding that "[i]n allowing Christophine to pronounce the curse on Rochester, Rhys reverses the current of determinism. What she does is to make the action of *Jane Eyre* the result of a West Indian obeah woman's curse" (23). The motif of the severed hand in *Wide Sargasso Sea* and *Jane Eyre* supports Erwin's and Newman's suggestions. Antoinette and Anna Morgan in *Voyage in the Dark* think stereotypically that "hands are obeah."[21] When Antoinette hears gossip about Christophine's Obeah practice she looks around Christophine's room, knowing, she says, "what I would find if I dared to look": "a dead man's dried hand, white chicken feathers, a cock with its throat cut, dying slowly, slowly" (*WSS* 26–27). In an early version of the story "Pioneers, O Pioneers" now in the British Library, white Creole Mrs. Cox plays the vigilante. She "had driven out the last obeah-man" by smoking him out of his room. "'There were hands,' she said, 'cut off dead people, hanging all over his room. It's hands are obeah.'" The newcomer to Dominica, Dr. Cox, a voice of British scientific authority, "had roared with laughter" (Add Mss 57859, folio 2). Rhys ambiguously admits Obeah powers into the cardboard walls of *Jane Eyre* in Rochester's injuries: "one eye was knocked out, and one hand so crushed that Mr Carter, the surgeon, had to amputate it directly. The other eye inflamed: he lost the sight of that also" (Brontë 454).

Who or what might release the powers in England is uncertain: it could be Christophine, using intercessionary powers of projective vision in Antoinette's third dream ("Other things I know," says Christophine, after acknowledging that her illiteracy will preclude written communication with Antoinette [*WSS* 133]), or the red dress, closeted in a black clothes press, the color of which is fire that seems to "spread across the room" (*WSS* 153), catalyzing the third installment of the serial dream. Christophine insists that Obeah is "not for *béké*. Bad, bad trouble come when *béké* meddle with that" (*WSS* 93). This is not, however, necessarily a judgment about the cultural specificity of "black ritual practices," as Spivak suggests ("Three Women's Texts" 252–53). It needs to be set alongside Christophine's comment: "If *béké* say it foolishness, then it foolishness" (*WSS* 97). In other words, she will tell *béké* what *béké* wants to hear about Obeah. Her earlier insistence may be a screen, a withholding. Like Friday in Spivak's reading of J. M. Coetzee's *Foe*, Christophine acts as the "curious guardian at the margin." "For every territorial space that is value coded by colonialism *and* every command of metropolitan anticolonialism for the native to yield his 'voice,' there is," writes Spivak, "a space of withholding, marked by a secret that may not be a secret but cannot be unlocked" ("Theory" 172).

The conceptual world of Obeah, as represented by Rhys, replete with sensational stereotypes she does not completely disavow, may be read into *Jane Eyre* past Antoinette/Bertha's physical death. Rhys's Rochester reads in the "Obeah" chapter of *The Glittering Coronet of Isles*: "'A zombi is a dead person who seems to be alive or a living person who is dead. A zombi can also be the spirit of a place, usually malignant but sometimes to be propitiated with sacrifices or offerings of flowers and fruit.' [. . .] "'They cry out in the wind that is their voice, they rage in the sea that is their anger.'"" (*WSS* 89). Brontë's Rochester "never was a mild man, but he got dangerous after he lost" Jane Eyre (Brontë 452). At Moor House, Jane Eyre hears the voice of Rochester speaking "in pain and woe, wildly, eerily, urgently" (445), as if in the wind. When Jane runs into the garden, "[t]he wind sighed low in the firs: all was moorland loneliness and midnight hush." "'Down superstition!'" comments Jane, "as that spectre rose up black by the black yew at the gate. 'This is not thy deception, nor thy witchcraft: it is the work of nature. She was roused, and did—no miracle—but her best'" (445). Rhys's accounts of Obeah and zombis open several interpretive possibilities. Jane Eyre may get her man in marriage, but he may be a zombi. Antoinette has accused Rochester of exercising powers comparable to Obeah in renaming her Bertha. The cardboard walls of *Jane Eyre* and the gendered and racialized Englishness of Thornfield may be "malignant" zombi forces "to be propitiated with sacrifices or offerings of flowers or fruit." Rhys as vigilante, acting through Antoinette and authorized by Brontë's text, smokes out Rochester, the representative of that Englishness.

Christophine's criticism of the operation of the apprenticeship system that replaced slavery as an interim to full emancipation—between 1834 and 1838 in most British Caribbean colonies—is framed as a distinction between old and new, the former slaveowning plantocracy and newcomer plantation owners like the Luttrells: "No more slavery! She had to laugh! 'These new ones have Letter of the Law. Same thing. They got magistrate. They got fine. They got jail house and chain gang. They got tread machine to mash up people's feet. New ones worse than old ones—more cunning, that's all'" (*WSS* 22–23). The phrase "Letter of the Law" has a specific historical provenance in relation to the abolition of slavery and the operation of apprenticeship law during the 1830s. The "Letter of the Law" signifies in documents of the early to mid-1830s the efforts of local legislatures controlled by slaveowners and holders of apprenticed labor (the old rather than the new) to frustrate the spirit of amelioration and emancipatory reform directed by the British Parliament and the frustration of the British government at the recalcitrance of the legislatures and the colonial judicial system in honoring the spirit of reform. Spivak transfers the phrase to British divorce law and a question of reform in *Jane Eyre*, arguing that Brontë's blurring of the boundary between human and animal in her representation of Bertha Mason allows her to consider the question of "a good greater than the letter of the Law" ("Three Women's Texts" 247). In *Wide Sargasso Sea*, Rhys occludes Lockhart family history, specifically controversy over the manner in which the Letter of the Law was used when James Potter Lockhart, Rhys's maternal great-grandfather, was in command of Dominica during the apprenticeship period.[22]

In the early to mid-1830s, James Potter Lockhart was often president of the Dominican Legislative Council (the upper house of the then dual-chamber Dominican colonial parliament), a position held by its senior member, and in this capacity he occasionally assumed the acting lieutenant-governorship with the title president and commander-in-chief. The governor-in-chief over a "semi-federal arrangement" of Leeward Island colonies, including Dominica, resided in Antigua (Honychurch 129); a lieutenant-governor resided in Dominica. The Crown-nominated members of the council also functioned as privy councillors of the governor. On the death of Lieutenant-Governor Sir Charles Schomberg in January 1835, Lockhart was president and commander-in-chief of Dominica for most of 1835. On his arrival in Dominica in the late eighteenth century he had worked as a plantation manager; he purchased Geneva estate in 1824 (Angier 7). In 1832 Lockhart's signature authorized the Report of a Joint Committee resisting Provisions of Orders in Council and proposed Resolutions for the Abolition of Colonial Slavery. The language is unequivocally opposed to abolition: the "slave owner is justly entitled to the property he has acquired, and . . . he cannot lawfully be dispossessed of it without compensation," and the "total annihilation of Colonial property" (a circumlocution for the abolition) is "an evil" (Report of the Joint Committee 135). In 1831 a Brown Privilege Bill was passed that enfranchised colored men of property—"freehold of ten acres of land, or a leasehold worth twenty pounds a year in land, or twenty pounds a year in building" (Trouillot 100)—and permitted them to stand for election to the Assembly (the lower house of the colonial parliament). By 1838 men of the colored elite dominated the Assembly. In 1835 and in 1837 (the year Lockhart died), one of their number, Joseph Fadelle, challenged Lockhart in his role as ultimate Dominican upholder of the manner in which the Letter of the Law was abused under his command. Abolitionists Sturge and Harvey comment in 1838 on Fadelle's renown "in England for his fearless exposure of colonial wickedness in high places" (93).

The cases elaborated by Fadelle highlight an official reluctance to accept the dismantling of the punitive "culture of terror" (the term is Michael Taussig's) that had structured master/slave relations and propped up the authority of the master. In 1835 two female apprentices, Dongouse and Mary Clarke, both convicted of receiving stolen goods, were sentenced to thirty-nine and thirty stripes respectively, the whipping to be carried out in the public market-place; and a free person, Xiste, convicted of common assault, was sentenced to labor in a chain gang (MacGregor, despatch to Aberdeen). In 1837 Fadelle referred to the secretary of state for the colonies, Lord Glenelg, among other cases, the matter of a violation of "the rights of the apprentices" under Lockhart's charge as master of Geneva estate and attorney of neighboring Coulibri estate (Glenelg to Colebrooke, 29 April 1837). (The Jamaican estate of the Cosways in *Wide Sargasso Sea* is called Coulibri.) Lord Bathurst had recommended to the governors on 28 May 1823 "an absolute prohibition to inflict the punishment of flogging under any circumstances on female Slaves," a measure which "cannot fail to raise this unfortunate Class generally above their present degraded level, and to restore to the female Slaves that sense of shame which is at once the ornament and protection of their Sex, and which their present mode of punishment has tended so unfortunately to weaken, if not to obliterate" (despatch to Murray). The legal opinion of John Shiell, the acting attorney-general of Antigua, was that as Dongouse and Mary Clarke were convicted under general law and not apprenticeship law the sentence was legitimate, but reprehensible (Opinion). In the case of Xiste, Fadelle asserted as "an axiom of the English law, that no ignominious punishment should be appended to a crime which is not in itself ignominious" (letter to MacGregor).

On 27 February 1835, Governor Sir E.J.M. MacGregor wrote to Lockhart to "earnestly recommend" that he "prevent" the whipping of women "by the intervention of the prerogative of pardon, in all future cases, when females may be sentenced to be so punished," and on 13 May 1835 he suggested to Lockhart that the "punishment of working in the chain-gang" (as a means of enforcing hard labor) be abolished; Lockhart recommended the measure to the assembly on 6 July 1835 (letter to MacGregor). The whipping of the apprentices was brought to the attention of the British House of Commons on 19 August 1835, and of abolitionists, being cited in Sturge and Harvey's *The West Indies in 1837*;[23] and it was evidently one of the myriad cases referred to the Select Committee of the House of Commons "appointed to inquire into the APPRENTICESHIP SYSTEM in the COLONIES, the Condition of the APPRENTICES, and the Laws and Regulations affecting them which have been passed," which reported in August 1836. Its task was to examine the gaps between the "Letter" of recently enacted colonial "Law" and the spirit "of the Imperial Parliament, as expressed in the Act of Emancipation." The committee reported that time constraint led them to "limit their investigation to Jamaica" (Report from the Select Committee on

Negro Apprenticeship [iii]). This decision of the committee had the effect of
curtailing further investigation of the case involving Dongouse and Mary Clarke,
casting into greater obscurity the relation between Lockhart "family history and
the larger history of the English colony of Dominica" (Hulme, "Locked Hearts"
23).

On 20 November 1835 an act "for abolishing the punishment of females by
whipping" was passed by the legislature of Dominica (MacGregor, despatch to
Glenelg, 13 January 1836). Fadelle's charge in 1837 that while Lockhart was "in
the administration of the Government of the Island" he demanded that the apprentices on Geneva and Coulibri estates carry passes authorized by him when they
left the estates on Saturdays and Sundays, days having been declared normally
free of labor, led Glenelg to lament to Governor Colebrooke on the "system
which places persons not conversant with public business in the occasional administration of colonial Governments." Apprentices without passes "suffered the
punishment of the dark hole at their return" to the estates. Lockhart had acted on
the "suggestion of Mr Saile, the Stipendiary Magistrate," in instituting the pass
system; Glenelg disputed Saile's interpretation of the law and Colebrooke's support of it, couched in terms of the "'the spirit of the law.'" Saile's interpretation
was based on deeming "wander[ing]" from the "direct road" to church on Sundays
or market on Saturdays, or "think[ing] fit, as free agents, neither to go to market
or to Church" acts of vagabondage (Glenelg, despatch to Colebrooke, 29 April
1837). Glenelg found that the "regulations respecting passes" were "not war-
ranted in Law" and demanded that Colebrooke "take such steps as may be necessary to cause them to be rescinded" (Colebrooke, letter to Light, 10 June 1837).
Interestingly, but without specific knowledge of Lockhart's practice, Moira Ferguson argues that the final part of *Wide Sargasso Sea* "recapitulates the lives of
slaves who were locked in cellars, victims of systematic abuse. The attic of
Thornfield Hall, Rochester's estate, provides an analogue to conditions of existence that continually punctuated the pages of periodicals, such as the *Anti-
Slavery Reporter*, during slavery" (14).

Christophine's references to prison reform in the British Caribbean between
c. 1835 in Jamaica and the early 1840s in Dominica—"No chain gang, no tread
machine, no dark jail either" (*WSS* 131)—suggest that Rhys knows at least part
of her great-grandfather's political career. The "dark jail" could also be a term for
the "punishment of the dark hole." Spivak reads these references, with Christophine's comment "This is free country and I am free woman," as an invocation
of the freeing of Jamaican slaves (253). Some prison reforms were also recommended by the Select Committee that enquired into the apprenticeship system in
Jamaica, and Governor Colebrooke was urging reforms on Lieutenant-Governor
Light in August 1837. In November 1837, Colebrooke sent Light a circular
from Glenelg announcing the appointment of Captain Pringle "to enquire into
the state of the Prisons and Workhouses in the West Indies." Christophine,
Rhys's feisty critic of colonialism, is comparatively more forgiving of old
slaveowners than those who settled after 1834, compensation indeed for James

Potter Lockhart's desire to exact the Letter of the Law when placed in positions of authority during the 1830s. Diana Paton, drawing in part on the work of Karen Haltunnen, argues that in the course of the eighteenth century, when the experiencing of pain became unacceptable and watching it was constructed as morally dangerous, a historical shift that worked to bring about the calls for the abolition of flogging as a punishment for slaves, the taboos on the infliction and spectacle of pain eroticized them as a central theme of pornography (170). The whipping of females as summary punishment in the Caribbean colonies leaves transgenerational traces in the Lockhart family history in Rhys's memories of having been whipped by her mother and in Rhys's vulnerability to Mr. Howard's sadomasochistic storytelling.

The deconstructive maxims that circulate in Spivak's analysis of Christophine as sufficient points of explanatory reference occlude the historical meanings of specific signs, local colonial histories, Lockhart family investment in a particular kind of representation of old slaveowners, and, indeed, colonial negotiations of what Spivak presupposes are at stake for "feminist individualism" in the imperialist era ("Three Women's Texts" 244)—"domestic-society-through-sexual-reproduction cathected as 'companionate love'" (one possible reading of "let us live lovingly") and the imperial soul-making project "cathected as civil-society-through-social-mission," twisted up in the turn-of-the-century Dominican moral panic over Obeah.

"THEY FOOL YOU WELL ABOUT THAT GIRL"

Daniel Cosway or Boyd (his right to the patronym Cosway is questioned by Antoinette) makes a series of allegations to Rochester about the sexual morality, Christian decency, and mental history of the Cosway family and suggests that the family "'fool[ed]'" him about Antoinette (*WSS* 103). His words are read and heard in Rochester's narrative in two letters and in Rochester's account of a meeting with him. The instability of Rochester's memories of the meeting— "'Give my love to your wife—my sister [. . .] You are not the first to kiss her pretty face'" (*WSS* 104) becomes "'Give my sister your wife a kiss from me. Love her as I did—oh yes I did'" (*WSS* 130)—suggests that Rochester is an unreliable narrator of the meeting and that the unreliability is produced by Daniel's speaking of the breaching of a "miscegenation taboo" that determines the "circulation of women among white men and black men" in a colonial context. The taboo "ordains that white men have access to black women but that black men must be denied access to white women" (Bergner 81). If Daniel's speaking of a breach involving Antoinette destabilizes the masculine racial hierarchy kept in place by the taboo, Rochester reinforces it again by having sex with Amélie. "My Mr Rochester as I see him becomes as fierce as Heathcliff and as jealous as Othello," Rhys wrote to Diana Athill on 28 April 1964, describing "the *Breakthrough*" in her reinscription of Rochester (Rhys, *Letters* 269), the "clue" to which was given by her writing of the poem "Obeah Night" (Rhys, *Letters* 262).

In *Wuthering Heights*, Emily Brontë codes the ferocity of Heathcliff's desire for Catherine as hunger; Rhys's Rochester speaks of the fierceness of his desire for Antoinette as "breathless and savage" (78), later as "thirst and longing" (141) and for "revenge" against her as a "hurricane" (135–36). "'What I see is nothing—I want what it *hides*—that is not nothing,'" thinks Rochester in *Wide Sargasso Sea* (73). To him Antoinette's tears are "nothing," her words are "less than nothing," and the "happiness" he gives her is "worse than nothing" (78). Daniel's allegations about the Cosway family and innuendos about Antoinette's relationship with Sandi, son of her "illegitimate" colored half-brother, Alexander, confirm, give form to Rochester's racialized sexual anxieties and porno-tropic imagination as they play themselves out in his sense of what might be hidden. Daniel plays Iago to Rochester's Othello and Antoinette's Desdemona in Rhys's elaboration of themes of jealousy, vengeance, racism, xenophobia, and misogyny. In elaborating these themes and developing the character Daniel, Rhys also draws on motifs from stories surrounding the historical Thomas ("Indian") Warner.

Spivak's explanation of Rochester draws on Lacanian psychoanalysis. She cites "the letter not written" and "the letter not sent" by Rochester to his father ("Three Women's Texts" 251), and her earlier reading of "castration and suppressed letters" in "The Letter as Cutting Edge" (261, n. 20) in support of her contention that "the thematics of Oedipus" played out in his relationship with his father provide the "'correct' explanation of the tragedy of the book" (251). In Spivak's reading of Antoinette's narcissistic desire there is a slippage from mythological to Lacanian psychoanalytic reference points. Spivak stories the pool at Coulibri, Antoinette's desire to be like Tia, and the settings of the second and third installments of Antoinette's serial dream with classical mythological import—they are Ovidian pools. John Brenkman, in an essay Spivak cites in an endnote, describes the pool in which Ovid's Narcissus gazes at himself "as the place where Narcissus' transgression will be answered . . . the scene of a punishment. Nemesis is not so much the actual agent of justice here as an emblematic rubric placed over the description of the pool to pin down the meaning of the episode that will take place there even before it unfolds" (304). In Spivak's reading of Antoinette's self/Other relations the emblematic rubrics, Nemesis, are "the fracture of imperialism" ("Three Women's Texts" 250) and a deconstructive maxim: "No perspective *critical* of imperialism can turn the Other into a self, because the project of imperialism has always already historically refracted what might have been the absolutely Other into a domesticated Other that consolidates the imperialist self" (253). Spivak herself has noted more recently that "Narcissus was a boy!" ("Echo" 176) and the commonness of the theme of women and "non-European cultures being stuck in varieties of narcissism and its vicissitudes[.] . . . Their growth is arrested on the civilizational scale" (177).[24] Her own reading of white Creole culture and the white Creole woman, Antoinette, in *Wide Sargasso Sea*, however, is complicit with, and perpetuates this theme. In "Three Women's Texts," Antoinette's suppressed letter to Richard, which she tells Grace Poole she has hidden from Grace's "beastly eyes" and possibly "[i]n the pocket" of her "red dress" (*WSS* 149), and Daniel's letters to Rochester, who takes the place of Cosway, the father as desired "benefactor," are not analyzed.

The location of Granbois in the near vicinity of Massacre is given as much by the historical significance of the village's name and a widely believed motive for the massacre, which occurred in 1674, as by its having been singled out as an area of intense Obeah activity in 1904. "'And who was massacred here? Slaves?'" Rochester asks Antoinette. "'Oh no.' She sounded shocked. 'Not slaves. Something must have happened a long time ago. Nobody remembers now'" (55). A set of stories surrounding Massacre features, like *Wide Sargasso Sea*, the betrayal of a half-sibling, racial tension exacerbated by the shame of miscegenation and illegitimacy, vengeance, and doubt over the paternity of the mixed-race illegitimate child. At Massacre, Thomas Warner, the reputed son of "Sir Thomas Warner, Governor of St Kitts, and a Carib woman" from Dominica (Hulme and Whitehead 89), and usually called "Indian" Warner, and his Carib party were murdered. The order to kill "Indian" Warner and his party was reportedly given by Philip Warner, Sir Thomas Warner's legitimate son.[25] Initially imprisoned in the Tower of London, Philip Warner was tried for the murders in Barbados in 1676 and acquitted. According to William Dampier, one of the reasons given for Philip Warner's "inhumane Action" was that he "was ashamed to be related to an Indian" (Hulme and Whitehead 90). "Indian" Warner's relations with the English, especially those on Antigua, were antipathetic (Hulme and Whitehead 95). In Dampier's account, "finding himself despised by his English Kindred, he forsook his Father's House" (Hulme and Whitehead 90); in du Tertre's, after Sir Thomas Warner's death, his wife "began to persecute him ['Indian' Warner] & treat him with such inhumanity that she made him work in the fields with the slaves of the household" (Hulme and Whitehead 91). Depositions presented in defence of Philip Warner (accused of fratricide) questioned the paternity of "Indian" Warner: he was a slave and "not reputed the child of Sir Thos. Warner," having acquired the name Warner "because he was the first-born slave in the General's family in St Christopher's" (Hulme and Whitehead 103–104).

In *A Grammar of Motives*, Kenneth Burke argues that "Iago, to arouse Othello, must talk a language that Othello knows as well as he, a language implicit in the nature of Othello's love as the idealization of his private property in Desdemona. This language is the dialectical opposite of Othello's; but it so thoroughly shares a common ground with Othello's language that its insinuations are never for one moment irrelevant to Othello's thinking" (414). There are several areas of common ground in the discourses of Rochester and Daniel: rationalization of xenophobic racism and vengeance through appeals to Christian duty; invocation of an English stereotype of the degenerate white creole; misogynistic fear of excessive feminine appetite and of loss of masculine self-command in heterosexual relationships; the sense of themselves as sons scorned by wealthy fathers. In part Daniel is manipulating the biases and prejudices of colonial discourse as part of a blackmail attempt; in the last two areas there is an intensity and consistency of disgust that suggest depth of libidinal investment in a worldview. In the dialogue with Daniel reported by Rochester, Daniel constructs women as "demons incarnate" in their demanding appetite ("[b]uy me this and buy me that"), which robs a man of his autonomous desire "to please" himself (103); old Cosway, old Mason, Daniel's half-brother Alexander, and Rochester are, in Daniel's reported narrative, bewitched by women. His account of old Cosway assumes the sexual "availability of the bodies of the slave/black/mulatto women" (Gregg 111). His mother becomes a "cipher in conflicts between men" (Clark 49) over paternity, legitimacy, rightful expectation, and racial and class exploitation. Daniel, like Iago, "suffers from the devouring resentment of a man cheated of his place," and Rochester, like Othello, "is threatened from the beginning with the even more radical insecurity of placelessness" (Neill, "Changing Places"). The name Daniel was conferred by old Cosway; he says that his name is Esau. The name Esau works, through Biblical allusion, to suggest his perceived loss of a birthright (monetary inheritance and financial support) and his father's blessing.

Robert Kendrick argues persuasively that Daniel is, as scorned son, Rochester's "illegitimate" double (242). Othello's position in Venetian society is secured only by his success as a mercenary soldier of the state. He is marked culturally as a stranger and is the object of xenophobia based on racial difference. Rochester's displacement and disorientation in Jamaica are emblematized by his fever, in Dominica by his dizziness. As Iago purportedly offers Othello local "knowledge" of the sexual mores of Venetian ladies, so Daniel purports to offer Rochester the common local "knowledge" of the Cosway family and to report a conspiracy to conceal it from him. Michael Neill argues that *Othello* "thinks abomination into being and then taunts the audience with the knowledge that it can never be *un*thought" ("Unproper Beds" 395). Daniel's scandalous local "knowledge" and insinuation that Antoinette has broken the miscegenation taboo with the son of her half-brother also cannot be unthought. Gregg insists that "his story contradicts Antoinette's and remains a probability" (114). The credibility attributed to Daniel's story, though, is a function of its confirmation of the racial, ethnic, and sexual prejudices and anxieties of Rochester and of its making available confessionally to Rochester and the reader the "nature" of the skeletons in the Cosway family closet.

That closet demarcates in Rochester's narrative the line between "bad blood" (81) and "good race" that is integral to his family property (Brontë 332); his anxieties over the hidden are structured by fears of contamination and degeneration. The rationale for Rochester's arranged marriage to Antoinette is the acquisition of private property, the thirty thousand pound dowry, to capitalize the younger son; Rochester's grim satisfaction with the exchange, however, is haunted by the anxiety that he has been purchased with the money, losing his autonomy over disposition of his own body (intertextually "good race") as private property. Rochester implies a sexual slavery. Like Othello, but through

different processes of acculturation, he is "representative and upholder of a rigorous sexual code which prohibits desire and defines it even within marriage as
adulterous, . . . and yet also the sign of a different, unbridled sexuality" (Karen
Newman 150). Rochester racializes his lust for Antoinette as savage, as uncontrollable animal craving. Sexual appetite is coded as feminine, not-white, not-
English. Rochester's fears of his own racial degeneration through contiguity and
congress with the foreign are projected obliquely in his narrative. The "golden-
brown flowers" of the orchid, like other flowers in his narrative, are "displaced
objects for masculine gender and sexual anxieties" (Looby 112). Looby points
out in his study of the ways that flowers were "saturated with the erotics of race"
in the nineteenth century, that "*orchis* is Greek for testicle, the orchid was an
antique aphrodisiac" (128, 126). After reading Daniel's letter, Rochester goes for
a walk during which, he says, he could not "force" himself "to think. Then I
passed an orchid with long sprays of golden-brown flowers. One of them touched
my cheek and I remembered picking some for her one day. 'They are like you,' I
told her. Now I stopped, broke a spray off and trampled it into the mud. This
brought me to my senses" (82).

The action suggests Rochester's rejection of Antoinette's destabilizing aphrodisiac effect on him. He tramples it into the (red) mud.[26] In the symbolic register
of Rochester's account, mud acquires moral connotations of filth. Rochester
naturalizes his senses of Antoinette's effect on him and its filthy origins in the
Dominican soil and racializes his senses of her alienness and the alienness of the
sexual passion she excites in him to his acculturated upper-class English masculinity in the golden-brown color of the fleshy orchid flowers. "The boundary of
the body as well as the distinction between internal and external," Judith Butler
suggests, drawing on Julia Kristeva's *Powers of Horror*, "is established through
the ejection and transvaluation of something originally part of identity into a
defiling otherness" (*Gender Trouble* 133). In Rochester's account of his socialization as upper-class white English man, sexual desire and intensity are ideally
expelled from "inner" space to stabilize and consolidate, control "the coherent
subject" (*Gender Trouble* 134). Daniel exacerbates Rochester's sense of Antoinette's contamination of his cleansed inner space in writing of Antoinette to
Rochester as "in your blood and your bones," "you bewitch with her" (81).
Rochester's abjection at his loss of control is reprojected as disgust at Antoinette
as adulterating. Her determining characteristic, according to Daniel, is "bad blood
[. . .] from both sides" of her family (81). The scandal assumes the proportion
of truth in Francis Wyndham's explanation of the "bad blood" as a product of
inbreeding and decadence (11). An implicit assumption here is that "bad blood"
causes promiscuity, especially across socially constructed racial barriers.

Remembering his departure from Daniel's home, Rochester recalls a "world
given up to heat and to flies, the light was dazzling after his little dark room. A
black and white goat tethered nearby was staring at me and for what seemed minutes I stared back into its slanting yellow-green eyes" (104). He then rides away
as fast as possible. The flies are emblems of decay and filth, the light of a

"dazzling" knowledge of himself as goat: fool, lecher, scapegoated by Daniel to carry the moral burden of the plantocracy (just as Daniel is scapegoated to carry the moral, emotional, and economic burden of illegitimacy). The goat, too, was popularly associated with sin and the devil. Othello, insisting to Iago that he will "see" signs of her adultery before he "doubt[s]" Desdemona (III.3.188), declares, "Exchange me for a goat,/When I shall turn the business of my soul/To such exsufflicate and blown surmises,/Matching thy inference" (III.3.178–81). Rhys's allusion implies that Rochester has by contrast turned the "business" of his soul to "exsufflicate and blown surmises" "[m]atching" Daniel's "inference." Kenneth Muir glosses "exsufflicate and blown" as "inflated and blown up (but some think the words mean 'spat out and fly-blown')" (202).

The scene with Rochester and the goat parallels that in which Antoinette stares at the rats on the windowsill of her bedroom at Granbois, recounted second-hand by Rochester, but, as Kendrick suggests, there "[t]he act of reflection says nothing about either her or the rats" (241). The black and white coloring of the goat signifies in the nonliteral register of Rochester's memory moral and racial admixture. Esau, Daniel's preferred name, means literally "hairy man." In Genesis, Esau's brother, Jacob, impersonates him to gain their father's blessing and property by wearing kid skin "upon his hands and, and upon the smooth of his neck" (Genesis 27.16). The stare exchanged between Rochester and the goat may, then, also acknowledge the doubling of Rochester and Daniel, but it is significant that in that acknowledgement on Rochester's part the Daniel figure is an animal.

Stephen Greenblatt argues persuasively that Othello wants to "ward off" the "shame" of an "excess" of erotic ardor, that "pleasure itself becomes for Othello pollution, a defilement of his property in Desdemona and in himself" (249–51). He

unleases [sic] upon Cassio . . . the fear of pollution, defilement, brutish violence that is bound up with his own experience of sexual pleasure, while he must destroy Desdemona both for her excessive experience of pleasure and for awakening such sensations in himself. . . . Othello's identity is entirely caught up in the narrative structure that drives him to turn Desdemona into a being incapable of pleasure, a piece of "monumental alabaster," so that he will at last be able to love her without the taint of adultery:

Be thus, when thou art dead, and I will kill thee,
And love thee after. (V.2.18–19) (250–52)

These arguments have helped me think through specific aspects of Rhys's representation of Rochester: his object in calling Antoinette "Marionette"; his bruising of her body on the night she tries to use Christophine's Obeah on him; his drawing "the sheet over her gently as if" he "covered a dead girl" the next morning (*WSS* 114); and his "zombification" of Antoinette. As with Desdemona, Antoinette's "confidence in her love's future has been reduced" by her husband's changing attitude towards her "to . . . a morbid preoccupation with unrequited love, and a fatalistic desire to recapture the experience of the wedding night" (Snow 238). In V.2, Othello declares, equivocating over his murderous intent towards Desdemona:

Yet I'll not shed her blood,
Nor scar that whiter skin of hers than snow,
and smooth as monumental alabaster . . . (3–5)

Rochester remembers little of what transpired on the night Rhys writes about in a poem as "Obeah Night"; in her confrontation with him, Christophine recalls to him the bruises he made on Antoinette's body ("'All you want to do is break her up'") and that he "'start[ed] calling her names. Marionette. Some word so.'

'Yes, I remember, I did.'
(*Marionette, Antoinette, Marionetta, Antoinetta*)
'That word mean doll, eh? Because she don't speak. You want to force her to cry and to speak.'" (127)

Rochester unleashes on Antoinette the fear of adulteration and the violence "bound up with his own experience of sexual pleasure, while he must destroy" her "both for her excessive experience of pleasure and for awakening such sensations in himself." Antoinette may be at this stage in their relationship either Marionette, "a being incapable of pleasure" he will "be able to love . . . without the taint of adultery," or Bertha, the sexually promiscuous madwoman, who will "moan and cry and give herself as no sane woman would—or could" (*WSS* 136). The names Marionette (a diminutive of Mary) and Bertha invoke a virgin/whore dichotomy. In spite of Rochester's reduction of her by the time of their departure from Granbois to the level of an emotional automaton with features marked as zombie-like indifference and as a "doll's voice" (140) and "doll's smile" (141), he fears the capacity for dissimulation, which he thinks is the "truth" of her "nature." As Marionette, she excites his hatred rather than the desire he is still working to suppress in himself.

That work of suppression is cross-cut with anxieties focused around pity and developed principally through allusion to Shakespeare's *Macbeth*. Rochester images his own violence as "contemptuous wind" (135), "the blast of hurricanes" (136). The word "[p]ity" gives him "no rest," and he recalls the words of Macbeth "contemplating the consequences of killing a person of patent innocence such as Duncan" (Little 42), "Pity like a naked new-born babe striding the blast" (*WSS* 135). The allusion "emphasizes the issue of judgment" (Little 42). Macbeth fears that Duncan's

virtues
Will plead like angels trumpet-tongued against
The deep damnation of his taking-off;
And Pity, like a naked new-born babe,

Striding the blast, or heaven's cherubin, horsed
Upon the sightless couriers of the air,
Shall blow the horrid deed in every eye,
That tears shall drown the wind. (I.7.18–25)

Judy Little has argued that "[t]he naked babe of pity . . . comes to the symbolic aid of Antoinette," whose "fundamental innocence" will arouse reader sympathy, and that "Rochester . . . seems to acknowledge that he has placed himself beyond most people's capacity for pity, and certainly beyond his own capacity to love or respect himself" (43). Rochester certainly feels self-pity, being "[t]ied to a lunatic for life—a drunken lying lunatic" (135); his vision of gently comforting "Antoinetta" in his pitying arms is animated by a desire to claim exclusive possession of her. Rochester insistently uses the possessive pronouns "my" and "*mine*": "my lunatic. She's mad but *mine, mine*"; "My lunatic. My mad girl." He waits in vain for her "human" "smiles" or tears "or both," which will "drown" his violence and occasion his pity, because they will be, as he puts it, "*For me*" (136). For Rochester even compassion is predicated on him winning hers first, being able to claim it as an exclusive emotional property. Rhys represents his pity for Antoinette as being like the pity "'one is justified in hurling back in the teeth of those who offer it'" that Brontë's Rochester disparages as he accepts Jane's pity, which is "'the suffering mother of love.'" The "'noxious and insulting'" sort of pity he despises is "'native to callous, selfish hearts; it is a hybrid, egotistical pain at hearing of woes, crossed with ignorant contempt for those who have endured them'" (Brontë 334).

Othello's tragedy entails a fall from noble estimation—"noble General Othello" (II.2.11). In the final scene Emilia declares of Desdemona and Othello: "O, the more angel she,/And you the blacker devil" (V.2.131–32). In the letter in which Rhys mentions Othello having been a reference point for her Rochester, she questions Brontë's Rochester: "this noble character! Noble!!" Several characters in *Wide Sargasso Sea* come to estimate Rochester a "devil" in his treatment of Antoinette. In the major confrontation scene between Antoinette and Rochester in *Wide Sargasso Sea*, Antoinette, talking about "justice" as a "lie," compares Rochester's kiss with the kiss of Annette's keeper: "'My mother whom you all talk about, what justice did she have? My mother sitting in the rocking-chair speaking about dead horses and dead grooms and a black devil kissing her sad mouth. Like you kissed mine'" (121). Christophine exclaims of Rochester's desire to have Antoinette declared mad: "'You do that for money? But you wicked like Satan self!'" (132). Grace Poole remembers declaring to Mrs. Eff, "'*I don't serve the devil for no money*'" (145), but is placated by Mrs. Eff's defense of Rochester as having been "'*gentle, generous, brave*'" before his "'*stay in the West Indies,*'" which "'*has changed him out of all knowledge*'" (145), a doubling of her salary, and by the "*thick walls*" that "*shelter*" her "*from the world outside which, say what you like, can be a black and cruel world to a woman,*" "*keeping away all the things that you have fought till you can fight no more*" (146).

The plantation house architecture of Jamaica in *Jane Eyre* and of Dominica in *Wide Sargasso Sea* is, by contrast, characterized by "thin partitions" (Brontë 335), or "thin partition" (*WSS* 115), through which Brontë's Rochester hears Bertha's "wolfish cries" (Brontë 335) and Rhys's Rochester calculates Antoinette will be able to hear his and Amélie's sexual "encounter" (*WSS* 115). For the foreign Antoinette the walls of Thornfield Hall are not "*thick*" enough to provide shelter and protection; they are "cardboard" (148), and in the final installment of her serial dream, in which her Aunt Cora, disgusted by Richard Mason's refusal to demand a marriage settlement for Antoinette, turns her face to a wall, saying "'The Lord has forsaken us'" (95), she looks to a wall of fire for protection. In *Jane Eyre*, Rochester suggests that Bertha is "hell" and carries it with her (322, 335) and "a demon" (322). *Wide Sargasso Sea* works to transfer such damnation to Rochester, Daniel, and "old devil" Cosway (80). Edward Fairfax Rochester is denied his *Christian* name and his patronym in both Antoinette's and Grace Poole's narratives. To his servants in England he is "*the master of the house*" (145).

Rochester himself customarily denies one character his Christian name, and the staging of the forgetting of the name exposes an unspeakable subject in his narrative. Rochester remembers Antoinette having introduced him to a servant named Bertrand on his arrival at Granbois (60). In recalling the scenes of leave-taking (Christophine's and his own) Rochester describes Bertrand as "the boy who helped with the horses" (132), "[t]hat boy" (137), "the nameless boy" whom he "could have strangled [. . .] with pleasure" because of his sobbing (140), "God! A half-savage boy as well as . . . as well as . . ." (140), and "[t]hat stupid boy" ([142]). The unspeakable covered by the ellipses, which also occasions an angry blasphemy, is suggested by Rochester's memory of what preceded it, a sexual gesture Antoinette made in telling him why Bertrand is crying as Rochester prepares to leave: "'Because—' she stopped and ran her tongue over her lips, 'he loves you very much'" (140). Rochester, in recalling his leavetaking, has already construed Baptiste's "dislike and contempt" as a questioning of his manliness comparable to Christophine's "'Taste my bull's blood'" (138). Antoinette implies that Rochester is the object of homosexual desire on Bertrand's part. Rochester says that his own desire for Bertrand is "nothing. Nothing. . . ." ([142]). It is this denial of a reciprocation of imputed homosexual feeling with a word that he has also used to signify the quality of his contempt for Antoinette and the hidden secret of Granbois that closes Rochester's narrative.

"WE STARED AT EACH OTHER, BLOOD ON MY FACE, TEARS ON HERS"

Spivak opens out her theoretical reading of self/Other relationships in *Wide Sargasso Sea* with a discussion of Antoinette's desire to "live with" and "be like" Tia. This desire is Antoinette's initial response to the major implication for her of the firing of Coulibri by local black people:

As I ran, I thought, I will live with Tia and I will be like her. Not to leave Coulibri.
Not to go. Not. When I was close I saw the jagged stone in her hand but I did not see
her throw it. I did not feel it either, only something wet, running down my face. I
looked at her and I saw her face crumple up as she began to cry. We stared at each
other, blood on my face, tears on hers. It was as if I saw myself. Like in a looking-
glass. (*WSS* 38)

As an instance of mirroring that frustrates Antoinette's narcissism, Spivak cites
this passage with two ellipses. Spivak cuts "Not to leave Coulibri. Not to go.
Not" and "I did not feel it either, only something wet, running down my face. I
looked at her and I saw her face crumple up as she began to cry." That first ellipsis erases the meanings of the lost place to Antoinette, a topic discussed interestingly and at length by Emery. The second ellipsis has the effect of shielding a
reader's attention from some of the gore and distress of a moment usually read as
one of recognition. For Spivak it is recognition of "the fracture of imperialism"
(250) that frustrates Antoinette's narcissistic desire to self her Other, a desire
metonymic of the "project of imperialism" (253). In Spivak's reading the monster in Antoinette's mirror is "the imperialist narrativization of history" (244).
The third installment of Antoinette's serial dream, which prefigures her firing of
Thornfield Hall and leap from the leads to her death, closes with "hard stones"
turning into the bathing pool at Coulibri at which Tia is present and beckoning
with a taunt, a dare for Antoinette to jump. Antoinette's vision of Coulibri
resonates with detail from the night it was burnt down: the red sky (Antoinette
says "all" her "life was in it") and the domesticated parrot, whose clipped wings
led to its death. Readings of the relationship between Antoinette and Tia have
occluded the pre-scription of Antoinette's desire to live with and be like Tia in
the gazes of various people at her wearing Tia's dress.[27] Attending to that pre-
scription, I work to unravel some of the twisting up of a thematic of domesticity. I return briefly first to a fragment of the history of colonial pornography
inscribed with difficulty in Rhys's Black Exercise Book.

On 11 June 1959, Rhys wrote to Diana Athill, explaining her slow progress
on the novel that would become *Wide Sargasso Sea*: "I'd been writing an autobiography, and imagined I could 'lift' whole passages from it. This wasn't so at
all. The time and mood were quite different" (*Letters* 167). Several motifs from
the Mr. Howard narrative are recontextualized in the Tia/Antoinette relationship
in *Wide Sargasso Sea*: the moralization of the white creole child by mother and
servant; the mother apparently sensing something alien in the daughter; the
"dirtying" of the white creole child/woman, especially by English eyes, which
places her at a racial threshold; sexual danger; a movement over an "edge" or
"border" beyond which might lie "Madness," "Death," or "Paralysis" (BEB). Antoinette dreams the first installment of her serial dream after she is forced to wear
Tia's dress rather than return home in only underwear and Christophine has
commented on the punitive culture of terror upheld by the Letter of the Law. The
second installment of the dream is, as I elaborated in chapter 2, a close reworking
of a dream of sexual menace that is part of the Mr. Howard narrative. Rhys re-

works from the Mr. Howard narrative some of the mother's solicitude for the child frightened by the nightmare to Annette's comforting of Antoinette after she dreams the first installment. As a nuptial dream the second installment catches up Antoinette's anxiety and her Aunt Cora's reassurance about a possible scar from the cut made by the stone Tia threw. Antoinette is concerned about a permanent "mark" on her face; Aunt Cora reassures her that it "'is healing very nicely. It won't spoil you on your wedding day'" (*WSS* 39).

The cut is subtextually characterized as a possible sexual violation. Rochester reports Antoinette having said, "'But I think it did spoil me for my wedding day and all the other days and nights'" (110). Rochester says that he responded to Antoinette's doubt of her aunt's emphasis on surface appearance with the advice to "'put the sad things away. Don't think about them and nothing will be spoiled, I promise you'" (110). Later Rochester reports that Antoinette called him a "stone" during their confrontation after he has had sex with Amelié (122). In the short term Rhys says that her relationship with Mr. Howard "went out" of her "memory like a stone" (BEB). In chapter 2 I elucidated the description with reference to the passing of urinary tract calculus. The stone that ruptures Antoinette's fantasy of living with and being like Tia does not pass out of her memory.[28]

A disjointed fragment of the Mr. Howard narrative that deals with what was evidently a very traumatic event (from which a strip of paper has been deliberately torn, withheld from the gaze of posterity, withdrawn from Rhys's own) is encrypted in the Tia/Antoinette relationship. The fragment is between draft material for the fragmentary story "Mr Howard's House./CREOLE," the title in the typescript annotated "Dont [sic] on any account put this name a real one," and an account of experiencing a moment of disembodied "bliss" while walking in France—"I was the wind the trees the sea the warm earth & left behind a prison a horrible dream of prison" (BEB). The fragment (I note the tear):

    Carreses [sic] me & how he
w[torn out   ] ush me
[3 lines torn out]
[torn out]nd the [torn out]
near the fragipanni [sic] tree—
the day I bet sixpence
Id[sic] turn a somnersault [sic]
under water & did it too.
But I nearly got drowned.
because I could nt [sic] stop turning—

Rhys's spellings of frangipani and somersault realize their pronunciation with nasal congestion, suggesting the immediacy of the return in memory to the moment of near drowning. The caress suggests that the fragment could be a memory of a second touch by Mr. Howard.

White plantocratic femininity in *Wide Sargasso Sea* is constructed around maintaining cultural standards of domestic cleanliness and personal toilet (including clothes). It is part of a bounded gender system modeled on the body, which expresses a social and economic relation to property and the labor of servants (apprentices and freed slaves), and policed by vigilance over racial and class boundaries. The continuity of that gender system is represented by the female child and the preservation of her "pure" exchange value through socialization. Her worth will be measured in her "bloodlines" (Pettman 37) and an unbroken hymen at marriage. The comments of "Jamaican ladies" on Annette's marriage to Cosway are instructive: her age and ethnic difference (she is young and from Martinique, which implies a French family background) offend their values (15); and they are scandalized by her apparently complaisant attitude to Cosway's sexual relationships with "those women!" and his siring of children by them. Their public disgust at cross-racial sex and what they are reading as contamination of bloodlines is brought out in the unspeakables attached to their generic terms "women" and "bastards" (24).

Before Antoinette's mother, Annette, meets Mr. Mason, Antoinette used to spend most of her time at Coulibri in the kitchen with Christophine. Antoinette explains this with reference to her mother's indifference, self-absorption, and neglect of her in favor of disabled son Pierre. Christophine introduces Antoinette to Tia, daughter of her friend Maillotte, who may have been the child who followed Antoinette singing, "'Go away white cockroach, go away, go away. [. . .] White cockroach, go away, go away. Nobody want you. Go away'" (20). The friendship between Antoinette and Tia, screened from Annette, is focused on activities at the bathing pool. After a falling out between them over Tia's bet on Antoinette turning somersaults during which racial insults ("cheating nigger," "white nigger") are exchanged, Tia takes Antoinette's "dress, starched, ironed, clean that morning," leaving her hers to wear (21).

Tia taunts Antoinette with her family's loss of prestige, expressed in the breaking down of racialized class boundaries: their eating the kind of food their former slaves eat and inability to have a leaky roof repaired. As Gregg observes, "[t]he name-calling, the verbal abuse, and the theft/switch dramatize the violence that inheres in the system of domination upon which the West Indian plantation society was constructed" (91). "Forced to put on Tia's dress, Antoinette, the poor white, takes on the mantle of the nigger" (Gregg 90). Wearing Tia's dress, Antoinette meets an English family, the Luttrells, through whom Annette will meet Mr. Mason. Because of the contrast between their beauty and "beautiful clothes" and her own appearance Antoinette cannot return their gaze at her, instead "looking away down at the flagstones" (*WSS* 21). She becomes an object of the Luttrells' derisive laughter prompted by her transgression of aestheticized class distinctions expressed in dress and demeanor. After the Luttrells leave, Annette tells Antoinette that she has "behaved very oddly" and that her "dress was even dirtier than usual" (22). On learning that it is Tia's dress, Annette, now racializing the dirty "matter out of place" (Douglas 35), orders Christophine to burn it. In the subsequent quarrel between Annette and Christophine, Christophine, deflecting attention from Antoinette's play with Tia and her own encouragement of it, shames Annette's domestic management and neglect, making the dirty dress synonymous with the "fact" that Antoinette "run wild, she grow up worthless. And nobody care" (*WSS* 22). Annette, Antoinette speculates, sells a ring in order to buy new dress material, and she and Christophine begin "mending and sewing" (23), preparing Annette and Antoinette to meet the approving gaze of English gentlemen and their families.

The notions of dirt, neglect, worth, repair, and renewal cited by the characters are part of "a systematic ordering and classification of matter, in so far as ordering involves rejecting inappropriate elements" (Douglas 35). The ordering instantiates the racial, class, ethnic, and gender hierarchies of the plantocracy. The fastidious effort to keep cockroaches out of the house is cross-cut with the anxious desire of the family not to be seen as "white cockroaches" (*WSS* 20), socially "low" white people. Rochester's upper-class English notions of dirt and cleanliness structure his sense of Antoinette's laxness as the mistress of the house at Granbois. He marks as inappropriate such things as Antoinette's scented hair, the frangipani wreath, Christophine's (and later Antoinette's) bad language, Antoinette's extravagance and feeding of "faces" "unfamilar" to him (75). When Antoinette does try to save herself and her family from Daniel's imputations by telling her side of the story, Rochester hears her "imitating a Negro's voice, singing and insolent": "'I might never be able to tell you in any other place or at any other time. No other time, now. You frightened?'" (106). (In the third installment of her dream Antoinette hears Tia say, "You frightened?" [155]).

Soiled clothes feature in the first and second installments of Antoinette's serial dream, and through intertextual allusion to the nondescriptly clothed, vampiric, or on-all-fours Bertha Mason of *Jane Eyre* in the third installment. In each dream Antoinette is being stalked: in the first by the "heavy footsteps" of a hater, who avoids her gaze; in the second, a nuptial dream, by a man whose face is "black" with hatred (50), recalling Bertha Mason's "blackened inflation of . . . lineaments" in *Jane Eyre* [Brontë 311]); in the third by the rumoured ghost of Thornfield Hall, Bertha Mason. In the last installment "the man who hated" her speaks in Rochester's voice, calling "Bertha! Bertha!" (155). Emery summarizes well the Freudian (and stock post-Freudian) view of "the dynamics of dream work":

a specific dream logic creates images, symbols, and stories that condense or displace other images and events, those from our unconscious minds and those from our everyday experience. Dream symbols thus become "overdetermined," resistant to exhaustive explanation or any exclusive meaning because of their multiple associations. In this dream logic, spatial relations may indicate relations ordinarily temporal or causal, so that our usual sense of history and event no longer explains the meaning of a dream. (55)

Given the premonitory quality of the second and third installments of Antoinette's dream and Antoinette's labeling as Obeah Rochester's change of her name, they may be read as mantic communication with departed spirits, understood by Rhys on the model of a form of Obeah practiced in early twentieth-century Dominica (Steber, "What Is Obeah?" [3]).

In the first dream Antoinette is "walking in the forest" (23). The stalking compresses aspects of her having been followed by a mocking "little girl," a "strange negro" (20). Tia's verbal attack, the gentleman's attack through laughter, and her mother's passive aggressive refusal to "speak to" or "look at" her after the incident of the dirty dress are transmuted into a physical attack, in which "though" she "struggled and screamed" she "could not move." The disheveling of her clothes is registered in the "covering sheet" being "on the floor" when she wakes "crying" (23). The anxieties excited by the little girl's taunt "white cockroach" (20) and the gazes that say "white nigger" (21, 109) are later caught up in Antoinette's response to Amelié's mockery of her as a "white cockroach" (83). Rochester observes that Antoinette "took a pair of scissors from the round table, cut through the hem and tore the sheet in half, then each half into strips" (84). The intact sheet may be read as metonymic of Antoinette's honeymoon ideal of a unified upper-class white creole feminine subjectivity, her action as externalizing the violent anger accompanying its collapse and the psychological and epistemic violence integral to the intertwined racial, class, and sexual tension between Amelié and Antoinette. The cut-up sheet (part of the bedclothes) takes the place of the disheveled clothes in the first dream.

Antoinette dreams the second installment in the convent after Mr. Mason hints at his marriage plans for her; the dream anticipates her body becoming, as Asha Varadharajan argues Douloti's does in Mahasweta Devi's "Douloti the Beautiful," "the brutalized terrain for the circulation of capital" (109). The dream is, Antoinette says, "mixed up" with the "thought" of Annette, her death and her recognition of Antoinette in an attempted wave from "the head of the cobblestoned road at Coulibri" when she is wearing "her mended habit riding a borrowed horse" (*WSS* [51]) on her way to "a dance or a moonlight picnic" before the remarriage (23). This characterization of the dream suggests that it may be a communication with Annette's spirit. In the dream Antoinette walks towards the forest in what is seemingly a bridal dress ("white and beautiful"), "holding up the skirt" because she does not "wish to get it soiled." Confronted by the man's gaze, "black with hatred," and now crying, Antoinette "do[es] not try to hold up" her "dress" and it "trails in the dirt" (50). Later in the novel Rochester, disgusted by what he thinks a "'very dirty'" habit, recalls Antoinette telling him that when nonwhite local women "'don't hold their dress up it's for respect [. . .] [o]r for feast days or going to Mass. [. . .] [I]t shows it isn't the only dress they have'" (71).

The gaze of the man in the dream brings about a racialized transformation of sumptuary habit. In an enclosed garden (a symbol of the Virgin), among unfamiliar trees (English shade and mordantly ironized protection), Antoinette stumbles over the dress and "cannot get up" when she thinks that "it" will happen "[a]t the top" of the steps (50). As terrified object of the man's malevolent intent, Antoinette is past caring about upholding racialized cultural distinctions among women. That she is unused to the erasure of the desire to preserve distinctions in the immediacy of a moment, to walking with a trailing skirt, hobbles her, Rhys implies. The cognate scene with Rochester is the one in which he finds the overgrown garden of the priest and becomes lost in the forest, with the "green menace" (123) of "undergrowth and creepers" threatening to trip him up (87). Baptiste, one of a search party, rescues Rochester. The tree in which the dream Antoinette takes refuge may be read as a dream symbol of Christophine, whose last name, Dubois, means literally, as Rodríguez points out, "of the forest" (9).

Several spatial and temporal settings, from Antoinette's Caribbean past and from *Jane Eyre*, are compressed in the third dream: Thornfield Hall; Jane's bedroom in Thornfield Hall,[29] redecorated in the style of the red room of Jane's childhood, a place of punishment for insubordination, which metamorphoses into Aunt Cora's room from a scene in which Aunt Cora, with her face to the wall, has said to Antoinette, "'The Lord has forsaken us'" (95); Coulibri, a loved Caribbean place that Rochester has not "spoilt" for her as he has Granbois (121); the stalking of Antoinette in her first dream; the man and the flight of stairs from her second dream; her earlier appeals to Christophine for salvation; her own voice taunting Rochester with "You frightened?"; and details from the inn host's account of Bertha's death in *Jane Eyre*. The red sky in which Antoinette sees all her life twists up the firing of Coulibri; Brontë's Rochester's nightmarish description of the contaminating effect of Bertha, "a world quivering with the ferment of tempest" (335), which makes him suicidal; and, Wilson Harris suggests, the food-bearing tree of the Arawak Indians fired "by the Caribs at a time of war when the Arawaks seek refuge in its branches" (143). Antoinette's look at the "hard stones" below the leads of Thornfield Hall after the hating man calls "Bertha! Bertha!" (155) recalls her refusal, while wearing Tia's dress, to meet the mocking gaze of the English Luttrells as she looks "away down at the flagstones" (21), which metamorphose into the pool at Coulibri. Antoinette does not seek or find a reflection of herself in the pool. The stone that Tia throws is also compressed in the dream look. Tia, recognized in childhood "through the racialist stereotype of the hardy, physically superior, animallike, lazy negro" (Gregg 88), and the various kinds of business at the pool are, in Antoinette's earlier narrative, sites of racialized class threshold for her.

The dream may be read as a mantic communication with the spirit of Aunt Cora and with the "ghost of a woman" said to haunt Thornfield Hall whom Antoinette thinks is "following" her, "chasing" her (*WSS* 153). "'There are always two deaths, the real one and the one people know about,'" says Antoinette of her mother's life (106). The "ghost of a woman" she sees in her dream is, then, interpretable as Antoinette herself in England, as she writes in her letter to Richard "'dying because it is so cold and dark'" (150), as much as the incarcerated Annette or Brontë's Bertha Mason.

In recent critical accounts of Antoinette's leap from the roof of Thornfield Hall, "the possibility of a unified self and an integrated consciousness that can transcend material circumstance is represented as the fulfilment of desire" (Kaplan 152) on Antoinette's part. This possibility assumes a liberal humanist desire. Brathwaite finds the implied transcendence of the socioeconomic power structures of a "race-founded & race-foundered" colonial culture unrealistic, a "figment" ("Post-Cautionary Tale" 74). Spivak describes the leap towards Tia and the pool in language that implies that Antoinette desires a self-consolidating mirror ("Three Women's Texts" 250). She reads Antoinette's desire for a self-consolidating mirror as imperialist ideology, but by collapsing a colonial into an imperial project of subject-constitution. She notes that Antoinette, occupies a position "between the English imperialist and the black native" (250), but this observation does not inform her reading of Antoinette's narcissism. Antoinette's whiteness is "set outside [the] history and geography" of the racialization of differences among "white" peoples (Bonnett 180). Gregg writes of a "jump into the mirror image of Tia and Coulibri," which scripts "[t]he cathexis between Antoinette and Tia, as Self/Other, Narcissus/Echo" as "the construction and de(con)struction of the white Creole woman (99–100).

Tiffin speaks of Antoinette and Tia: "Victims of history, one is the true sacrificial mirror image of the other. . . . Here at last is a mirror in which Antoinette can perceive herself, not the English distortion of self" ("Mirror and Mask" 338). To read Tia's appearance in the third installment of the dream as the summoning of a mirror is to privilege one earlier moment in their relationship and to reduce the complexity of the ways in which Tia is twisted up in the dream and divinatory "logic" of Antoinette's narrative. In Erwin's formulation, Antoinette fantasizes a "merging of 'Antoinette' with 'Tia,' or blackness," produced in the novel by placing her "life under English eyes, in an attempt to construct an identity for it impossible in the colonial setting itself" (155–56). For Emery, Antoinette's "choice" of "flight" can be made "not because she has consolidated her character, but because she has lost and multiplied it, become [sexually] enslaved, and thus joined the history of the blacks on the islands, learning from them traditional means of resistance. . . . [S]he joins a community of black women in her final leap, while borrowing from all of black and native cultures in her quest for place" (59). Emery does not broach the question of reciprocation of Antoinette's communal identification on the part of the black women she cites, the question of a "shared feeling of belonging or merging" (Dorothy Allison, qtd. in Iris Young 309).

I borrow my chapter title, "A Place-to-Be-From" from Erwin's fine essay "'Like in a Looking-Glass': History and Narrative in Wide Sargasso Sea." She poses questions about the way the "subject of a narrative . . . reads itself into history by means of that narrative" ([143]). Rhys reads and writes Wide Sargasso Sea into history through engagement with a range of canonical and (from a European perspective) recondite intertexts: Dominican autoethnographic discourses of nature and place; Froude's *The English in the West Indies*; a European ethnographic discourse of white creole degeneracy; an early twentieth-century Dominican moral panic over Obeah; the "Letter of the Law" in the British Caribbean of the 1830s; stories about "Indian" Warner; *Othello*; *Jane Eyre*; and the Mr. Howard narrative. These are some of "the 'materials' that went into the writing of *Wide Sargasso Sea*" and Rhys's representations of self/Other relationships that "throw light on the dense particularity of that novel" (Hulme, "Locked Heart" 23).

Christophine explicitly comments on shifts in the culture of terror and bondedness that structured master/slave relations. Rhys marks the shift, too, in her treatment of the response of servants to Rochester's sexual act with Amélie, constructed in the text as a repetition of the exploitative conduct of male slaveowners. Rose, the cook, departs immediately, leaving Baptiste to tell Rochester: "'She won't stay in this house'" (117). Baptiste refuses Rochester the appellations "'sir' or 'master,'" but remains attached to his socioeconomic status as overseer (117). Christophine confronts Rochester directly over his behavior with Antoinette and Amélie in the matter, telling him "'Don't think I frightened of you either'" (124). Antoinette, the white creole woman, however, has divinatory dreams of terror generated from the changing social and economic relations between racial communities and an imperial imparting of a gendered, "moral, cultural and territorial content to Whiteness" through "a triple conflation of 'White,' 'Europe' and 'Christian'" (Bonnett 175) that seizes on signs of perceived colonial degeneracy. Rochester himself is terrorized by the "green menace," his xenophobia, misogyny, racialization of sexual desire, and fears of emasculation. Rhys engages in close intellectual, imaginative, and narrative work with and on her intertexts to relocate the lives of Brontë's Bertha Mason and Edward Fairfax Rochester in and as a product of a colonial interregnum. By attending to that work, one may begin to comprehend the historical and political situatedness of Rhys's authorial and narrative voices in the novel.

NOTES

1. I elucidate these references and their implications in "The Tropical Extravagance of Bertha Mason."

2. Emery's characterization of the apprenticeship period as neocolonial is anachronistic.

3. Ileana Rodríguez argues that "when garden goes wild, bush, this image as represesentation of white psychic disorder also stands for maroonage, for guerilla warfare under colonialism, and therefore as metaphor for liberation, self-determination, and national formation" (128).

4. Antoinette says, "it was as if a door opened and I was somewhere else, something else. Not myself any longer" (24).

5. Moira Ferguson, by contrast, in her reading of *Wide Sargasso Sea* locates subaltern being in insurgency. The "unassailable power" of the "community" of African-Caribbeans "dominates" the novel "despite the white creole author's transparent in-

tention to heroinize a victimized Antoinette" (13).

6. "Murder and Superstition" [3].

7. There have been several fine readings of Obeah in *Wide Sargasso Sea*: Emery's chapter on the novel in *Jean Rhys at "World's End,"* Wilson Harris's "Carnival of Psyche," Elaine Campbell's "Reflections of Obeah in Jean Rhys' Fiction," and Elaine Savory's "'Another Poor Devil of a Human Being . . .': Jean Rhys and the novel as Obeah." Obeah becomes in Harris's and Campbell's readings a sign of Rhys's transcendence of a white creole consciousness, of a catholicity of imaginative vision, and for Emery a mark of Antoinette's identification with Caribbean difference that multiplies rather than consolidates her character (59), giving her an elsewhere from which to counter dominant imperial discourse (62). Savory argues, in speaking of Rhys writing "'the novel as obeah,'" that Rhys "thought of writing as summoning spirits or drawing on a level of consciousness far beyond the logical or rational, which gave her the free space in which to survive her difficult life and to deserve a proper death" (26–27). She concludes that the Caribbeanness of the ways in which "the spiritual saturates" Rhys's "writing" lies in their "linking of defiance towards an oppressive use of community with spiritual forms of subversion. Obeah was one, and witchcraft, in Europe, another" (36).

8. [Steber], "Obeah Legislation."

9. Leeward Islands. No. 6 of 1904.

10. Judith R. Walkowitz notes that the "'imaginary' solution" to the threat integral to the "classic moral panic" entails "tougher laws, moral isolation, and symbolic court action" (121).

11. In the news report Ann Tuitt is said to have stated in her defense: "With regard to the grave yard, at night time I go to the Judge's yard to clean out the latrine. I never went to the cemetery. The phial containing the white liquid I use for headache. I am never without these things in case of sickness. Sometime in July last I was applied to for smelling salt for a dying person, which I keep. I have the 'luck' seed for a long time. But the roast potatoe [sic] with grass I keep for bodily disease. I cannot account for the balance of the things. My house and trunk are always kept unlocked." Evidence of her "respectable" character was called. The Rees Williamses did not appear as character witnesses.

12. Leeward Islands. No. 6 of 1904.

13. "AN ACT to Consolidate and Amend the LAWS Relating to SLAVES," 122.

14. The phrase "part of the creed of most Dominicans" is used in "Superstition," "right thinking" in "Murder and Superstition."

15. The term "masses" is drawn from "What Is Obeah?" and the concept of "real" Christianity from "Superstition."

16. In his narrative he becomes the heroic campaigner for a further emancipation of the "masses," with whom he can identify himself only through the figures of "black ancestors" and the great-grandparents "kidnapped from the West Coast of Africa," and the possessor of the cultural capital (civilization, humanity, real Christianity, education, right thinking, good mind, and noble heart) his "masses" lack. He does draw a distinction between the Obeah of the great-grandparents' generation ("whatever that was") and the "present practice" of Obeah ("a sure species of humbug," one of the signs of which is "the proposition for human sacrifices for propitiatory offerings").

17. Both letters are reprinted by Steber in "The Obeah Correspondence."

18. Both Righton and Steber linked the speaking of patois (and poor literacy) and the credulity of believers in Obeah. [Righton], Editorial, *Dominican* 12 Nov. 1903: [2]; [Steber], "What is Obeah?" [3].

19. Rhys's story, "The Bishop's Feast," a narrator's reminiscence of a girlhood in Dominica published in *Sleep It Off Lady*, features a newly arrived Catholic bishop. The prospective change in the order of nuns referred to in the story occurred in 1937, the Order of the Faithful Virgin being replaced by the Missionary Canonesses of St Augustin (Honychurch 177).

20. Erwin's quotation is from p. 132 of the Penguin edition of *Wide Sargasso Sea*.

21. Anna remembers of Anne Chewett that "she had been in gaol for obeah (obeah-women who dig up dead people and cut their fingers off and go to gaol for it—it's hands that are obeah)—but can't they do damned funny things—Oh if you lived here you wouldn't take them so seriously as all that—" (*Voyage* 139).

22. I discuss this in more detail, and the manner in which the Letter of the Law was used against Lockhart's estate and his heirs, in "James Potter Lockhart and the 'Letter of the Law.'"

23. Sturge and Harvey write: "Nothing can be said in praise of the Legislative Council, which is nominated by the Crown; and it would be difficult to reprobate too strongly the appointment or retention, in the most responsible offices, of men who perpetuate the worst Colonial abuses" (Appendix xviii).

24. One of her prime objects in rereading Ovid and the circulation of the story of Narcissus in Western critical and psychoanalytic archives "to 'give woman' to Echo" (176) is to do for Freud's "race-, class-, and gender-specificity" what she did for Charlotte Brontë's in "Three Women's Texts and a Critique of Imperialism": "incite a degree of rage against the gendered/imperialist narrativization of history, that it should produce so abject a script for him" (177–78).

25. Honychurch also discusses "Indian" Warner (44–45).

26. The orchid is possibly Epidendrum anceps, which may be epiphitic or lithphytic (grow on trees or rocks). See Hodgson, Paine and Anderson 126.

27. Gregg discusses the exchange of clothes (89–91) but does not make the links that I do.

28. Hulme examines the complex ways "matters of race are negotiated" in relation to the Lockhart family's implication in Dominica's 1844 census riots, the "guerre nègre," in Rhys's representations of the burning of Coulibri and Tia's wounding of Antoinette with a stone ("Locked Hearts" 27). In the aftermath of the "guerre nègre," "Jean Philip Motard was executed for throwing a stone at the head of a white planter called Bremner. The following year (1845) Bremner's son married Cora Lockhart, daughter of the 'old' Lockhart who, as the original for Cosway, stands as father to Antoinette in *Wide Sargasso Sea*"(29).

29. The inn host who tells Jane the story of the "conflagration" at Thornfield Hall (Brontë 450) says that Bertha proceeded to a lower story and set fire to Jane's room.

Works Cited

PRIMARY

The Jean Rhys Papers and the David Plante Papers are held by the Department of Special Collections, McFarlin Library, University of Tulsa, Oklahoma.

Rhys, Jean. Add. Mss. 57856. Department of Manuscripts. British Library, London.
———. Add. Mss. 57859, folio 2. Department of Manuscripts. British Library, London.
———. *After Leaving Mr Mackenzie*. 1930. Harmondsworth: Penguin, 1971.
———. "Again the Antilles." *The Left Bank and Other Stories*. 1927. Freeport, NY: Books for Libraries P, 1970. 93–97.
———. "The Birthday." Ts. Jean Rhys Papers.
———. Black Exercise Book. Ms. Jean Rhys Papers.
———. "The Cardboard Dolls'-House." Ts. Jean Rhys Papers.
———. *Good Morning, Midnight*. 1939. Harmondsworth: Penguin, 1969.
———. "Good-bye Marcus, Good-bye Rose." *Sleep It Off Lady: Stories*. 1976. Harmondsworth: Penguin, 1979. 23–30.
———. "The Imperial Road." Ts. Jean Rhys Papers.
———. *The Left Bank and Other Stories*. 1927. Freeport, NY: Books for Libraries P, 1970.
———. Letter to Oliver Stoner. 7 Aug. 1970. Jean Rhys Papers.
———. Letter to Peggy Kirkaldy. 30 July [1957]. Jean Rhys Papers.
———. *Letters 1931–66*. Ed. Francis Wyndham and Diana Melly. 1984. Harmondsworth: Penguin, 1985.
———. "Lost Island. A Childhood: Fragments of Autobiography." Ts. Jean Rhys Papers.
———. "Love." Ts. David Plante Papers.
———. "Mr Howard's House./CREOLE." Ts. Jean Rhys Papers.
———. "Mixing Cocktails." *The Left Bank and Other Stories*. 1927. Freeport, NY: Books for Libraries P, 1970. 87–92.

————. *Quartet.* 1928. Harmondsworth: Penguin, 1973.

————. *Smile Please: An Unfinished Autobiography.* 1979. Harmondsworth: Penguin, 1981.

————. *Tales of the Wide Caribbean.* Ed. Kenneth Ramchand. London: Heinemann, [1986].

————. "Temps Perdi." *Tales of the Wide Caribbean.* Ed. Kenneth Ramchand. London: Heinemann, [1986]. 144–61.

————. *Tigers Are Better-Looking: With a Selection from* The Left Bank. 1968. Harmondsworth: Penguin, 1972.

————. "Trio." *The Left Bank and Other Stories.* 1927. Freeport, NY: Books for Libraries P, 1970. 83–85.

————. "Triple Sec." Ts. Jean Rhys Papers.

————. "Vienne." 1924. *The Gender of Modernism: A Critical Anthology.* Ed. Bonnie Kime Scott. Bloomington: Indiana UP, 1990. 377–81.

————. "Vienne." *The Left Bank and Other Stories.* 1927. Freeport, NY: Books for Libraries P, 1970. 193–256.

————. *Voyage in the Dark.* 1934. Harmondsworth: Penguin, 1969.

————. "*Voyage in the Dark.* Part IV (Original Version)." Ed. Nancy Hemond Brown. *The Gender of Modernism: A Critical Anthology.* Ed. Bonnie Kime Scott. Bloomington: Indiana UP, 1990. 381–89.

————. *Wide Sargasso Sea.* 1966. Harmondsworth: Penguin, 1969.

SECONDARY

"Acrostics." *Dominican* 31 July 1880: [3].

AN ACT to Consolidate and Amend the LAWS Relating to SLAVES. Enclosure in despatch from J. P. Lockhart to Viscount Goderich, 6 July 1831. *British Parliamentary Papers: Reports from Protectors of Slaves in British Colonies Together with the Proceedings and Decisions in Each Case of Complaint between Masters and Slaves 1830–31.* Slave Trade. Vol. 79. Shannon: Irish UP, 1969.

Review of *After Leaving Mr Mackenzie,* by Jean Rhys. *Times Literary Supplement* 5 March 1931: 180.

Alexander, Sally. "Becoming a woman in the 1920s and 1930s." *Metropolis London: Histories and Representations since 1800.* Ed. David Feldman and Gareth Stedman Jones. London: Routledge, 1989. 245–71.

Allen, Walter. "Bertha the Doomed." Rev. of *Wide Sargasso Sea,* by Jean Rhys. *New York Times Book Review* 18 June 1967: 5.

Allfrey, Phyllis Shand. *The Orchid House.* 1953. London: Virago, 1982.

Anderson, Benedict. *Imagined Communities: Reflections on the Origin and Spread of Nationalism.* Rev. ed. London: Verso, 1991.

Angier, Carole. *Jean Rhys: Life and Work.* Rev. ed. Harmondsworth: Penguin, 1992.

"The Approaching Carnival." *Dominica Guardian* 25 Feb. 1905: [2].

Arata, Stephen D. "The Occidental Tourist: *Dracula* and the Anxiety of Reverse Colonization." *Victorian Studies* 33 (1989/90): 621–45.

Armstrong, Nancy. *Desire and Domestic Fiction: A Political History of the Novel.* New York: Oxford U.P., 1987.

"Arrival of the New Bishop of Roseau." *Dominica Guardian* 4 & 11 June 1902: [2]–[3].

Ashcroft, Bill, Gareth Griffiths, and Helen Tiffin. *Key Concepts in Post-Colonial Studies*. London: Routledge, 1998.

Bailey, Peter. "Conspiracies of Meaning: Music-Hall and the Knowingness of Popular Culture." *Past and Present: A Journal of Historical Studies* 144 (Aug. 1994): 138–70.

Baker, Patrick. *Centring the Periphery: Chaos, Order and the Ethnohistory of Dominica*. Montreal: McGill-Queen's UP, 1994.

Bathurst, Lord. Despatch to Murray [copy]. 28 May 1823. Despatches from Secretary of State 1821–1825. Dominica National Archives, Roseau, Dominica.

Bell, Hesketh J. *Administrator Bell to Mr. Chamberlain*, Cd. 1298 (29 July 1902).

———. *Glimpses of a Governor's Life from Diaries, Letters and Memoranda*. London: Sampson, Low, Marston, [1946].

———. "The Imperial Road in Dominica." *West India Committee Circular* 19 (1904): 257–60.

———. *Obeah; Witchcraft in the West Indies*. 1889. Westport, CT: Negro Universities P, 1970.

Bell, Shannon. *Reading, Writing and Rewriting the Prostitute Body*. Bloomington: Indiana UP, 1994.

Bergner, Gwen. "Who Is That Masked Woman? or, The Role of Gender in Fanon's *Black Skin, White Masks*." *PMLA* 110 (1995): 75–88.

Bernheimer, Charles. *Figures of Ill-Repute: Representing Prostitution in Nineteenth-Century France*. Cambridge, MA: Harvard UP, 1989.

Bernstein, Susan David. "Dirty Reading: Sensation Fiction, Women, and Primitivism." *Criticism* 36 (1994): 213–41.

Bhabha, Homi K. *The Location of Culture*. London: Routledge, 1994.

———. "'Race', Time and the Revision of Modernity." *Oxford Literary Review* 13.1–2 (1991): 193–219.

———. "Representation and the Colonial Text: A Critical Exploration of Some Forms of Mimeticism." *The Theory of Reading*. Ed. Frank Gloversmith. Brighton: Harvester, 1984.

Billington-Greig, Teresa. "The Truth about White Slavery." *English Review* June 1913: 428–46.

Bland, Lucy. "'Guardians of the Race,' or 'Vampires upon the Nation's Health'?: Female Sexuality and Its Regulation in Early Twentieth-Century Britain." *The Changing Experience of Women*. Ed. Elizabeth Whitelegg, et al. Oxford: Basil Blackwell in conjunction with the Open U, 1982. 373–88.

Bland, Lucy, and Frank Mort. "Look Out for the 'Good Time' Girl: Dangerous Sexualities as a Threat to National Health." *Formations of Nation and People*. Ed. Formations Editorial Collective. London: Routledge & Kegan Paul, 1984. 131–51.

Bonnett, Alastair. "Constructions of Whiteness in European and American Anti-racism." *Debating Cultural Hybridity: Multi-cultural Identities and the Politics of Anti-racism*. Ed. Pnina Werbner and Tariq Modood. London: Zed, 1997. 173–92.

Boromé, Joseph A. "How Crown Colony Government Came to Dominica by 1898." *Caribbean Studies* 9.3 (Oct. 1969): 26–67.

Boucé, Paul-Gabriel. "Imagination, Pregnant Women, and Monsters, in Eighteenth-Century England and France." *Sexual Underworlds of the Enlightenment*. Manchester: Manchester UP, 1987. 86–100.

Bowen, Stella. *Drawn from Life: Reminiscences*. London: Collins, 1941.

Bowlby, Rachel. *Still Crazy after All These Years: Women, Writing & Psychoanalysis*. London: Routledge, 1992.

Brathwaite, [Edward] Kamau. *The Colonial Encounter: Language*. N.p.: Centre for Commonwealth Literature and Research, 1984.

———. "A Post-Cautionary Tale of the Helen of Our Wars." *Wasafiri* 22 (Autumn 1995): 69–81.

Brenkman, John. "Narcissus in the Text." *Georgia Review* 30 (1976): 293–327.

British Parliamentary Papers: West India Royal Commission. Appendix C. Volumes III and IV (1898). Colonies. West Indies 8. Shannon: Irish UP, 1971.

Brontë, Charlotte. *Jane Eyre*. 1847. Harmondsworth: Penguin, 1966.

Brydon, Diana, and Helen Tiffin. *Decolonising Fictions*. Sydney: Dangaroo, 1993.

Buck-Morss, Susan. "The Flaneur [sic], the Sandwichman and the Whore: The Politics of Loitering." *New German Critique* 39 (Fall 1986): 99–140.

Bullough, Vern, and Bonnie Bullough. *Women and Prostitution: A Social History*. Buffalo: Prometheus, 1987.

Burke, Kenneth. *A Grammar of Motives*. 1945. Berkeley: U of California P, 1969.

Butler, Judith. *Bodies That Matter: On the Discursive Limits of "Sex."* New York: Routledge, 1993.

———. *Gender Trouble: Feminism and the Subversion of Identity*. New York: Routledge, 1990.

Campbell, Elaine. "Reflections of Obeah in Jean Rhys's Fiction." *Kunapipi* 4.2 (1982): 42–50.

Carlyle, Thomas. "Signs of the Times." 1829. *A Carlyle Reader: Selections from the Writings of Thomas Carlyle*. Ed. G. B. Tennyson. New York: Modern Library, 1969. 31–54.

Carr, Helen. *Jean Rhys*. Plymouth: Northcote House in assoc. with the British Council, 1996.

"Cases for the Circuit Court." *Dominica Guardian* 7 May 1909: [3].

Chandler, Arthur. "Paris 1937." *Historical Dictionary of World's Fairs and Expositions, 1851–1988*. Ed. John E. Findling and Kimberly D. Pelle. Westport, CT: Greenwood, 1990. 283–90.

Chrisman, Laura. "The Imperial Unconscious? Representations of Imperial Discourse." *Colonial Discourse and Post-Colonial Theory: A Reader*. Ed. Patrick Williams and Laura Chrisman. Hemel Hempstead: Harvester Wheatsheaf, 1993. 498–516.

Cixous, Hélène. "Sorties: Out and Out: Attacks/Ways Out/Forays." *The Newly Born Woman*. By Hélène Cixous and Catherine Clément. 1975. Trans. Betsy Wing. Manchester: Manchester UP, 1986. 63–132.

Cixous, Hélène, and Catherine Clément. *The Newly Born Woman*. Trans. Betsy Wing. Manchester: Manchester UP, 1986.

Clark, Anna. "The Politics of Seduction in English Popular Culture, 1748–1848." *The Progress of Romance: The Politics of Popular Fiction*. Ed. Jean Radford. London: Routledge & Kegan Paul, 1986. 46–70.

Cliff, Michelle. "Caliban's Daughter: The Tempest and the Teapot." *Frontiers* 12.2 (1991): 36–51.

Colebrooke, Sir W.M.G. Letter to Lieutenant-Governor Henry Light [copy]. 10 June 1837. Despatches from Secretary of State 1837. Dominica National Archives, Roseau, Dominica.

————. Letter to Lieutenant-Governor Henry Light [copy]. 10 Aug. 1837. Despatches from Secretary of State 1837. Dominica National Archives, Roseau, Dominica.

————. Letter to Lieutenant-Governor Henry Light [copy]. 24 Aug. 1837. Despatches from Secretary of State 1837. Dominica National Archives, Roseau, Dominica.

————. Letter to Lieutenant-Governor Henry Light [copy]. 13 Nov. 1837. Despatches from Secretary of State 1837. Dominica National Archives, Roseau, Dominica.

Conley, Verena Andermatt. *Hélène Cixous*. Hemel Hempstead: Harvester Wheatsheaf, 1992.

————. *Hélène Cixous: Writing the Feminine*. Rev. ed. Lincoln: U of Nebraska P, 1991.

Conrad, Joseph. *Almayer's Folly: A Story of an Eastern River*. Ed. Floyd Eugene Eddleman and David Leon Higdon. Cambridge: Cambridge UP, 1994.

————. *Heart of Darkness*. 1902. Harmondsworth: Penguin, 1973.

Corke, Helen. *Lawrence & Apocalypse*. London: William Heinemann, 1933.

————. *Neutral Ground*. London: Arthur Barker, 1933.

Courtney, W. L. *The Feminine Note in Fiction*. London: Chapman & Hall, 1904.

Cracknell, Basil. *Dominica*. Newton Abbot: David & Charles, 1973.

Creed, Barbara. *The Monstrous-Feminine: Film, Feminism, Psychoanalysis*. London: Routledge, 1993.

"Creole." *The Encyclopedia Brittanica: A Dictionary of Arts, Sciences, and General Literature* Vol VI. 9th. ed. Edinburgh: Adam and Charles Black, 1877.

Crosby, Earnest H. "The Real 'White Man's Burden.'" *Dominica Guardian* 26 April 1899: [3].

————. "The Real 'White Man's Burden.'" *Swords and Ploughshares*. London: Grant Richards, 1903. 33–35.

Dabydeen, David. "On Not Being Milton: Nigger Talk in England Today." *Crisis and Creativity in the New Literatures in English*. Ed. Geoffrey V. Davis and Hena Maes-Jelinek. Amsterdam: Rodopi, 1990. 61–74.

Dalton, Anne B. "The Devil and the Virgin: Writing Sexual Abuse in *Incidents in the Life of a Slave Girl*." *Violence, Silence, and Anger: Women's Writing as Transgression*. Ed. Deirdre Lashgari. Charlottesville: UP of Virginia, 1995. 38–61.

Davidson, Arnold E. *Jean Rhys*. New York: Frederick Ungar, 1985.

Davies, Michele L. "Healing Sylvia: Accounting for the Textual 'Discovery' of the Unconscious." *Sociology* 27.1 (Feb. 1993): 110–20.

[Davies, William.] "1887: A Retrospect." *Dominica Dial* 7 Jan. 1888: [2].

————. "Froude Localised." *Dominica Dial* 17 Mar. 1888: [2].

————. "Mr Froude's Friends." *Dominica Dial* 14 Apr. 1888: [3].

————. "The *Mot d'Ordre*." *Dominica Guardian* 22 June 1898: [3].

————. "Negrophobia: A Review." *Dominica Dial* 10 Nov. 1888: [3].

————. "Patriots Wanted." *Dominica Guardian* 15 July 1893: [2].

————. "Rubbish on the West Indies, or Froude's Long Bow." *Dominica Dial* 19 Mar. 1888: [3].

————. "Their Photographs." *Dominica Dial* 30 Oct. 1886: [3]–[4].

————. "An Ungrateful Munchausen [sic]." *Dominica Dial* 24 Mar. 1888: [2].

Davin, Anna. "Imperialism and Motherhood." *History Workshop* 5 (Sping 1978): 9–65.

Davis, Tracy C. *Actresses as Working Women: Their Social Identity in Victorian Culture*. London: Routledge, 1991.

Destination Dominica: The Official Visitor Magazine of the Dominica Hotel & Tourism Association. North Miami, FL: Ulrich Communications for the Dominica Hotel & Tourism Association, 1996.

Dijkstra, Bram. *Idols of Perversity: Fantasies of Feminine Evil in Fin-de-Siècle Culture*. New York: Oxford UP, 1986.

A Disgusted Dominican [pseudonym]. "C'est Manicou." Letter. *Dominica Guardian* 5 Aug. 1893: [2].

Dominica [pseudonym]. "Superstition." Letter. *Dominica Guardian* 14 May 1904: [2].

Dominica Guardian [special edition] 11 Dec. 1893.

Dominica Guardian [special edition] 22 Dec. 1893.

A Dominican [pseudonym]. "An Unmerited Attack." Letter. *Dominican* 6 Nov. 1902: 2.

Douglas, Mary. *Purity and Danger: An Analysis of the Concepts of Pollution and Taboo*. 1966. London: Ark, 1984.

Draper, R. P., ed. *D. H. Lawrence: The Critical Heritage*. London: Routledge & Kegan Paul, 1970.

"An Editor's Complete Apology to Another." *Trinidad Mirror*. Rpt. *Dominica Guardian* 26 Mar. 1904: [3].

Edwards, Bryan. *The History, Civil and Commercial, of the British Colonies in the West Indies*. 2 vols. 1793. Rpt. from 5th ed., 1818–19. New York: Arno, 1972.

Eliot, E. C. *Broken Atoms*. London: Geoffrey Bles, 1938.

Emery, Mary Lou. *Jean Rhys at "World's End": Novels of Colonial and Sexual Exile*. Austin: U of Texas P, 1990.

Review of *The English in the West Indies*, by James Anthony Froude. *Voice* (St. Lucia). Rpt. *Dominica Dial* 5 May 1888: [4].

Erwin, Lee. "'Like in a Looking-Glass': History and Narrative in *Wide Sargasso Sea*." *Novel: A Forum on Fiction* 22.2 (Winter 1989): 143–58.

Faber, Richard. *High Road to England*. London: Faber, 1985.

Fadelle, Joseph. Letter to Sir E.J.M. MacGregor [extract]. 9 Feb. 1835. Enclosure No. 8, despatch No. 361. *British Parliamentary Papers: Papers Relating to the Slave Trade and the Abolition of Slavery in the West India Colonies 1836*. Slave Trade. Vol. 83. Shannon: Irish UP, 1969. 354.

Fanon, Frantz. *Black Skin, White Masks*. Trans. Charles Lam Markmann. 1967. London: Pluto, 1986.

Febvre, Lucien, and Henri-Jean Martin. *The Coming of the Book: The Impact of Printing 1450–1800*. Trans. David Gerard. Ed. Geoffrey Nowell-Smith and David Wootton. London: NLB, 1976.

Felski, Rita. *The Gender of Modernity*. Cambridge, MA: Harvard UP, 1995.

Ferguson, Moira. "Sending the Younger Son across the Wide Sargasso Sea: The New Colonizer Arrives." *Jean Rhys Review* 6.1 (1993): 2–16.

Fisher, H.A.L. *A History of Europe. Volume II. From the Beginning of the Eighteenth Century to 1935*. 1935. London: Collins, 1960.

Ford, Ford Madox. Preface: Rive Gauche. *The Left Bank and Other Stories*. By Jean Rhys. 1927. Freeport, NY: Books for Libraries P, 1970. 7–27.

———. Extract from *The Spirit of the People*. *Writing Englishness 1900–1950: An Introductory Sourcebook on National Identity*. Ed. Judy Giles and Tim Middleton. London: Routledge, 1995. 46–52.

Foucault, Michel. "The Art of Telling the Truth." *Politics, Philosophy, Culture: Interviews and Other Writings 1977–1984*. Ed. Lawrence D. Kritzman. Trans. Alan Sheridan, et al. New York: Routledge, 1988. 86–95.

Fraser, Sylvia. *My Father's House: A Memoir of Incest and of Healing*. Toronto: Doubleday Canada, 1987.

"Free Will or Compulsion?" *Dominica Guardian* 22 June 1898: [2].

Freeman, Judi. *Picasso and the Weeping Women: The Years of Marie Thérèse Walter & Dora Maar*. Los Angeles: Los Angeles County Museum and New York: Rizzoli, 1994.

Freud, Sigmund. "On the History of the Psycho-analytic Movement." *Collected Papers*. Vol. 1. Trans. Joan Riviere. 1924. New York: Basic, 1959. 287–359.

Frickey, Pierrette M., ed. *Critical Perspectives on Jean Rhys*. Washington, DC: Three Continents, 1990.

Froude, James Anthony. *The English in the West Indies or, The Bow of Ulysses*. 1888. New York: Negro Universities P, 1988.

Frow, John. "Intertextuality and Ontology." *Intertextuality: Theories and Practices*. Ed. Michael Worton and Judith Still. Manchester: Manchester UP, 1990. 45–55.

Fussell, Paul. *Abroad: British Literary Traveling between the Wars*. New York: Oxford UP, 1980.

Gallop, Jane. *Around 1981: Academic Feminist Literary Theory*. New York: Routledge, 1992.

———. *The Daughter's Seduction: Feminism and Psychoanalysis*. 1982. Ithaca: Cornell UP, 1984.

Gardiner, Judith Kegan. "Good Morning, Midnight; Good Night, Modernism." *Boundary 2* 11 (Fall–Winter 1982–83): 233–52.

———. *Rhys, Stead, Lessing, and the Politics of Empathy*. Bloomington: Indiana UP, 1989.

"The Garrison on Parade." *Dominica Guardian* [special edition] 11 Dec. 1893: [2].

Gates, Henry Louis, Jr. *Figures in Black: Words, Signs, and the "Racial" Self*. New York: Oxford UP, 1987.

Gilman, Sander L. *Difference and Pathology: Stereotypes of Sexuality, Race, and Madness*. Ithaca, NY: Cornell UP, 1985.

———. *Disease and Representation: Images of Illness from Madness to AIDS*. Ithaca, NY: Cornell UP, 1988.

———. "Sexology, Psychoanalysis, and Degeneration: From a Theory of Race to a Race for Theory." *Degeneration: The Dark Side of Progress*. Ed. J. Edward Chamberlin and Sander L. Gilman. New York: Columbia UP, 1985. 72–96.

Glenelg, Lord. Despatch to Sir W.M.G. Colebrooke [copy]. 29 Apr. 1837. Despatches from Secretary of State 1837. Dominica National Archives, Roseau, Dominica.

———. Despatch to Sir W.M.G. Colebrooke [copy]. 24 Oct. 1837. Despatches from Secretary of State 1837. Dominica National Archives, Roseau, Dominica.

Gordimer, Nadine. *The Essential Gesture: Writing, Politics and Places*. Ed. Stephen Clingman. 1988. Harmondsworth: Penguin, 1989.

Gould, Gerald. Review of *After Leaving Mr Mackenzie*, by Jean Rhys. *Observer* 8 Feb. 1931: 6.

Greenblatt, Stephen. *Renaissance Self-Fashioning from More to Shakespeare*. Chicago: U of Chicago P, 1980.

Gregg, Veronica Marie. *Jean Rhys's Historical Imagination: Reading and Writing the Creole*. Chapel Hill: U of North Carolina P, 1995.

Grosz, Elizabeth. "Inscriptions and Body-Maps." *Feminine/Masculine and Representation*. Ed. Terry Threadgold and Anne Cranny-Francis. Sydney: Allen & Unwin, 1990. 62–74.

———. "The In(ter)vention of Feminist Knowledges." *Crossing Boundaries: Feminisms and the Critique of Knowledges*. Ed. Barbara Caine, E.A. Grosz, and Marie de Lepervanche. Sydney: Allen & Unwin, 1988. 92–104.

———. *Volatile Bodies: Toward a Corporeal Feminism*. St Leonards: Allen & Unwin, 1994.

Grudin, Peter. "Jane and the Other Mrs Rochester: Excess and Restraint in *Jane Eyre*." *Novel* 10 (1977): 145–57.

Guide to the Jean Rhys Papers, Department of Special Collections, McFarlin Library, University of Tulsa, Oklahoma.

Hacking, Ian. "The Making and Molding of Child Abuse." *Critical Inquiry* 17 (1991): 253–88.

Haldane, Charlotte. *Motherhood and Its Enemies*. London: Chatto & Windus, 1927.

Hall, Douglas. *Modigliani*. Rev. ed. Oxford: Phaidon, 1984.

Hamilton, Sir R. *Report of the Royal Commission (appointed in September, 1893) to Inquire into the Condition and Affairs of the Island of Dominica and Correspondence Relating Thereto*, C. 7477 (1894).

Haraway, Donna J. *Simians, Cyborgs, and Women: The Reinvention of Nature*. New York: Routledge, 1991.

Harris, Wilson. "Carnival of Psyche: Jean Rhys's *Wide Sargasso Sea*." *Kunapipi* 2 (1980): 142–50.

Harrison, Nancy R. *Jean Rhys and the Novel as Women's Text*. Chapel Hill: U of North Carolina P, 1988.

Heath, Jane. "Helen Corke and D. H. Lawrence: Sexual Identity and Literary Relations." *D. H. Lawrence: Critical Assessments, Volume II*. Ed. David Ellis and Ornella De Zordo. Mountfield: Helm Information, 1992. 43–63.

Herman, Judith Lewis. *Trauma and Recovery*. New York: Basic, 1992.

Hodgson, Margaret, Roland Paine, and Neville Anderson. *A Guide to Orchids of the World*. North Ryde: Angus & Robertson, 1991.

Hollander, Martien Kappers-den. "A Gloomy Child and Its Devoted Godmother: *Barred, Sous les Verrous*, and *In de Strik*." *Jean Rhys Review* 1.2 (Spring 1987): 20–30.

———. "Measure for Measure: *Quartet* and *When the Wicked Man*." *Jean Rhys Review* 2.2 (Spring 1988): 2–17.

Honychurch, Lennox. *The Dominica Story: A History of the Island*. London: Macmillan, 1995.

Hopwood, Mr., and Sir Richard Webster. In debate on the Criminal Law Amendment Bill. House of Commons. 31 July 1885. *Hansard's Parliamentary Debates: Third Series*. Vol. 300. 1885. New York: Klaus Reprint, 1971.

Howells, Coral Ann. *Jean Rhys*. Hemel Hempstead: Harvester Wheatsheaf, 1991.

Hughes, Richard. *A High Wind in Jamaica*. 1929. London: Chatto & Windus, 1965.

Hulme, Peter. *Colonial Encounters: Europe and the Native Caribbean, 1492–1797*. London: Methuen, 1986.

————. "The Locked Heart: The Creole Family Romance of *Wide Sargasso Sea*—An Historical and Biographical Analysis." *Jean Rhys Review* 6.1 (1993): 20–36.

————. "Polytropic Man: Tropes of Sexuality and Mobility in Early Colonial Discourse." *Europe and Its Others.* Vol. II. Ed. Francis Barker, Peter Hulme, Margaret Iversen and Diana Loxley. Colchester: U of Essex, 1985. 17–32.

Hulme, Peter, and Neil L. Whitehead, ed. *Wild Majesty: Encounters with Caribs from Columbus to the Present Day. An Anthology.* Oxford: Clarendon P, 1992.

Huston, Nancy. "Tales of War and Tears of Women." *Women's Studies International Forum* 5.3–4 (1982): 271–82.

Huyssen, Andreas. *After the Great Divide: Modernism, Mass Culture, Postmodernism.* Bloomington: Indiana UP, 1986.

Impartial [pseudonym]. "The Colour Question." Letter. *Dominica Guardian* 8 Oct. 1902: [2].

————. "Colour Question Dying Hard." Letter. *Dominica Guardian* 24 Sept. 1902: [2].

Irele, Abiola. *The African Experience in Literature and Ideology.* 1981. Bloomington: Indiana UP, 1990.

Irigaray, Luce. "Is the Subject of Science Sexed?" Trans. Carol Mastroangelo Bové. *Feminism and Science.* Ed. Nancy Tuana. Bloomington: Indiana UP, 1989. 58–68.

————. *Speculum of the Other Woman.* Trans. Gillian C. Gill. Ithaca, NY: Cornell UP, 1985.

————. *This Sex Which Is Not One.* Trans. Catherine Porter and Carolyn Burke. Ithaca, NY: Cornell UP, 1985.

Jackson, Rosemary. *Fantasy: The Literature of Subversion.* London: Methuen, 1981.

JanMohamed, Abdul R. "The Economy of Manichean Allegory: The Function of Racial Difference in Colonialist Literature." *Critical Inquiry* 12 (Autumn 1985): 59–87.

Jeffreys, Sheila. *The Spinster and Her Enemies: Feminism and Sexuality 1880–1930.* London: Pandora, 1985.

Joyce, James. *Ulysses.* 1922. Harmondsworth: Penguin, 1971.

Kaplan, Cora. "Pandora's Box: Subjectivity, Class and Sexuality in Socialist Feminist Criticism." *Sea Changes: Essays on Culture and Feminism.* London: Verso, 1986. 147–76.

Kendrick, Robert. "Edward Rochester and the Margins of Masculinity in *Jane Eyre* and *Wide Sargasso Sea.*" *Papers on Language & Literature* 30 (1994): 235–56.

Kent, Susan Kingsley. "The Politics of Sexual Difference: World War I and the Demise of British Feminism." *Journal of British Studies* 27 (1988): 232–53.

Kernfeld, Barry, ed. *The New Grove Dictionary of Jazz.* London: Macmillan, 1988.

Kincaid, James R. *Child-Loving: The Erotic Child and Victorian Culture.* New York: Routledge, 1992.

Kristeva, Julia. *Black Sun: Depression and Melancholia.* Trans. Leon S. Roudiez. New York: Columbia UP, 1989.

————. "Giotto's Joy." *Desire in Language: A Semiotic Approach to Literature and Art.* Ed. Leon S. Roudiez. Trans. Thomas Gora, Alice Jardine and Leon S. Roudiez. Oxford: Basil Blackwell, 1980. 210–36.

————. *The Portable Kristeva.* Ed. Kelly Oliver. New York: Columbia UP, 1997.

————. *Powers of Horror: An Essay on Abjection.* Trans. Leon S. Roudiez. New

York: Columbia UP, 1982.

Laffin, John. *The French Foreign Legion*. London: J.M. Dent, 1974.

Language of Flowers. Illus. Kate Greenaway. London: George Routledge & Sons, n.d.

"Last Week's Carnival." *Dominica Guardian* 17 Apr. 1901: [3].

Lawrence, D. H. *The Letters of D. H. Lawrence. Volume 1. September 1901–May 1913*. Ed. James T. Boulton. Cambridge: Cambridge UP, 1979.

———. *The Trespasser*. Ed. Elizabeth Mansfield. Cambridge: Cambridge UP, 1981.

———. "The Witch *a la Mode*." *The Complete Short Stories*. Vol. 1. New York: Viking, 1961. 54–70.

Leeward Islands. No. 6 of 1904. *Dominica Guardian* 7 May 1904: [2].

Review of *The Left Bank and Other Stories*, by Jean Rhys. *Irish Statesman* 22 Oct. 1927: 162.

Review of *The Left Bank and Other Stories*, by Jean Rhys. *Nation and Athenaeum* 25 June 1927: 424.

Review of *The Left Bank and Other Stories*, by Jean Rhys. *New Statesman* 30 Apr. 1927: 90.

Review of *The Left Bank and Other Stories*, by Jean Rhys. *New York Times Book Review* 11 Dec. 1927: 28+.

Review of *The Left Bank and Other Stories*, by Jean Rhys. *Saturday Review of Literature* 5 Nov. 1927: 287.

Review of *The Left Bank and Other Stories*, by Jean Rhys. *Spectator* 30 Apr. 1927: 772.

Le Gallez, Paula. *The Rhys Woman*. Basingstoke: Macmillan, 1990.

Leiss, William. "Technology and Degeneration: The Sublime Machine." *Degeneration: The Dark Side of Progress*. Ed. J. Edward Chamberlin and Sander L. Gilman. New York: Columbia UP, 1985. 145–64.

Lent, John A. *Third World Mass Media and Their Search for Modernity: The Case of Commonwealth Caribbean, 1717–1976*. Lewisburg: Bucknell UP, 1977.

Light, Alison. *Forever England: Femininity, Literature and Conservatism between the Wars*. London: Routledge, 1991.

Little, Judy. "Signifying Nothing: A Shakespearean Deconstruction of Rhys's Rochester." *Jean Rhys Review* 7.1-2 (1996): 39–46.

"Local." *Dominica Dial* 24 Mar. 1888: [2].

"Local." *Dominica Dial* 14 Apr. 1888: [3].

[Lockhart, Alexander Rumsey]. Editorial. *Dominican* 1 Dec. 1877: [3].

———. "Death of Mr. Righton." *Leeward Islands Free Press* 23 Feb. 1907: [2].

———. Editorial Introduction. "Dominica & Its Boiling Lake." By H. A. Alford Nicholls and Edmund Watt. *Dominican* 15 May 1880: [2]–[3].

———. "In Memoriam!" *Dominican* 28 Aug. 1880: [3].

———. "No Crown Colony: Views of an Elective on the Question of the Hour." Letter. *Dominican* 12 May 1898: [2]–[3].

Lockhart, J[ames]. P[otter]. Letter to Sir E. J. M. MacGregor. 17 July 1835. Enclosure No. 1, Despatch No. 363 from Sir E.J.M. MacGregor to Lord Glenelg. *British Parliamentary Papers: Papers Relating to the Slave Trade and the Abolition of Slavery in the West India Colonies 1836*. Slave Trade. Vol. 83. Shannon: Irish UP, 1969. 357.

"Lockhart *v.* Shillingford." *Dominican* 4 Oct. 1879: [2]–[3].

Looby, Christopher. "Flowers of Manhood: Race, Sex and Floriculture from Thomas

Wentworth Higginson to Robert Mapplethorpe." *Criticism* 37.1 (Winter 1995): 109–56.

Low, Gail Ching-Liang. "White Skin/Black Masks: The Pleasures and Politics of Imperialism." *New Formations* 9 (1989): 83–103.

McClintock, Anne. *Imperial Leather: Race, Gender and Sexuality in the Colonial Contest*. New York: Routledge, 1995.

MacGregor, Sir E[van]. J[ohn]. Murray. Appendix, No. 143. Enclosure in Despatch to Lord Glenelg, 13 Jan. 1836, No. 366. *British Parliamentary Papers: Papers Relating to the Slave Trade and the Abolition of Slavery in the West India Colonies 1836*. Slave Trade. Vol. 83. Shannon: Irish UP, 1969. 360.

———. Despatch No. 361, to the Earl of Aberdeen, 13 May 1835 [extract], and Enclosures. *British Parliamentary Papers: Papers Relating to the Slave Trade and the Abolition of Slavery in the West India Colonies 1836*. Slave Trade. Vol. 83. Shannon: Irish UP, 1969. 352–57.

———. Letter to His Honor the President of Dominica [extract]. 27 Feb. 1835. Enclosure No. 9, Despatch No. 361, to the Earl of Aberdeen. *British Parliamentary Papers: Papers Relating to the Slave Trade and the Abolition of Slavery in the West India Colonies 1836*. Slave Trade. Vol. 83. Shannon: Irish UP, 1969. 354–55.

———. Letter to His Honor the President of Dominica. 13 May 1835. Enclosure No. 14, Despatch No. 361. *British Parliamentary Papers: Papers Relating to the Slave Trade and the Abolition of Slavery in the West India Colonies 1836*. Slave Trade. Vol. 83. Shannon: Irish UP, 1969. 356.

McKay, Claude. *Banjo: A Story without a Plot*. 1929. New York: Harcourt Brace Jovanovich, 1957.

Macquarie Dictionary. McMahons Point: Macquarie Library, 1981.

Mair, John. Rev. of *Good Morning, Midnight*, by Jean Rhys. *New Statesman and Nation* 22 Apr. 1939: 614.

Malcolm, Cheryl Alexander, and David Malcolm. *Jean Rhys: A Study of the Short Fiction*. New York: Twayne, 1996.

Mansfield, Elizabeth. Introduction. *The Trespasser*. By D. H. Lawrence. Cambridge: Cambridge UP, 1981.

Marholm, Laura. *Studies in the Psychology of Woman*. Trans. Georgia A. Etchison. Chicago: Herbert S. Stone, 1899.

Maxwell, Anne. "The Debate on Current Theories of Colonial Discourse." *Kunapipi* 13.3 (1991): 70–84.

M.D. [pseudonym]. "Venereal Disease: Sources of Infection." Letter. *Times* 14 Dec. 1917: 12.

Meister, Father. Letter. *Dominican* 9 Mar. 1904. Rpt. in "The Obeah Correspondence." *Dominica Guardian* 21 May 1904: [3].

Metz, Christian. "Photography and Fetish." *October* 34 (1985): 82–90.

Miller, Nancy K. *Subject to Change: Reading Feminist Writing*. New York: Columbia UP, 1988.

Milltown, Earl of Milltown. In debate on the Criminal Law Amendment Bill. House of Lords. 25 June 1883. *Hansard's Parliamentary Debates: Third Series*. Vol. 280. 1883. New York: Klaus Reprint, 1971.

Ministry of Health, Great Britain. *Report of an Investigation into Maternal Mortality*. London: HMSO, 1937.

————. *Report of the Inter-Departmental Committee on Abortion*. 1939. London: HMSO, 1965.

Moi, Toril. *Sexual/Textual Politics*. London: Methuen, 1985.

Molesworth, Sir W. Speech. House of Commons. 25 July 1848. *Hansard's Parliamentary Debates: Third Series*. Vol. 100. 1848. New York: Klaus Reprint, 1971.

"Moralizing." *Dominica Guardian* 19 Aug. 1893: [2]–[3].

Moretti, Franco. "The Dialectic of Fear." *New Left Review* 136 (1982): 67–85.

Morris, Mervyn. "Oh, Give the Girl a Chance: Jean Rhys and *Voyage in the Dark*." *Journal of West Indian Literature* 3.2 (Sept. 1989): 1–8.

Morrison, Toni. *Playing in the Dark: Whiteness and the Literary Imagination*. Cambridge, MA: Harvard UP, 1992.

Mount Temple, Lord. In debate on the Criminal Law Amendment Bill. House of Lords. 15 May 1884. *Hansard's Parliamentary Debates: Third Series*. Vol. 288. 1884. New York: Klaus Reprint, 1971.

Muir, Kenneth, ed. *Othello*. By William Shakespeare. Harmondsworth: Penguin, 1968.

Narain, Denise de Caires. Rev. of *Motherlands: Black Women's Writing from Africa, the Caribbean and South Asia*, ed. Susheila Nasta. *Journal of West Indian Literature* 6.2 (May 1994): 112–15.

"Negrophobia." Rev. of *Mr. Froude's Negrophobia, or Don Quixote as a Cook's Tourist*. By Darnell Davis. *Dominica Dial* 10 Nov. 1888: [3].

Neill, Michael. "Changing Places in *Othello*." *Shakespeare Survey* 37 (1984): 115–31.

————. "Unproper Beds: Race, Adultery, and the Hideous in *Othello*." *Shakespeare Quarterly* 40 (1989): 383–412.

Review of *Neutral Ground*, by Helen Corke. *Times Literary Supplement* 10 Aug. 1933: 538.

Newman, Judie. *The Ballistic Bard: Postcolonial Fictions*. London: Arnold, 1995.

Newman, Karen. "'And wash the Ethiop white': Femininity and the Monstrous in *Othello*." *Shakespeare Reproduced: The Text in History and Ideology*. Ed. Jean E. Howard and Marion F. O'Connor. New York: Methuen, 1987. 143–62.

Nicholls, H. A. Alford. *Report on Yaws in Tobago, Grenada, St Vincent, St Lucia, and the Windward Islands, Addressed to the Right Honourable Lord Knutsford, G.C.M.G., Her Majesty's Principal Secretary of State for the Colonies*. London: H.M.S.O., 1894.

————. *A Text-book of Tropical Agriculture*. London: Macmillan, 1914.

Nicholls, H. A. Alford, and Edmund Watt. "Dominica & Its Boiling Lake." *Dominican* 15 May 1880: [2]–[3].

Nicholls, Peter. *Modernisms: A Literary Guide*. Houndsmills: Macmillan, 1995.

O'Connor, Teresa F. "Jean Rhys, Paul Theroux, and the Imperial Road." *Twentieth Century Literature* 38 (1992): 404–14.

————. *Jean Rhys: The West Indian Novels*. New York: New York UP, 1986.

Ong, Walter. *Orality and Literacy*. 1982. London: Routledge, 1988.

Osborne, Harold, ed. *The Oxford Companion to Art*. Oxford: Oxford UP, 1970.

Ovid. *The Metamorphoses*. Trans. Mary M. Innes. Harmondsworth: Penguin, 1955.

Owen, Nancy H. "Land, Politics, and Ethnicity in a Carib Indian Community." *Ethnology* 14 (1975): 385–93.

Parry, Benita. "Problems in Current Theories of Colonial Discourse." *Oxford Literary*

Review 9 (1987): 27–58.

Paton, Diana. "Decency, Dependency and the Lash: Gender and British Debate over Slave Emancipation, 1830–34." *Slavery and Abolition: A Journal of Slave and Post-Slave Studies* 17.3 (Dec. 1996).

Pefanis, Julian. *Heterology and the Postmodern: Bataille, Baudrillard, and Lyotard.* Sydney: Allen & Unwin, 1991.

Perry, L. A. *Criminal Abortion.* London: John Bale, Sons & Danielsson, 1932.

Pettman, Jan Jindy. *Worlding Women: A Feminist International Politics.* St. Leonards: Allen & Unwin, 1996.

Plante, David. "Jean Rhys: A Remembrance." *Paris Review* 76 (1979): 238–84.

Pound, [Ezra]. "Vortex." *Blast* 1 (1914): 153–54.

Pratt, Mary Louise. *Imperial Eyes: Travel Writing and Transculturation.* London: Routledge, 1992.

Protection of Mentally Defective Persons Bill. *Parliamentary Papers, Commons, Bills Public. Vol. 5. Session 10 Feb. 1920–23 Dec. 1920.* London: HMSO, 1920. Bill 105.

Proust, Marcel. *Time Regained.* Trans. Stephen Hudson. London: Chatto and Windus, 1966.

"The Queen's Jubilee." *Dominican* 30 June 1887: [3].

Quinones, Ricardo J. *Mapping Literary Modernism: Time and Development.* Princeton, NJ: Princeton UP, 1985.

Radden, Jennifer. "Melancholy and Melancholia." *Pathologies of the Modern Self: Postmodern Studies on Narcissism, Schizophrenia, and Depression.* Ed. David Michael Levin. New York: New York UP, 1987. 231–50.

Rae, J. Stanley, and Sydney A. Armitage-Smith. *Conditions in the Carib Reserve, and the Disturbance of 19th September, 1930, Dominica.* Cmd. 3990. London: HMSO, 1932.

Raiskin, Judith L. *Snow on the Cane Fields: Women's Writing and Creole Subjectivity.* Minneapolis: U of Minnesota P, 1996.

Ramchand, Kenneth. Introduction. *Tales of the Wide Caribbean.* London: Heinemann, 1985. 1–21.

Rat, J. Numa. "A Paper on Yaws." *Journal of Tropical Medicine* 1 July 1902: 205–12.

Rauch, Angelika. "The *Trauerspiel* of the Prostituted Body, or Woman as Allegory of Modernity." *Cultural Critique* 10 (1989): 77–88.

Read, Herbert. "Guernica: A Modern Calvary." *Picasso's Guernica: Illustrations, Introductory Essay, Documents, Poetry, Criticism, Analysis.* Ed. Ellen C. Oppler. New York: W. W. Norton, 1988. 217–18.

Rees, Abraham, comp. *The Cyclopaedia; or Universal Dictionary of Arts, Sciences and Literature.* London: Longman, 1819.

Reid, Fred. "The Disintegration of Liberalism, 1895–1931." *The Context of English Literature 1900–1930.* Ed. Michael Bell. London: Methuen, 1980. 94–125.

Report of the Joint Committee Appointed to Investigate and Report Their Opinion as to the Alternative to Be Taken, Whether of Unconditionally Adopting or Absolutely Rejecting the Order in Council of 2d November Last, and How Far the Provisions of the Order in Council Are Met by the Slave Act Passed in June Last; and Also How Far the Said Order in Council May Be Adopted with Safety to the Colony, and without Infringing Unnecessarily on Private Property. Enclosure No. 3. Despatch from Sir E.M. MacGregor to Viscount Goderich. 28 March 1832. *Brit-*

ish Parliamentary Papers: Reports from Protectors of Slaves in British Colonies Together with the Proceedings and Decisions in Each Case of Complaint between Masters and Slaves 1830–31. Slave Trade. Vol. 79. Shannon: Irish UP, 1969.

Report of the Royal Commission on the Care and Control of the Feeble-Minded (Minutes of Evidence). Vol. VIII. *Reports from Commissioners, Inspectors and Others. 1908.* Vol. 26. [London: HMSO], 1908.

Report from the Select Committee on Negro Apprenticeship in the Colonies. *British Parliamentary Papers: Reports from Select Committees Appointed to Enquire into the Working of the Apprenticeship System in the Colonies with Minutes of Evidence, Appendix and Index.* Slave Trade. Vol. 3. Shannon: Irish UP, 1968.

Rich, Adrienne. "Compulsory Heterosexuality and Lesbian Existence." *Signs* 5 (1980): 631–60.

Rich, Paul B. *Race and Empire in British Politics.* Cambridge: Cambridge UP, 1986.

Riddell, Lord. "Abortion and Maternal Mortality." *Journal of Obstretrics and Gynæcology of the British Empire* 38. n.s. 1 (Spring 1931): [1]–6.

[Righton, A. Theodore]. "Another Obeah Case." *Dominican* 26 Jan. 1905: [3].

———. Editorial. *Dominican* 3 July 1880: [2]–[3].

———. Editorial. *Dominican* 12 Nov. 1903: [2].

———. Editorial. *Dominican* 2 June 1904: [2].

———. Obituary of Joseph Fadelle. *Dominican* 17 Sept. 1896: [2].

R.M.C. Review of *After Leaving Mr Mackenzie*, by Jean Rhys. *New Yorker* 4 July 1931: 53.

Rodríguez, Ileana. *House/Garden/Nation: Space, Gender, and Ethnicity in Postcolonial Latin American Literatures by Women.* Trans. Robert Carr and Ileana Rodríguez. Durham, NC: Duke UP, 1994.

Rose, Jacqueline. *States of Fantasy.* Oxford: Clarendon, 1996.

Rose, Phyllis. *Writing of Women: Essays in a Renaissance.* Middletown, CT: Wesleyan UP, 1985.

"The Roseau River Embankment." *Dominica Guardian* 25 May 1906: [3].

Rothfield, Philippa. "Alternative Epistemologies, Politics and Feminism." *Social Analysis* 30 (Dec. 1991): 54–67.

Rowbotham, Sheila. *A New World for Women. Stella Browne, Socialist Feminist.* London: Pluto, 1977.

Russo, Mary. "Female Grotesques: Carnival and Theory". *Feminist Studies/Critical Studies.* Ed. Teresa de Lauretis. Bloomington: Indiana UP, 1986. 213–29.

"Safer Motherhood." *Times* 9 May 1934: 16.

"The Saint; the Sawbones and the Speculator." *Dominica Guardian* 27 July 1898: [3].

Saleeby, Caleb Williams. *Parenthood and Race Culture: An Outline of Eugenics.* London: Cassell, 1909.

Sargeant, Winthrop. *Jazz, Hot and Hybrid.* 3rd ed. New York: Da Capo, 1975.

Satchell, William. "Humility and Ostentation." *Dominica Colonist* 21 Dec. 1839: [4].

Savory, Elaine. "'Another Poor Devil of a Human Being . . .': Jean Rhys and the Novel as Obeah." *Jean Rhys Review* 7.1–2 (1996): 26–38.

Schiesari, Juliana. *The Gendering of Melancholia: Feminism, Psychoanalysis, and the Symbolics of Loss in Renaissance Literature.* Ithaca, NY: Cornell UP, 1992.

Scott, Joan W. "'Experience.'" *Feminists Theorize the Political.* Ed. Judith Butler and Joan W. Scott. New York: Routledge, 1992. 22–40.

Sedgwick, Eve Kosofsky. "The Beast in the Closet: James and the Writing of Homosexual Panic." *Speaking of Gender*. Ed. Elaine Showalter. New York: Routledge, 1989. 243–68.

Shakespeare, William. *Macbeth*. Ed. D. R. Elloway. Houndsmills: Macmillan Education, 1971.

———. *Othello*. Ed. Kenneth Muir. Harmondsworth: Penguin, 1968.

Shiell, John. Opinion. Enclosure No. 10. Despatch No. 361, to the Earl of Aberdeen, 13 May 1835 [extract], and Enclosures. *British Parliamentary Papers: Papers Relating to the Slave Trade and the Abolition of Slavery in the West India Colonies 1836*. Slave Trade. Vol. 83. Shannon: Irish UP, 1969. 355.

Shorter, Clement. *The Brontës: Life and Letters*. 1908. New York: Haskell, 1969.

Showalter, Elaine. *The Female Malady: Women, Madness and English Culture, 1830–1980*. 1985. London: Virago, 1987.

Simpson, Archibald H. *A Treatise on the Law and Practice Relating to Infants*. 3rd. ed. By Edgar J. Elgood. London: Stevens and Haynes, 1909.

Simpson, Hilary. *D. H. Lawrence and Feminism*. London: Croom Helm, 1982.

Smith, Tony, Richard Robinson, and Peter Arnold. *Reader's Digest Encyclopedia of Family Health*. Sydney: Reader's Digest, 1994.

Snow, Edward A. "Sexual Anxiety and the Male Order of Things in *Othello*." Othello: *Critical Essays*. Ed. Susan Snyder. New York: Garland, 1988. 213–49.

Soyinka, Wole. *Myth, Literature and the African World*. 1976. Cambridge: Cambridge UP, 1990.

"The Special Inquiry." *Dominica Guardian* [special edition] 29 Nov. 1893.

Spivak, Gayatri Chakravorty. "Can the Subaltern Speak?" *Marxism and the Interpretation of Culture*. Ed. Cary Nelson and Lawrence Grossberg. London: Macmillan, 1988. 271–313.

———. "Echo." *The Spivak Reader: Selected Works of Gayatri Chakravorty Spivak*. Ed. Donna Landry and Gerald MacLean. New York: Routledge, 1996. 175–202.

———. "The Rani of Sirmur." *Europe and Its Others*. Vol. I. Ed. Francis Barker, Peter Hulme, Margaret Iversen and Diana Loxley. Colchester: U of Essex, 1985. 128–51.

———. "Theory in the Margin: Coetzee's *Foe* Reading Defoe's *Crusoe/Roxana*." *Consequences of Theory: Selected Papers from the English Institute, 1987–88*. Ed. Jonathan Arac and Barbara Johnson. Baltimore: Johns Hopkins UP, 1991. 154–80.

———. "Three Women's Texts and a Critique of Imperialism." *Critical Inquiry* 12 (1985/86): 243–61.

Squier, Susan Merrill. *Babies in Bottles: Twentieth-Century Visions of Reproductive Technology*. New Brunswick, NJ: Rutgers UP, 1994.

Staley, Thomas F. *Jean Rhys: A Critical Study*. Austin: U of Texas P, 1979.

Stallybrass, Peter, and Allon White. *The Politics and Poetics of Transgression* London: Methuen, 1986.

Stanton, Domna C. "Difference on Trial: A Critique of the Maternal Metaphor i n Cixous, Irigaray, and Kristeva." *The Poetics of Gender*. Ed. Nancy K. Miller. New York: Columbia UP, 1986. 157–82.

[Steber, Joseph Hilton]. "The Civil Service List." *Dominica Guardian* 29 Oct. 1902: [3].

———. "The Colour Question." *Dominica Guardian* 24 Sept. 1902: [2].

————. "Juvenile Lawlessness and the Compulsory Education Act." *Dominica Guard-ian* 28 Aug. 1901: [2].

————. "Moralizing." *Dominica Guardian*. 27 Dec. 1899: [1].

————. "Murder and Superstition." *Dominica Guardian* 29 Oct. 1904: [3].

————. "The Obeah Correspondence." *Dominica Guardian* 21 May 1904: [3].

————. "Obeah Legislation." *Dominica Guardian* 7 May 1904: [2].

————. "The Obeah Question." *Dominica Guardian* 16 Aug. 1907: [2].

————. Paragraph. *Dominica Guardian* 8 Nov. 1902: [3].

————. "A Public Nuisance." *Dominica Guardian* 7 Nov. 1894: [3].

————. "Up to Date." *Dominica Guardian* 22 Oct. 1902: [2]–[3].

————. "What Is Obeah?" *Dominica Guardian* 5 Nov. 1904: [3].

Stekel, Wilhelm. *Frigidity in Woman in Relation to Her Love Life*. 2 vols. Trans. James S. van Teslaar. New York: Boni and Liveright, 1926.

Stepan, Nancy. "Biology: Races and Proper Places." *Degeneration: The Dark Side of Progress*. Ed. J. Edward Chamberlin and Sander L. Gilman. New York: Columbia UP, 1985. 97–120.

Stouck, Jordan. "Locating Other Subjectivities in Jean Rhys's 'Again the Antilles.'" *Jean Rhys Review* 8.1–2 (1997): 1–5.

Streip, Katharine. "'Just a Cérébrale': Jean Rhys, Women's Humor, and Ressenti-ment." *Representations* 45 (Winter 1994): 117–44.

Sturge, Joseph, and Thomas Harvey. *The West Indies in 1837*. 1838. Introduction by Philip Wright. London: Dawsons, 1968.

Swinnerton, Frank. "All Sorts." Rev. of *Good Morning, Midnight*, by Jean Rhys. *Observer* 23 April 1939.

Taussig, Michael. *Shamanism, Colonialism, and the Wild Man: A Study in Terror and Healing*. Chicago: U of Chicago P, 1987.

Taylor, Helen. *Gender, Race, and Region in the Writings of Grace King, Ruth McEn-ery Stuart, and Kate Chopin*. Baton Rouge: Louisiana State UP, 1989.

Taylor, Rachel Annand. *The Hours of Fiammetta: A Sonnet Sequence*. London: Elkin Mathews, 1910.

Thomas, J. J. *Froudacity: West Indian Fables by James Anthony Froude*. 1889. Lon-don: New Beacon, 1969.

Thomas, Sue. "Battlefield and Sky: Sex-Consciousness in *A Room of One's Own*." *Women: A Cultural Review* 7.2 (Autumn 1996): 160–75.

————. "Conflicted Textual Affiliations: Jean Rhys's 'The Insect [World]' and 'Heat.'" *A Talent(ed) Digger: Creations, Cameos, and Essays in Honour of Anna Rutherford*. Ed. Hena Maes-Jelinek, Gordon Collier, and Geoffrey V. Davis. Am-sterdam: Rodopi, 1996. 287–94.

————. "Difference, Intersubjectivity and Agency in the Colonial and Decolonizing Spaces of Hélène Cixous's 'Sorties.'" *Hypatia: A Journal of Feminist Philoso-phy* 9.1 (Winter 1994): 53–69.

————. "James Potter Lockhart and the 'Letter of the Law.'" *Jean Rhys Review* 9.1–2 (1998): 36–43.

————. "Jean Rhys, 'Human Ants,' and the Production of Expatriate Creole Identi-ties." Constructing British Identities: Texts, Sub-texts, and Contexts. National University of Singapore. 11–13 Sept. 1997.

————. "Modernity, Voice and Window-Breaking: Jean Rhys's 'Let Them Call It Jazz.'" *De-scribing Empire: Post-colonialism and Textuality*. Ed. Alan Lawson and Chris Tiffin. London: Routledge, 1994. 185–200.

———. "The Tropical Extravagance of Bertha Mason." *Victorian Literature and Culture* 27.1 (1999): 1-17.

———. "William Rees Williams in Dominica." *Jean Rhys Review* 7.1-2 (1996): 3–14.

Tiffin, Helen. "Metaphor and Mortality: The 'Life-Cycle(s)' of Malaria." *Meridian: The La Trobe University English Review* 12 (1993): 46–58.

———. "Mirror and Mask: Colonial Motifs in the Novels of Jean Rhys." *World Literature Written in English* 17 (1978): 328–41.

———. "Rite of Reply—Shorter Fictions of Jean Rhys." *Re-Siting Queen's English: Text and Context in Post-colonial Literatures.* Ed. Gillian Whitlock and Helen Tiffin. Amsterdam: Rodopi, 1992. 67–79.

———. "Rites of Resistance: Counter-Discourse and West Indian Biography." *Journal of West Indian Literature* 3.1 (Jan. 1989): 28–46.

Torgovnick, Marianna. *Gone Primitive: Savage Intellects, Modern Lives.* Chicago: U of Chicago P, 1990.

"Treatment in Hospitals." *Times* 26 July 1932: 7.

Trollope, Anthony. *The West Indies and the Spanish Main.* 1859. London: Frank Cass, 1968.

Trouillot, Michel-Rolph. *Peasants and Capital: Dominica in the World Economy.* Baltimore: Johns Hopkins UP, 1988.

Turnbull, Patrick. *The Foreign Legion: A History of the Foreign Legion.* London: Heinemann, 1964.

Valverde, Mariana. "The Love of Finery: Fashion and the Fallen Woman in Nineteenth-Century Social Discourse." *Victorian Studies* 32.2 (Winter 1989): 168–88.

Varadharajan, Asha. *Exotic Parodies: Subjectivity in Adorno, Said, and Spivak.* Minneapolis: U of Minnesota P, 1995.

"Venereal Diseases." *The Encyclopædia Brittanica: A Dictionary of Arts, Sciences, Literature and General Information.* 11th. ed. Cambridge: Cambridge UP, 1910–11.

Walkowitz, Judith R. *City of Dreadful Delight: Narratives of Sexual Danger in Late-Victorian London.* London: Virago, 1992.

Ward, Fannie D. "In Drowsy Dominica." *Dominican* 1 Nov. 1894: [3].

Ward, Frazer. "Foreign and Familiar Bodies." *Dirt & Domesticity: Constructions of the Feminine.* By Jesús Fuenmayor, Kate Haug and Frazer Ward. New York: Whitney Museum of American Art, 1992. 8–37.

Watkins, Kathleen Blake. "Dominica." *Daily Mail and Empire.* Rpt. in *Dominican* 18 Apr. 1895: [3].

Weiskel, Thomas. *The Romantic Sublime: Studies in the Structure and Psychology of Transcendence.* Baltimore: Johns Hopkins UP, 1976.

West, Mr. In debate on the Criminal Law Amendment Bill. House of Commons. 31 July 1885. *Hansard's Parliamentary Debates: Third Series.* Vol. 300. 1885. New York: Klaus Reprint, 1971.

West, Rebecca. *The Young Rebecca: Writings of Rebecca West 1911-17.* Ed. Jane Marcus. London: Macmillan in assoc. with Virago, 1982.

Whitaker, Arthur P. *The United States and the Southern Cone: Argentina, Chile, and Uruguay.* Cambridge, MA: Harvard UP, 1976.

Whitford, Margaret. *Luce Irigaray: Philosophy in the Feminine*. London: Routledge, 1991.

Wilcocks, Charles. *Health and Disease in the Tropics*. Oxford: Oxford UP, 1950.

Williamson, Janice. "'I Peel Myself out of My Own Skin': Reading *Don't: A Woman's Word*." *Essays on Life Writing: From Genre to Critical Practice*. Ed. Marlene Kadar. Toronto: U of Toronto P, 1992. 133–51.

Wilson, Lucy. "'Women Must Have Spunks': Jean Rhys's West Indian Outcasts." *Critical Perspectives on Jean Rhys*. Ed. Pierrette Frickey. Washington, DC: Three Continents, 1990. 67–74.

Wilton, Andrew. *Turner and the Sublime*. London: British Museum Publications, 1980.

Wolfe, Peter. *Jean Rhys*. Boston: Twayne, 1980.

Woolf, Virginia. *A Room of One's Own*. 1929. Uniform ed. London: Hogarth, 1935.

"Wyllis v. Steber." *Dominica Guardian* 19 Nov. 1904: [3].

"Wyllis v. Steber (Concluded)." *Dominica Guardian* 26 Nov. 1904: [3].

Wyndham, Francis. Introduction. *Wide Sargasso Sea*. By Jean Rhys. Harmondsworth: Penguin, 1968. 5–11.

Wyndham-Lewis, D.B. "Hinterland of Bohemia." Rev. of *The Left Bank and Other Stories*, by Jean Rhys. *Saturday Review* 23 Apr. 1927: 637.

Young, Filson. *The Sands of Pleasure*. London: E. Grant Richards, 1905.

Young, Iris Marion. "The Ideal of Community and the Politics of Difference." *Feminism/Postmodernism*. Ed. Linda J. Nicholson. New York: Routledge, 1990. 300–23.

Zimmeck, Meta. "Jobs for the Girls: The Expansion of Clerical Work for Women, 1850–1914." *Unequal Opportunities: Women's Employment in England 1800–1918*. Ed. Angela V. John. Oxford: Basil Blackwell, 1986. 153–77.

Zonana, Joyce. "The Sultan and the Slave: Feminist Orientalism and the Structure of *Jane Eyre*." *Signs* 18 (1993): 592–617.

Works Consulted

This list is highly selective. I include uncited primary sources, important work on Rhys to which I have not referred and material that helped shape my argument or provided historical or theoretical background.

PRIMARY

David Plante Papers, Department of Special Collections, McFarlin Library, University of Tulsa, Oklahoma.

Jean Rhys Papers, Department of Special Collections, McFarlin Library, University of Tulsa, Oklahoma.

Rhys, Jean. Add. Mss. 57856-57859. Department of Manuscripts. British Library, London.

———. "The Christmas Presents of Mynheer Van Rooz." *Time and Tide* 28 Nov. 1931: 1360–61.

———. "I Spy a Stranger." *Penguin Modern Stories*. London: Penguin, 1969.

———. "The Joey Blagstock Smile. September 7, 1974." *New Statesman* 94 (23–30 Dec. 1977): 890.

———. *Smile Please: An Unfinished Autobiography*. New York: Harper & Row, 1980. 142–48. ["The Cottage" and "My Day."]

———. "Whistling Bird." *New Yorker* 11 Sept. 1978: 38–39.

SECONDARY

Abel, Elizabeth. "Women and Schizophrenia: The Fiction of Jean Rhys." *Contemporary Literature* 20 (1979): 155–77.

Atwood, Thomas. *The History of the Island of Dominica*. 1791. London: Frank Cass, 1971.

Benstock, Shari. *Women of the Left Bank: Paris 1900–1940*. London: Virago, 1987.

Black, Clinton V. *The History of Jamaica*. London: Collins, 1983.

Blackburn, Robin. *The Overthrow of Colonial Slavery 1776–1848*. London: Verso, 1988.

Brathwaite, Edward. *Contradictory Omens: Cultural Diversity and Integration in the Caribbean*. Kingston: Savacou, 1974.

Carco, Francis. *Perversity*. Trans. Ford Madox Ford. Chicago: Pascal Covici, 1928. [Rhys was the actual translator.]

Choudhury, Romita. "'Is there a ghost, a zombie there?' Postcolonial Intertextuality in Jean Rhys's *Wide Sargasso Sea*." *Textual Practice* 10.2 (1996): 315–27.

Curtin, Philip D. *Two Jamaicas: The Role of Ideas in a Tropical Colony 1830–1865*. Cambridge, MA: Harvard UP, 1955.

Curtis, Jan. "The Secret of *Wide Sargasso Sea*." *Critique: Studies in Contemporary Literature* 31 (1990): 185–97.

Davy, John. *The West Indies before and since Slave Emancipation*. 1854. London: Frank Cass, 1971.

Ford, Ford Madox. *When the Wicked Man*. London: Jonathan Cape, 1932.

Forrester, Faizal. "Who Stole the Soul in *Wide Sargasso Sea*." *Journal of West Indian Literature* 6.2 (May 1994): 32–42.

Gaines, Nora, ed. *Jean Rhys Review* 1.1 (Fall 1986)–9.1–2 (1998).

Hite, Molly. *The Other Side of the Story: Structures and Strategies of Contemporary Feminist Fiction*. Ithaca, NY: Cornell UP, 1989.

James, Louis. *Jean Rhys*. London: Longman, 1978.

Jenny, Laurent. "The Strategy of Form." *French Literary Theory Today: A Reader*. Ed. Tzvetan Todorov. Trans. R. Carter. Cambridge: Cambridge UP, 1982. 34–63.

Kloepfer, Deborah Kelly. *The Unspeakable Mother: Forbidden Discourse in Jean Rhys and H. D.* Ithaca, NY: Cornell UP, 1989.

Mellown, Elgin W. *Jean Rhys: A Descriptive and Annotated Bibliography of Works and Criticism*. New York: Gale, 1984.

Mezei, Kathy. "'And it Kept its secret': Narration, Memory, and Madness in Jean Rhys' *Wide Sargasso Sea*." *Critique: Studies in Contemporary Literature* 28 (1987): 195–209.

Myers, Robert A. *Dominica*. World Bibliographical Series 82. Oxford: Clio, 1987.

Nasta, Susheila, ed. *Motherlands: Black Women's Writing from Africa, the Caribbean and South Asia*. London: Women's, 1991.

Nebeker, Helen. *Jean Rhys: Woman in Passage: A Critical Study of the Novels of Jean Rhys*. Montreal: Eden, 1981.

Nève, Edward de. *Barred*. Trans. Jean Rhys. London: Desmond Harmsworth, 1932.

Ober, Frederick A. *Our West Indian Neighbours: The Islands of the Caribbean Sea, "America's Mediterranean": Their Picturesque Features, Fascinating History, and Attractions for the Traveler, Nature-lover, Settler and Pleasure-seeker*. New York: James Pott, 1904.

O'Callaghan, Evelyn. *Woman Version: Theoretical Approaches to West Indian Fiction by Women*. New York: St Martin's, 1993.

Olaussen, Maria. "Jean Rhys's Construction of Blackness as Escape from White Femininity in *Wide Sargasso Sea*." *Ariel: A Review of International English Literature* 24.2 (April 1993): 65–82.

Oppenheim, Janet. *"Shattered Nerves": Doctors, Patients, and Depression in Victorian England*. New York: Oxford UP, 1991.

Paravisini-Gebert, Lizabeth. *Phyllis Shand Allfrey: A Caribbean Life*. New Brunswick, NJ: Rutgers UP, 1996.

Paton, William Agnew. *Down the Islands: A Voyage to the Caribbees*. New York: Charles Scribner's Sons, 1887.

Plante, David. *Difficult Women: A Memoir of Three*. London: Victor Gollancz, 1983.

Ragatz, Lowell Joseph. *The Fall of the Planter Class in the British Caribbean, 1763–1833: A Study in Social and Economic History*. New York: Century, 1928.

Ramchand, Kenneth. *The West Indian Novel and Its Background*. 2nd ed. London: Heinemann, 1983.

Roe, Sue. "The Shadow of Light: The Symbolic Underworld of Jean Rhys." *Women Reading Women Writing*. Ed. Sue Roe. Brighton: Harvester, 1987. 227–62.

Sternlicht, Sanford. *Jean Rhys*. New York: Twayne, 1997.

Stoddard, Charles Augustus. *Cruising among the Caribbees: Summer Days in Winter Months*. New York: Charles Scribner's Sons, 1895.

Sypher, Wylie. "The West-Indian as a 'Character' in the Eighteenth Century." *Studies in Philology* 38 (1939): 503–20.

Index

Abortion, 113 n.25, 113 n.26

Abortion, representations of: in "Triple Sec," 72, 75–76; in *Voyage in the Dark*, 109–10

Adam, H. Pearl, 5

After Leaving Mr Mackenzie (Rhys): as an engagement with discourses about amateur prostitutes, 67–68, 84–91, 117, 138; bachelor types in, 86–88; burial alive as motif in, 85–88; indifference as motif in, 85–90; reception of, in 1931, 84–85; reduplication in, 85, 89–90; representation of depression in, 85–90

"Again the Antilles" (Rhys), 10, 52–53, 56–61; allusion to *The Canterbury Tales* (Chaucer) in, 57, 59–60; knowingness as thematic and structural device in, 58–59; misrepresentation of Augustus Theodore Righton in, 57; references to William Shakespeare in, 59–60

Amateur prostitution, 35, 62, 67–70; definition of, 67; moral panics around, 67–70; Rhys's engagements with discourses about, 67–68, 71–93, 104–5, 108–9, 138

Angier, Carole, 3, 37, 51, 99

Arata, Stephen D., 73–74

Autoethnography, definition of, 9

Baker, Patrick, 20, 160

Bell, Henry Hesketh, 13, 15, 84, 106, 144–45

Benjamin, Walter, 63–64, 77, 79, 83

Bhabha, Homi, 3, 146–47, 154 n.7

"The Birthday" (Rhys): as a reworking of material in the Black Exercise Book, 41–43; Francine figure in, 41–43; horticultural tropology in, 20

"The Bishop's Feast" (Rhys), 189 n.19

Black Exercise Book, autobiographical narrative in the. *See* Black Exercise Book (Rhys), seduction narrative in the

Black Exercise Book (Rhys), seduction narrative in the: 24; as intertext of *Wide Sargasso Sea*, 180–81; as recovered memory of sexual trauma, 27–41, 45–46; as reply to Sigmund Freud's renunciation of his seduction theory of hysteria, 28, 45–46; figurations of blackness in, 31; horticultural tropology in, 38–39; intertextual relation to *A High Wind in Jamaica* (Hughes), 34–35

Blackness, figurations of: in *Good Morning Midnight*, 126; in *Quartet*, 78, 83–84; in the seduction narrative

About the Author

SUE THOMAS is Senior Lecturer in English at La Trobe University. She has published extensively on Jean Rhys, late nineteenth- and twentieth-century women's writing, feminist theory, postcolonial writers, and Victorian and Edwardian periodicals. She is a member of the editorial boards of *Jean Rhys Review*, *Australasian Victorian Studies Journal*, and *Meridian*, and an advisory editor of *New Literatures Review: Decolonising Literatures*.